Shaping the Humanitarian World

Providing a critical introduction to the notion of humanitarianism in global politics, tracing the concept from its origins to the twenty-first century, this book examines how the so called international community works in response to humanitarian crises and the systems that bind and divide them.

By tracing the history on international humanitarian action from its early roots through the birth of the Red Cross to the beginning of the UN, Peter Walker and Daniel Maxwell examine the challenges humanitarian agencies face, from working alongside armies and terrorists to witnessing genocide. They argue that humanitarianism has a vital future, but only if those practicing it choose to make it so. Topics covered include:

- the rise in humanitarian action as a political tool
- the growing call for accountability of agencies
- the switch of NGOs from bit players to major trans-national actors
- the conflict between political action and humanitarian action when it comes to addressing causes as well as symptoms of crisis.

This book is essential reading for anyone with an interest in international human rights law, disaster management and international relations.

Peter Walker is Director at the Feinstein International Center at Tufts University. Dr Walker founded the World Disasters Report and was one of the founders of the Sphere humanitarian standards.

Daniel Maxwell is Associate Professor at the Friedman School of Nutrition Science and Policy, and a Research Director at Feinstein International Center at Tufts Univers

D1021878

Routledge Global Institutions

Edited by Thomas G. Weiss
The CUNY Graduate Center, New York, USA
and Rorden Wilkinson
University of Manchester, UK

About the Series

The Global Institutions Series is designed to provide readers with comprehensive, accessible, and informative guides to the history, structure, and activities of key international organizations. Every volume stands on its own as a thorough and insightful treatment of a particular topic, but the series as a whole contributes to a coherent and complementary portrait of the phenomenon of global institutions at the dawn of the millennium.

Books are written by recognized experts, conform to a similar structure, and cover a range of themes and debates common to the series. These areas of shared concern include the general purpose and rationale for organizations, developments over time, membership, structure, decision-making procedures, and key functions. Moreover, current debates are placed in historical perspective alongside informed analysis and critique. Each book also contains an annotated bibliography and guide to electronic information as well as any annexes appropriate to the subject matter at hand.

The volumes currently published or under contract include:

The United Nations and Human Rights (2005)
A guide for a new era
by Julie Mertus (American University)

The UN Secretary General and Secretariat (2005)
by Leon Gordenker (Princeton University)

United Nations Global Conferences (2005)
by Michael G. Schechter (Michigan State University)

The UN General Assembly (2005)
by M.J. Peterson (University of Massachusetts, Amherst)

Internal Displacement (2006)
Conceptualization and its consequences
by Thomas G. Weiss (The CUNY Graduate Center) and David A. Korn

Global Environmental Institutions (2006)
by Elizabeth R. DeSombre (Wellesley College)

African Economic Institutions
by Kwame Akonor (Seton Hall University)

The United Nations Development Programme (UNDP)
by Elizabeth A. Mandeville (Tufts University) and Craig N. Murphy (Wellesley College)

The Regional Development Banks
Lending with a regional flavor
by Jonathan R. Strand (University of Nevada, Las Vegas)

Multilateral Cooperation Against Terrorism
by Peter Romaniuk (John Jay College of Criminal Justice, CUNY)

Transnational Organized Crime
by Frank Madsen (University of Cambridge)

Peacebuilding
From concept to commission
by Robert Jenkins (University of London)

Governing Climate Change
by Peter Newell (University of East Anglia) and Harriet A. Bulkeley (Durham University)

Millennium Development Goals (MDGs)
For a people-centered development agenda?
by Sakiko Fukada-Parr (The New School)

Regional Security
The capacity of international organizations
by Rodrigo Tavares (United Nations University)

Human Development
by Maggie Black

Human Security
by Dan Hubert (University of Ottawa)

For further information regarding the series, please contact:

Craig Fowlie, Publisher, Politics & International Studies
Taylor & Francis
2 Park Square, Milton Park, Abingdon
Oxford OX14 4RN, UK

+44 (0)207 842 2057 Tel
+44 (0)207 842 2302 Fax

Craig.Fowlie@tandf.co.uk
www.routledge.com

Shaping the Humanitarian World

Peter Walker and
Daniel Maxwell

Routledge
Taylor & Francis Group

LONDON AND NEW YORK

First published 2009
by Routledge
2 Park Square, Milton Park, Abingdon, Oxon, OX14 4RN

Simultaneously published in the USA and Canada
by Routledge
270 Madison Avenue, New York, NY 10016

Routledge is an imprint of the Taylor & Francis Group, an informa business

Typeset in Times New Roman by
Taylor & Francis Books
Printed and bound in Great Britain by
TJ International Ltd, Padstow, Cornwall

British Library Cataloguing in Publication Data
A catalogue record for this book is available from the British
Library

Library of Congress Cataloging in Publication Data
  Walker, Peter, 1955-
    Shaping the humanitarian world / Peter Walker and Daniel G.
Maxwell.
    p. cm. – (Global institutions series)
    Includes bibliographical references and index.
    1. Humanitarian intervention. 2. Humanitarian assistance. I.
Maxwell, Daniel G. II. Title.
    JZ6369.W35 2008
    341.5'84–dc22
                        2008021884

ISBN 978-0-415-77370-6 (hbk)
ISBN 978-0-415-77371-3 (pbk)
ISBN 978-0-203-61453-2 (ebk)

Contents

List of illustrations

Figures

Tables

Foreword

The current volume is the thirtieth in a dynamic series on "global institutions." The series strives (and, based on the volumes published to date, succeeds) to provide readers with definitive guides to the most visible aspects of what many of us know as "global governance." Remarkable as it may seem, there exist relatively few books that offer in-depth treatments of prominent global bodies, processes, and associated issues, much less an entire series of concise and complementary volumes. Those that do exist are either out of date, inaccessible to the non-specialist reader, or seek to develop a specialized understanding of particular aspects of an institution or process rather than offer an overall account of its functioning. Similarly, existing books have often been written in highly technical language or have been crafted "in-house" and are notoriously self-serving and narrow.

The advent of electronic media has undoubtedly helped research and teaching by making data and primary documents of international organizations more widely available, but it has also complicated matters. The growing reliance on the Internet and other electronic methods of finding information about key international organizations and processes has served, ironically, to limit the educational and analytical materials to which most readers have ready access—namely, books. Public relations documents, raw data, and loosely refereed web sites do not make for intelligent analysis. Official publications compete with a vast amount of electronically available information, much of which is suspect because of its ideological or self-promoting slant. Paradoxically, a growing range of purportedly independent web sites offering analyses of the activities of particular organizations has emerged, but one inadvertent consequence has been to frustrate access to basic, authoritative, readable, critical, and well-researched texts. The market for such has actually been reduced by the ready availability of varying quality electronic materials.

For those of us who teach, research, and practice in the area, such limited access to information has been particularly frustrating. We were delighted when Routledge saw the value of a series that bucks this trend and provides key reference points to the most significant global institutions and issues. They are betting that serious students and professionals will want serious analyses. We have assembled a first-rate line-up of authors to address that market. Our intention, then, is to provide one-stop shopping for all readers—students (both undergraduate and postgraduate), negotiators, diplomats, practitioners from nongovernmental and intergovernmental organizations, and interested parties alike—seeking information about the most prominent institutional aspects of global governance.

Shaping the Humanitarian World

Humanitarian issues loom large for contemporary international relations. A number of books in the series have been devoted to human rights,[1] humanitarian action for internally displaced persons and for refugees,[2] and to one of the "gold standard" institutions in this field—the International Committee of the Red Cross (ICRC).[3] We are delighted to add this informative, polished, and well-argued volume on the overall shape of the humanitarian enterprise.

Dealing with the human debris from contemporary wars is anything except straightforward. Killing, maiming, raping, and displacing civilians are all-too-frequent features of the strategies of belligerents. Added to this is the "ethnic cleansing" and the reality of the "well-fed dead"—people who have been temporarily rescued by international efforts but then are abandoned to their fates afterwards—of the post–Cold War period.

The basic identity of humanitarians as straightforwardly life-savers is considerably more complicated today than it was in previous eras. Concerns over the impact of humanitarian action on military and political realities had surfaced routinely in the past, but so-called new wars and new humanitarianisms have led many observers—both insiders and outsiders—to lament the ongoing "crisis in humanitarianism." This debate has led to considerable weeping and gnashing of teeth, as well as many academic and policy analyses. Many observers believe that these debates have generated more heat than light and that it is time for evidence-based humanitarian action—thus, social scientists should closely examine the sector, and practitioners should help ensure that scholars are well grounded in real problems.[4]

Humanitarian organizations have been asked to include in their portfolios everything from peacebuilding to political transformation while they now routinely interact with military forces. Publicity about malfeasance by agencies and personnel has disparaged the enterprise. The titles of recent books on the issue characterize a downward spiral teeming with the sins of saints. Indeed, one of us recently co-authored an inquiry into "confronting new wars and humanitarian crises"[5] that ran together several recent book titles about humanitarianism to posit the following: "Deliver us from evil and the dark sides of virtue, or we are condemned to repeat famine crimes, bear witness to genocide, offer only a bed for the night, and pay the price of indifference along the road to hell."[6] In Afghanistan and Iraq in particular, the humanitarian mantle is in tatters.

As Sadako Ogata wrote in her autobiography of a decade as the UN High Commissioner for Refugees: "There are no humanitarian solutions to humanitarian problems."[7] Even temporary solutions require political will and international engagement.

Given the complexity of a book on the development of humanitarian values and standards, we required not only first-rate scholars with a track record in publishing the very best work in the area, but also people with practical exposure to the kinds of crises that arise routinely in contemporary crises. We were delighted when Peter Walker and Dan Maxwell accepted our invitation to write this book.

Peter Walker is Director of the Feinstein International Famine Center at the School of Nutrition, Tufts University with a long and distinguished career in the field designing and implementing early warning, disaster prevention, and emergency response strategies. As Director of the International Federation of Red Cross and Red Crescent Societies' (IFRC) Disaster Policy Department, he was instrumental in championing the need to professionalize the disaster response business, developing the Code of Conduct for disaster relief workers, lecturing on disaster response in a number of European universities and steering the development of the "Sphere Project," a major NGO collaborative effort to develop universal competence standards in humanitarian assistance. In 1993, Peter founded the annual *World Disasters Report*, which has now become one of the standard reference texts in the humanitarian business. In the past decade, Peter has published in the academic and popular press on themes as diverse as the relationship between the military and humanitarian efforts, the use of local knowledge and skills in relief, the coordination of international relief programs, and the humanitarian effects of economic sanctions.[8]

Dan Maxwell has also had a long and distinguished career in humanitarian programming and management. Currently Associate Professor at the Friedman School of Nutrition Science, and Policy and

Research Director of the Food Security and Livelihoods in Complex Emergencies program at the Feinstein International Center, Tufts University, Dan has 20 years of experience in inter-disciplinary applied social research with an emphasis on famine, food security, and livelihoods. His most recent co-authored works include "Why do Famines Persist in the Horn of Africa? Ethiopia 1999–2003" and *Food Aid After Fifty Years: Recasting its Role.*[9]

As always, we look forward to comments from first-time or veteran readers of the Global Institutions Series.

Thomas G. Weiss, The CUNY Graduate Center, New York, USA
Rorden Wilkinson, University of Manchester, UK August 2008

Acknowledgements

We are indebted to myriad colleagues and disaster victims who, over the past 30 years, have allowed us to work with them in humanitarian operations around the world. In the same vein, we would like to thank our families who have opted into this migratory and uncertain lifestyle. This book would not have got written without the cheerful and meticulous support of our research assistant, Elizabeth Mandeville, and the amazing editing skills of Tim Morris. We also need to thank Tom Weiss and Rorden Wilkinson, the Global Institutions series editors, for suggesting we write this book in the first place and for guidance along the way. Finally, a big thanks to all those at the Feinstein International Center who have reviewed earlier drafts, and to colleagues around the world who have provided material and comment to help complete this work.

Peter Walker and Dan Maxwell
March 2008

List of acronyms and weblink guide

The humanitarian community is increasingly complex and cannot be
described without reference to an, often baffling, array of acronyms.
Here are the key acronyms used in this book.

ALNAP   Active Learning Network for Accountability and
Performance in Humanitarian Action
www.alnap.org
Humanitarian network to improve learning and
accountability

ARC   American Red Cross
www.redcross.org
US national Red Cross Society

BPRM   Bureau for Population, Refugees and Migration
www.state.gov/g/prm
Branch of US State Dept administering US refugee
assistance programs

CAP   Consolidated Appeal Process
http://ochaonline.un.org/cap2005
UN financial appeal organization

CARE   Cooperative for Assistance www.care.org
Major INGO, with 13 national members

CERF   Central Emergency Response Fund
http://cerf.un.org
UN standby fund to provide quick access emergency
funding

CERP   Commander's Emergency Response Program
Funds for US military- led humanitarian assistance
in Iraq and Afghanistan

CEWARN   Conflict Early Warning and Response Mechanism
www.cewarn.org

	IGAD initiative to anticipate and respond to conflict in Horn and East Africa
CHF	Common Humanitarian Fund
	www.unsudanig.org/workplan/chf/index.html
	Country-specific UN pooled funding mechanism
DART	Disaster Assistance Response Team
	A rapidly deployable USAID disaster response unit
DEC	Disasters Emergency Committee
	www.dec.org.uk
	UK NGO fundraising coordination body
DFID	UK Dept. for International Development
	www.dfid.gov.uk
	UK govt. development and relief agency
DPKO	Dept of Peacekeeping Operations
	www.un.org/Depts/dpko/dpko
	UN peacekeeping coordination dept.
ECHO	European Community Humanitarian Aid Office
	http://ec.europa.eu/echo/ataglance_en.htm
	European Commission humanitarian aid department
EMOPS	Office of Emergency Programmes
	www.unicef.org/emerg/index_33578.html
	UNICEF's emergency department
ERC	Emergency Relief Coordinator
	UN humanitarian chief, head of OCHA
ERF	Emergency Response Fund
	UN fund to rapidly support NGO emergency responses
FAO	Food and Agriculture Organization
	www.fao.org
	UN agriculture agency
FEMA	Federal Emergency Management Authority
	www.fema.gov
	US federal government disaster response agency
FEWSNET	Famine Early Warning System Network
	www.fews.net
	USAID-funded global food insecurity forecasting network
FFP	Food for Peace Program
	www.usaid.gov/our_work/humanitarian_assistance/ffp/
	USAID food aid unit
GHD	Good Humanitarian Donorship
	www.goodhumanitariandonorship.org
	Donor governments' initiative to harmonize aid flows
GWOT	Global War on Terror

HAP   Humanitarian Accountability Partnership
                www.hapinternational.org
                Project to make humanitarian action accountable to its
                intended beneficiaries
HC   Humanitarian Coordinator
                In-country head of UN humanitarian response
HIC   Humanitarian Information Centre
                www.humanitarianinfo.org
                Information clearing house for crisis situations
HRR   Humanitarian Response Review
                www.unicef.org/emerg/files/ocha_hrr.pdf
                Independent 2005 UN-published report on humanitarian
                reform options
IASC   Inter-Agency Standing Committee
                www.humanitarianinfo.org/iasc
                Primary international humanitarian coordination
                mechanism
ICRC   International Committee of the Red Cross
                www.icrc.org
                Agency assisting prisoners, wounded, civilians affected
                by conflict
ICVA   International Council of Voluntary Agencies
                www.icva.ch
                Geneva-based umbrella group of NGOs: member of IASC
IDP   Internally Displaced Person
                www.internal-displacement.org
IFRC   International Federation of Red Cross and Red
                Crescent Societies
                www.icrc.org
                Federation of national Red Cross/ Crescent National
                Societies
IGAD   Intergovernmental Authority on Development
                www.igad.org
                Six- country regional development organization in
                Horn and East Africa
IHL   International Humanitarian Law
IMF   International Monetary Fund
                www.imf.org
                Together with World Bank comprises the Bretton Wood
                Institutions
INGO   international non-governmental organization

InterAction American Council for Voluntary International Action
www.interaction.org
Umbrella group of 150 US-based INGOs, member of IASC

IOM International Organization for Migration
www.iom.int
Inter-governmental organization promoting orderly migration

IRIN Integrated Regional Information Network
www.irinnews.org
Online UN humanitarian news agency

ISCA International Save the Children Alliance
www.savethechildren.net
Coalition of 28 child-focused NGOs

MDGs Millennium Development Goals
www.un.org/millenniumgoals
Eight UN goals to assist world's poorest

MSF Médecins Sans Frontières
www.msf.org
Coalition of NGOs

NFI non-food item

NGO non-governmental organization

OCHA Office for the Coordination of Humanitarian Affairs
http://ochaonline.un.org
UN agency to coordinate humanitarian response

ODA Official Development Assistance
Humanitarian/development funding provided by OECD member governments

OECD Organization for Economic Cooperation and Development
www.oecd.org
Organization of developed countries

OECD/DAC Development Assistance Committee, Organization for Economic Cooperation and Development
http://www.oecd.org/dac/
OECD unit for cooperation with developing countries, compiler of ODA statistics

OFDA Office of Foreign Disaster Assistance
www.usaid.gov/our_work/humanitarian_assistance/disaster_assistance/
Emergency response unit of USAID

OHCHR Office of the High Commissioner for Human Rights
www.ohchr.org
UN human rights agency

SC	Security Council
	www.un.org/sc/
	United Nations Security Council
SCHR	Steering Committee for Humanitarian Response
	www.humanitarianinfo.org/iasc/content/about/schr.asp
	Alliance of eight major INGOs, member of IASC
UNDP	United Nations Development Programme
	www.undp.org
	UN development agency
UNFPA	United Nations Population Fund
	www.unfpa.org
	UN population agency
UNHCR	Office of the UN High Commissioner for Refugees
	www.unhcr.org
	UN refugee agency
UNICEF	UN Children's Fund
	www.unicef.org
	UN child protection/assistance agency
UNOCHA	UN Office for the Coordination of Humanitarian Affairs
	http://ochaonline.un.org
	UN agency to coordinate humanitarian response
UNRWA	UN Relief and Works Agency for Palestine Refugees
	www.unrwa.org
	UN agency assisting Palestinian refugees
USAID	US Agency for International Development
	www.usaid.gov
	US government humanitarian / development agency
VOICE	Voluntary Organizations in Cooperation in Emergencies
	www.ngovoice.org
	Network of 90 European INGOs
WFP	UN World Food Programme
	www.wfp.org
	UN food aid agency
WHO	World Health Organization
	www.who.org
	UN health agency
WVI	World Vision International
	www.wvi.org
	International partnership of Christian INGOs

Introduction
Humanitarian response today

If one sought to account for the success of *homo sapiens* on earth over the past few million years, one could sum it up in one word—adaptation. Likewise, where the species has failed, it has been through its inability to adapt.

How people and societies react to disaster, war, and other cataclysmic events revolves around adaptation. The disaster happens and survivors adapt to cope with the new reality. Disasters happen and the national and international system adapts to cope with their changing pattern and the changing political and economic environment which allows for this or that adaptation.

The international humanitarian system, the subject of this book, is not a logical construct. It is the result of many, often competing, processes. Some driven by self-interest or national interest, some by ideology, some by altruism, but all about adaptation; adaptation to changing needs, as war shifts from predominantly international and between armies to predominantly civil and within populations; adaptation to improved knowledge and technology as we are better able to predict flooding, hurricane paths and extended periods of drought; adaptation to available resources as the national political expediency of reacting to someone else's tragedy waxes and wanes. Adaptation to new ways of organizing and communicating as once-national non-governmental organizations (NGOs) go transnational and previously government-focused UN agencies look to civil society and commerce for new partnerships and avenues to effect change.

The future will surely be shaped by how these and less understood processes of adaptation pan out. How will the system adapt to climate change? How will it adapt to the rise of Asia as an economic power focus? How will it adapt to the ever increasing ability of non-state actors to wield power for good—through mighty funding foundations and service provision—or power for destruction though terrorism and technology-fueled mass aggression?

The international humanitarian system

The international humanitarian system evolved. It was never designed, and like most products of evolution, it has its anomalies, redundancies, inefficiencies, and components evolved for one task being adapted to another. Evolution enables the system to adapt and continue to provide service as the political, social and economic environs change. Biological evolution is driven by the tendency of one generation of DNA to seek the most effective way of ensuring its survival into the next. The mechanisms it uses to ensure this are mutation and natural selection.

The international humanitarian system has its equivalents. Its driving tendency, one increasingly under threat, is to prevent and alleviate human suffering wherever it may be found. At heart, this is the principle of *humanity*—that humankind is one family and it is an intrinsic part of our humanity to both seek assistance and wish to provide assistance to those in need.

The international humanitarian system is a system that allows those caught up in crisis to articulate what they need to alleviate their suffering while allowing others in the human family, who are better off, to provide the resources to meet those needs. It is a people-to-people structure with governments, agencies and aid organizations as the go-betweens.

The principle of humanity, however, needs some caveats if it is to work in a world of finite resources and conflicting agendas. All suffering everywhere cannot be addressed instantly. The principle of *impartiality* evolved to address this conundrum. Impartiality, as used in the humanitarian context, encapsulates two concepts. First, that suffering is addressed without discrimination. Nationality, race, religious beliefs, class, or political opinions make no difference. Second, because resources are finite, priority is given to the most urgent cases of need. The system should function to alleviate the suffering of individuals, guided solely by the severity and urgency of their needs.

In order to do this, two operating principles have evolved—the notions of *neutrality* and *independence*.

To alleviate suffering the aid provider must have access to those in need. This often means accessing people in the midst of a conflict, a war or a politically fraught situation. To gain impartial access, the aid provider needs to be trusted. Those waging war, or seeking to drive a political agenda, need to be confident that the aid provider is motivated only by a desire to alleviate suffering and is not going to "interfere" in the conflict or political discourse. This is the principle of neutrality. It is a means to an end, a way to bolster impartiality and maximize the possibility of getting access to those who are suffering. However, it comes at a price. If one side in a conflict is committing mass atrocities, against an oppressed rival—and that oppression looks set to continue and to cause more suffering—is it morally defensible to claim neutrality and not take sides? Working through this dilemma, or finding a third way to both be neutral and address root causes of suffering, is an increasingly demanding agenda for humanitarian agencies and their staff.

The notion of independence seeks to support both impartiality and neutrality by ensuring that the humanitarian agency is able to make its own decisions free from undue coercion. Like neutrality, this is an increasingly difficult concept to put into practice. If an agency receives substantial funding from one government, is it still independent? If the majority of an agency's staff are of one nationality, religion, or political persuasion, are they still independent?

Seeking to alleviate suffering according to these principles, humanitarian agencies sit between those who are suffering and those who have the resources to alleviate that suffering. They are entrusted with resources by the donor community of governments, foundations, and the general public and trusted by the beneficiary community to provide appropriate, timely and impartial assistance. They therefore have multiple accountabilities: to the beneficiaries, the donors, standards of professionalism, and internally to their own governance.

These agencies broadly fall into four categories.

1 They may be subsets of an individual country's aid structures. For example, USAID—the US government body for funding and carrying out international development and humanitarian activities—has Disaster Assistance Response Teams (DART) for carrying out assessments in disasters.

2 They may be multilateral organizations, often agencies of the UN, like the World Food Programme (WFP) or UNICEF, or outside of the UN, like the International Organization for Migration (IOM).

3 They may be part of the Red Cross and Red Crescent Movement, which encompasses all 186 national Red Cross or Red Crescent Societies, a Federation which brings them together, and the International Committee of the Red Cross (ICRC).

4 They may be structured groups of private citizens: community-based organizations (CBOs), which tend to arise from within communities in crisis, or non-governmental organizations (NGOs), which are often external to, but wanting to assist the crisis-affected people.

In reality, the majority of international humanitarian assistance is ultimately delivered by the Red Cross and Red Crescent Movement along with NGOs around the world. Organizationally, this can mean anything from one-man shows to transnationals with budgets amounting to billions of dollars. UN agencies may pass funds and work on to NGOs and NGOs may partner with CBOs or local government structures. This complex system of actions and accountabilities is illustrated in Figure I.1.

Funds can flow directly from concerned individuals to these operational NGOs, or via governments in the shape of tax revenue passed on as grants and contracts. They can also flow from charitable foundations or from corporations, either as philanthropic donations or as contracts to deliver service. Government funds can flow to a UN agency and be passed on to an NGO, who can pass them on to a CBO. The cash flow of the humanitarian system is shown in Figure I.2.

We have a complex web of relationships, loosely guided by a set of principles, but principles which not all components of the web would accept and which may sometimes be subordinated to other agendas. We have dilemmas which create tension. Do we address suffering now or address the causes of suffering? Do we address the suffering we have funding for, and ignore the crises we cannot raise funds for? Do we work with organizations which are manifestly not neutral, when our

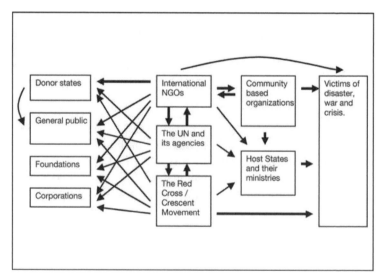

Figure I.1 Humanitarian accountabilities

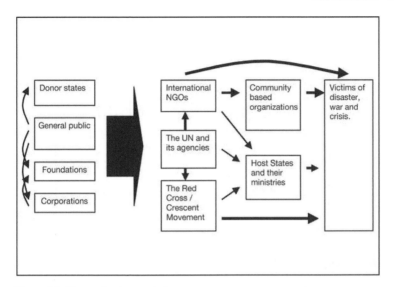

Figure I.2 Humanitarian cash flow

agendas seem to overlap, or do we preserve our independence? Do we accept any funds or are some attached strings too restrictive?

The humanitarian system sits within a causal environment, as shown in Figure I.3. Shocks and hazards act on vulnerable populations to cause a humanitarian crisis. Agencies intervene to drive outcomes which will hopefully alleviate suffering, promote human rights, and support livelihoods. In the best possible world, this assistance renders the population less vulnerable and more able to withstand shocks and hazards.

Thinking through, and dealing in a practical way, with these pressures, tensions and dilemmas is the story of the evolution of the international humanitarian system and its future trajectory. It is this story that we hope this book will tell.

Chapters 1–3 take us through history, showing how the system came into being. Chapters 4–6 describe the major components of the system and Chapter 7 looks to the future and how the system may have to evolve. Chapter 1 describes the early history, from ancient stirrings of humanitarianism through the formative years of the mid-1800s to mid-1900s when the main principles and institutions, that are now called the international humanitarian system, were established. Chapter 2 deals with the growth of humanitarianism during the Cold War years and covers some of the major formative operations of that time

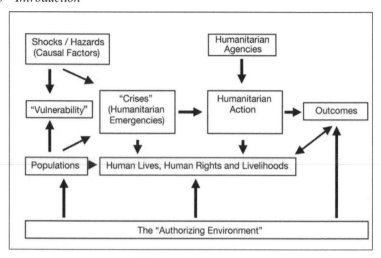

Figure I.3 The humanitarian world

including famine in Biafra, Cambodia, the Sahel and the Horn of Africa along with the birth of famine early warning systems. In Chapter 3, we look at the more recent history bringing us up and into the Global War on Terror. In particular, we examine the response to the Balkans crisis in the 1990s and the 1994 Rwanda Genocide, out of which flowed so many of the reforms to the system which are flagged in later chapters. The role and responsibilities of national states, both as responders at home and overseas, are analyzed in Chapter 4, with a handful of northern and southern state systems being described in some detail by way of illustration. Chapter 5 focuses on the inter-state institutions, principally the UN and its agencies, along with the more innovative recent systems they have put in place to improve humanitarian action. In Chapter 6, we seek to describe the world of the humanitarian NGOs, picking out a few of the larger ones for explicit description and also focusing on the collective improvements to the system which NGOs have led. Finally, in Chapter 7, we examine what we think are the key challenges to the humanitarian system today and where that system may need to go in the future.

Humanitarian action is organized to alleviate acute suffering in crises that usually take place outside of the aid giver's home community. Today this implies international action. It aims primarily to save lives, but increasingly looks to lay the foundations for rebuilding livelihoods. It is premised on the assumption that all lives are of equal worth and so seeks to act impartially. In order to do this, much of the humanitarian system believes it needs to be seen to be independent from the power brokers of the day—be they state, religious, corporate, or renegade—strongly emphasizing independence and neutrality.

One thing that changes little in this epic is the people under the system: those caught up in crisis that the system purports to support—from the sixteenth-century Huguenot refugees to the twenty-first-century tsunami victims.

Over 150 years ago, Ireland suffered a massive famine. Estimates vary, but between half a million and one million people died in 1846–1849. Maybe two million fled the country, to Great Britain, the United States, Canada, and Australia. The famine just about halved Ireland's population and today with a total population of around six million people in the Republic of Ireland and Northern Ireland, the island has still not reached pre-famine population levels. One hundred years later, Charles McGlinchey was in his nineties but with a clear memory of his youth and the stories from his father of how he and Charles' mother survived the Great Famine.[1] McGlinchey portrays destitute families walking from town to town looking for work. He describes women gathering herbs from the hedges to feed their children and when these are no longer to be had, making cookies out of mud and grass to at least fill them with something. He describes how normal it became to come across emaciated corpses in roadside ditches and how the price of grain, and indeed any food, skyrocketed as the price of land, the only thing the peasant had to sell, plummeted. Stories from Bengal in 1943, Biafra in 1968, and Ethiopia in 1973, 1985, 1991; from floods in Bangladesh in 1973 or New Orleans in 2005 all tell the same story. Families do everything in their power to survive crises. Famine foods, coping mechanisms, livelihood adaptation—all the lexicon of modern crisis research—just seek to describe and understand what people have done and will continue to do to protect their families and communities and survive.

Historians tell us that in Ireland a combination of centuries of subjugation under foreign rule, a divisive land tenure system, and poor and exploitative government had reduced the Irish peasantry to a near permanent state of destitution. Then the one food crop they controlled—potatoes, because they grew it in their back gardens—was wiped out in a matter of weeks by an epidemic of the potato blight *Phytophthora*.

A vulnerable population is impacted by a new hazard too heavy to bear and disaster ensues. This equation is at the heart of every crisis.

That is the humanitarian crisis writ large: a people rendered vulnerable by economics, politics or geography, a hazard that overwhelms normalcy, and a determined, inventive and harsh struggle to survive. Throughout most of human history that would have been the totality of describing such crises, but today there is a fourth element, intervention from outside to alleviate the suffering and, perhaps, support the strategies and aspirations of the survivors. Today we take it for granted that there is an intentional humanitarian system, but in truth it is a very new phenomenon. The next chapter will describe its early history, but even as that history evolved, the notion of the greater community acting for the greater good of the minority who were suffering was no foregone conclusion.

In the 1930s, the Great Depression raged across the United States. The stock market crash of 1929 wiped out the paper value of stock. Agricultural production fell by half as coincidental drought hit the Great Plains, creating the dust bowl so well captured in John Steinbeck's *Grapes of Wrath*. In the cities, unemployment soared to 25 percent. Fifteen million people were out of work across the nation and average wages were down 60 percent on their pre-crash levels. Today one can watch film, shot in New York City in 1931, showing people selling single apples on street corners, massive queues at soup kitchens in Manhattan, and children and women picking over the city's garbage dumps looking for food and anything sellable. In Central Park there were shanty towns built by the homeless and destitute—known as Hoovervilles after the then president who believed that recovery should largely be a "natural" process allowed to take its course.

Hoover's opponent in the 1932 presidential race had a radically different approach. Franklin D. Roosevelt proposed intervention, the New Deal, whereby the Federal government accepted responsibility to alleviate the worst of the suffering and manage the economy back to prosperity. The realization that is shocking to us today is that prior to Roosevelt's "radical" New Deal the notion that the state should intervene to curb suffering just didn't exist. The New Deal heralded America's national humanitarian system, as it were. A decade later, while much of the world staggered out of the devastation of World War II, it was the same Roosevelt and his wife, Eleanor, who were instrumental in starting the international mechanisms which would later become integral to the intentional humanitarian system—the United Nations, the Bretton Woods Institutions,[2] the Conventions on Human Rights and the rise of citizen action to both provide services and effect policy change.

The Reuters news agency runs a specialized website for humanitarian crises (www.alertnet.org). The headlines on the site today, as we write this chapter, are typical of the gamut of humanitarian crises and responders:

More rain hits flood stricken Indonesian capital.
Pakistan government plays down bird flu risk.
Church World Service latest situation report on Guinean civil strife.
UNHCR concerned about 400 people stuck on drifting ship off Africa.

Weather-induced disasters, civil war, refugees, UN agencies, government actors, NGOs and disaster victims, all caught in the fixated gaze of the international media.

The theory of how the international humanitarian system should work is quite simple. A crisis deepens to the point where massive suffering is imminent or a sudden disaster threatens the lives of many. Unable to cope with the rapidity or severity of the crisis, local authorities—usually government, but not always—appeal for international assistance. International bodies translate their own assessment of local needs, and the local appeal, into an international appeal and plan of action. The UN, through its Office for the Coordination of Humanitarian Affairs (OCHA) may issue an emergency appeal drawing on the projected plans of all the UN agencies. The Red Cross Movement may do the same. International NGOs, in groups or individually, will do likewise. Funds will be raised, supplies purchased and shipped, expert personnel flown out and all applied, in close coordination with the local authorities and community, to the task of alleviating suffering. The relief is effective, the crisis recedes and the international system stands down. This is the theory. In practice, it is far messier, far less effective and far more political.

Three days of torrential rain in February 2007 brought floods up to 3m deep to the metropolis of Jakarta, Indonesia's capital. The homes of nine million people were threatened as 340,000 people were rendered homeless. The city's Crisis Center organized inflatable boats and helicopters on rescue missions, field kitchens and tents to provide temporary accommodation and sustenance, and water pumps to try and bring vital hospitals back into action. The local Red Cross mobilized hundreds of local volunteer aid workers. The city authorities did not make an appeal for assistance, nor did the national government or the national Red Cross but, to quote from a UN press release at the time: "Though the Government has issued no formal request for international assistance, a wide range of countries and international non-governmental organizations (NGOs) are now providing assistance or stand ready to assist Indonesia."[3]

On the other side of the world, Malawi, one of the poorest countries in Africa, has faced a severe food crisis for two years. Forty percent of the population need food aid. When an international appeal was finally made, food aid flooded in but appeals for seeds, tools, and fertilizers to boost future food production were neglected. Crisis averted—until next year.

Every year Médecins Sans Frontières (MSF), an NGO regarded by some as a maverick—by others as the most consistently humanitarian non-governmental agency—publishes its list of "forgotten disasters." In 2006, its top 10 accounted for only 7.2 minutes of air time out of a total of over 14,000 minutes of nightly news coverage on the United States' top three TV networks.[4] Top of their list was the civil war in the Central African Republic (CAR) where fighting between government troops and various rebel groups forced tens of thousands of civilians to flee into the jungle, often into rebel-controlled areas where aid agencies had no access. In late 2005, the UN appealed for just under $47 million to address the crisis over the next year. By the end of 2005, however, donors had contributed just $25 million.[5]

In early 2007, USAID announced on its website:

> *USAID Awards National Capacity Development Program in Iraq*: The U.S. Agency for International Development (USAID) has awarded the cooperative agreement for the Iraq National Capacity Development Program (NCD) to Management Systems International, Inc. (MSI), a Washington, D.C. based consulting firm. NCD is a two year, plus one option year program valued up to $165 million.[6]

These developments in Indonesia, Malawi, CAR, and Iraq encapsulate the major challenges facing the international humanitarian system today. Challenges of being evidence-driven, and sufficiently resourced; of addressing cause as well as symptom and of being impartial and neutral in so doing.

These key challenges will resonate throughout the rest of this book as we examine the history, makeup and future of the international humanitarian system.

Before moving on to these issues, however, we need to address a fundamental and often overlooked problem. To put it bluntly, why bother? Why should people on one side of the planet go out of their way to alleviate the suffering of others in places where there is no obvious gain to be made—no market for one's trade to be developed, no useful alliances to be forged, no indispensable natural resources to be tapped?

Many look to moral philosophy or religious beliefs to justify such seemingly selfless behavior, but this reasoning is self-evidently flawed. If humanitarianism proposes to be universal, then one needs to find a universal driver for it, not one confined to a particular culture or religion. In 1859, Jean Henri Dunant, a Swiss businessman, witnessed the aftermath of the battle of Solferino in Italy. He organized local women to provide relief to the wounded on the battlefield and thus the International Red Cross was born. Why did he do this? In that same year, 1859, Charles Darwin, after many years of preparation, finally published his monumental work *On the Origin of Species*. Darwin reflected on the seemingly altruistic habits of social insects, like bees or ants, where sexless drones, who will never have offspring, lay down their lives for the greater good of the hive. Why are they altruistic?[7]

Two of Darwin's greatest early proponents obsessively, but in very different ways, drove forward this debate. Thomas Huxley, the free marketeering British Empire bulldog, well versed in both Darwin's and Russell's descriptions of the highly competitive ecologies of the tropics, was clear. For Huxley, altruism makes sense only in the context of family.[8] My brother shares a large proportion of my genes, so if I give up my life to save him, many of my genes will survive. A hundred years later, Richard Dawkins refers to this as the "Selfish Gene."[9] A continent away, Russian prince-turned-anarchist Peter Kropotkin, studying human and animal life in the desolate and only recently inhabited tundra of Siberia, sees things differently and believes that mutual aid and cooperation are as strong a driving force in evolution as competition is in ensuring the survival of the fittest.[10] Both men are, of course, mixing their scientific understanding with their political desires and both are trying to explain altruism.

Today the mathematical theorems which describe the role of altruism in evolution are well established[11] and at one level Huxley was right. The evidence from almost every species examined suggests that altruism is a family matter; it is strongest between genetically close individuals and weakens as their percentage of mutually shared genes decreases. The one examined species that challenges the theory is *Homo sapiens*. We show all the expected behavior of family-driven altruism: protection of children, significantly reduced care for adopted, non-genetically related children and so on, but *Homo sapiens* go further and appears to apply the evolutionary mechanism of altruism to the larger family of mankind, choosing, as it were, to conceive of mankind as the family, rather than be limited by the mechanisms of genes.

Robert Wright, in his provocative analysis of cultural evolution,[12] posits that mankind has demonstrated a propensity to drive social and cultural evolution in one direction—towards greater complexity of relationships and towards greater "win–win" situations where ever larger and more diverse groups, fueled by ever-improving communications and trust, mutually benefit from their relationships. In essence, Wright shows how the propensity to aid people at a distance, provided by the evolution of altruism, is developed beyond the family to the clan, the tribe, the city-state, the nation, and ultimately the international community. Humanitarianism, Wright might argue, is one small part of the logical extension of 15,000 years of human cultural evolution.

This is the crux of the matter. The urge to assist others, to behave altruistically, is an innate part of being human but what is important for this discussion is how humankind chooses to use this faculty. We choose to conceive of humankind as one family and to build systems which allow just about anybody to participate in humanitarian action. Individuals can participate directly as volunteers or paid staff of agencies, or indirectly by contributing funds to relief programs. Corporations can participate, states can participate.

Today, a veritable menagerie of individuals, civil society organizations, state institutions, international bodies, corporations, international treaties, and conventions make up the so-called system, more akin to an ecosystem, which seeks to act in times of crisis. The ideals outlined above are not a set of preconceived properties for the system, but rather a commonly agreed yardstick that has evolved against which components in the system, and the system as a whole, should be judged.

The modern history of humanitarianism is largely one of the struggle to keep the system on track. Darwin, as ever, foresaw this:

> As man advances in civilization, and small tribes are united into larger communities, the simplest reason would tell each individual that he ought to extend his social instincts and sympathies to all the members of the same nation, though personally unknown to him. This point being once reached, there is only an artificial barrier to prevent his sympathies extending to the men of all nations and races.[13]

1 Origins of the international humanitarian system

There is no simple history of humanitarianism, or the construction of a system to make that notion a reality. There are many strands to be followed, strands now woven together to form the system we recognize. Understanding the history of humanitarian action helps understand why it is the way it is today, and helps identify how it can, and maybe should, change in the future. All too often, we simply accept that the way things are is the way they have to be. History allows us to challenge this notion. It demonstrates that original founding ideals can become distorted as organizations develop. It shows us that apparently inseparable alliances are in reality temporary conveniences, and it shows us, particularly when we look at humanitarianism, that individuals can make a difference.

In this chapter, we will look at the early history of humanitarianism and some of its precursors in the form of charitable imperatives and actions in the major religions and cultures that have helped shape today's humanitarian system. In some ways the chapter tracks two separate histories. The history of humanitarian action for war victims, and the history of disaster response for victims of natural disaster. We track both because today, so many communities are afflicted by both, and the causal nature of today's crises, often labeled complex emergencies, makes the distinction between man-made and natural crises distinctly dubious. To the victim and the responder, it is the crisis and its effects, not the classification of its cause, that matters.

Historical and religious precursors

One of the earliest recordings we have of what might be, if not humanitarian, at least charitable action comes from the tomb inscriptions of Harkhuf, the governor of Upper Egypt in the twenty-third century BCE. The inscriptions on his tomb, which read like an over-zealous curriculum vitae, document his many trading ventures south into what we now know as Sudan ensuring the reader knows how well respected Harkhuf was by his rulers and peers. At the very beginning of his self-aggrandizement, he proclaims: "I gave bread to the hungry, clothing to the naked, I ferried him who had no boat."[1] Harkhuf is making it clear not only that he did these things, but by including them right at the beginning of his tomb inscription, we might deduce that in ancient Egyptian society such acts were meritorious.

On the other side of the world, and nearly two thousand years later, the Li Ki (usually known in English as the Book of Rites)—a collection of Chinese cultural and religious practices from the eighth to the fifth century BCE—records state support for widows and orphans.[2]

Now travel west and a little forward in time. Food scarcity, sometimes verging on famine, was a regular feature of urban life in the ancient Greek and Roman world. Between 330 and 320 BCE Cyrene, a Greek colony in present-day Libya, sent grain supplies to 41 communities in Greece to alleviate famine. In AD 6 during the reign of Emperor Augustus, and again in AD 12 and AD 32 during the reign of Tiberius, Rome was threatened with famine. The crisis of AD 6 was by far the most serious. Augustus reacted with a series of measures that would not seem unfamiliar today. He expelled "extraneous" personnel from Rome, including most foreigners and the retinues of most officials. He introduced grain rationing and appointed a senior senator to oversee the supply of grain and bread across the city. He doubled the grain handouts to the destitute. Unlike his successors, Tiberius and Nero, he did not resort to grain price-fixing.[3] Was this charitable action or self-interested defense of the state?

As we progress from archeology to history, the philosophy of charitable action becomes intimately tied up with the evolution of religious ideals and institutions. It is the monotheist religions of Judaism, Islam and Christianity that have most directly contributed to today's humanitarian system.

Notions of charity and support for those less well-off are central to the Christian faith. Prior to AD 325, when the Roman emperor Constantine effectively co-opted Christianity as a state religion, acts of charity were the business of the individual or the ruling elite. Constantine shifted this burden to the church, saving the Roman state tax money and paving the way for over a thousand years (till the Protestant Reformation) of Catholic Church domination of organized charity in Europe.

In the 1340s, the Black Death (the bubonic plague) killed between one- and two-thirds of Europe's population and irrevocably changed

European societies. Major changes in demographics led to changes in land tenure and the relationship between the landed elite and the working farmer. The pre-eminence of the church as spiritual guide and charitable giver, as provider of cure, treatment, and explanation, faded.[4] These social upheavals laid the foundation of discontent that gave birth to the reformation. In 1517, Martin Luther, in Germany, crystallized discontent across the old world order and paved the way for the creation of Protestant denominations. Under Protestantism, charity and social order were more firmly linked. For the burghers of the newly-formed Protestant states, poverty was not the enemy, but rather the unacceptable social face of destitution. Their object was not to wage war on poverty, which remained a fact of life, but to attack its distorted forms and disreputable causes—begging, vagrancy, and willful idleness. They strove to establish a stable, disciplined, and laborious society in which all people would work as much as they were able and find whatever care they needed from within their communities.[5] Many of the non-governmental organizations (NGOs) active today in humanitarian relief trace their origins to this Protestant ethic of charity.

Islam, founded in the early fifth century by the Prophet Muhammad in what is now Saudi Arabia, like Judaism, embodied a notion of charity as a duty. The notion of zakat, dutiful charitable giving—one of the five Pillars of Islam—is derived from a direct interpretation of the Quran. In contemporary Muslim societies zakat ranges across a spectrum from individual acts of charity to institutions fully incorporated into the state and tantamount to a national tax welfare system.[6] Some Islamic scholars have held that zakat is fundamentally different from the Christian concept of charity, being based on the premise that both individual need and class distinctions run counter to Islam and the good of society. They assert that the doctrine of zakat, where it was incorporated into state institutions, represented the first formal social security system.[7] The other Islamic tradition which is of importance to us here is waqf, the Islamic equivalent of a charitable foundation dating back to pre-Islamic days. It is often used to set up an endowment to fund the purchase of land for the construction of a building which will be used for charitable purposes—such as a mosque, school, hospital, or orphanage. At the start of the nineteenth century, at least half of the lands of the sprawling Ottoman empire were administered under waqf[8] and between the fourteenth and nineteenth centuries a vast system of public soup kitchens was established across the empire to hand out free food to the needy.[9]

What we should take away from this brief religious overview is that ideals of charity, the alleviation of the suffering of others, and the forming of organized bodies to carry out these acts, are not the pre-rogative of any one religious or philosophical tradition. Our present humanitarian system, historically dominated as it is by the patronage of the powerful states of the nineteenth and twentieth centuries, reflects the predominantly Christian, and particularly Protestant, philosophical heritage which has shaped the powerful states of Europe and North America. This is fundamentally important, as we look to the future of humanitarianism, we must acknowledge that the rationale and philosophy that underlies humanitarianism has its roots in universal altruistic human behavior. It is expressed and practiced in all major, and one might imagine most minor, world religions and philosophies. Humanitarianism does not have to be shackled by its past.

The beginnings of a system: refugees, earthquakes, and famine

The term "refugee," so closely associated today with humanitarian work, was first coined in seventeenth-century Europe to describe the wave of French and Walloon Protestants fleeing Catholic Europe to seek refuge in Protestant England. During the reign of Queen Elizabeth the First at the end of the sixteenth century, some 50,000 refugees fled to England. This was the first recorded instance of a major movement of people fleeing religious persecution—rather than economic deprivation—and being formally received and offered refuge by a state. Andrea Paras draws parallels between this period of history and today's complex emergencies.[10] The Protestants were being perse-cuted and killed in droves in Catholic Europe. England saw itself as a bastion of Protestantism and had the military power to intervene directly in support of the persecuted—while also furthering its own territorial ambitions. The state, the church, and individuals all assisted in helping those who fled from Europe to settle in England, a country with a long history of deep suspicions towards all foreigners.

We should not get too carried away with the analogy between modern refugee action and that of Elizabethan England. Good Queen Bess (who at the time was profiting handsomely from the early slave trade to the Americas) did not choose to assist the equally persecuted Jews, or, indeed, other less popular Protestant sects. England's actions were essentially political and its treatment of the arriving refugees, although better than the past norm for foreigners (hostility and mar-ginalization), was self-serving.

If the support for Huguenot refugees marks the first stirrings of humanitarian action in the face of conflict, the first recorded instance in modern history of a comprehensive disaster response strategy and post-disaster international relief operation was triggered by the earthquake which destroyed the Portuguese capital, Lisbon in 1755. Portugal's First Minister, the Marquês de Pombal, is credited with ordering the burial of the dead the day after the quake, the prompt distribution of food and freezing of grain prices, dispatch of peacekeeping troops and proclamation of a city rebuilding plan within a week of the quake—a response plan and operation which puts that of many modern cities to shame.[11] Both the Spanish Crown and the British Parliament, upon hearing of the disaster, sent aid. Writing three years after the event, Emmerich de Vattel notes that "the calamities of Portugal have given England an opportunity of fulfilling the duties of humanity." Drawing on this experience, de Vattel goes on to lay down what he sees as one of the precepts of good nationhood: "if a nation is afflicted with famine, all those who have provisions to spare aught to relieve her distress without, however, exposing themselves to want."[12] Humanitarian action, thought de Vattel, was an intrinsic property of sovereignty.

Even in these early stirrings we can see that the history of humanitarianism is effectively shaped by two of the four Horsemen of the Apocalypse: war and famine. The modern story of war and humanitarian action starts in 1859 in northern Italy, but the story of famine and humanitarian action starts in India and Ireland.

The beginnings of a global system

What is clear with hindsight is that something changed around the middle of the nineteenth century which galvanized humanitarian action, by states and private individuals, from a handful of disconnected instances to a more organized series of thought-through policies and activities with global connections.

It can surely be no coincidence that this period in history also marks the first true period of globalization. Under the European and Ottoman empires the globe was connected like never before and would not be so connected again from the end of World War I to the 1990s. The revolution of railways and telegraph had connected trading routes and travel across the world. Those from the imperial heartlands could travel with relative ease to every continent and, from their living rooms in the metropolitan centers of London, Paris or Istanbul, could summon goods from across the world.[13] For the first time, the enlightened, the philanthropic, and the politically ambitious had a global stage to play on and the wealth and tools to make a difference.

As the nineteenth century progressed, security concerns and suffering on the other side of the world were no longer "out there," remote and reported many weeks after the event. It was close to home, through the telegraph and mass circulation newspapers and growing familiarity with the names of countries supplying tea, coffee, and the raw materials of empire. It was this transformation of the world into its first manifestation of a global village that provided the fertile ground upon which notions of international humanitarian action could take seed.

The response to the famine of 1837–38 in India organized by the East India Company, the quintessential empire-machine, marked the first time that modern principles of relief emerge in the history of humanitarian action. Organized public works providing food or cash in return for work, coupled with free food distribution for the most destitute, were first experimented with in northern India—despite formal British adherence to the values of an unfettered free market economy. Historians have argued that a fear of public disorder, a sense of humanitarian responsibility, and simple pragmatic concerns over maintaining a governable nation, pushed the administration to act.

The language used to describe those seeking relief at the time is instructive. They were referred to as destitute, paupers, vagrants, and the "laboring poor"—terminology which essentially depicted them as a threat to law and order until they could be returned to their assigned role in agricultural and industrial workforces. Relief works not only sought to put the laboring poor back to work, but were seen as opportunities to encourage discipline and obedience to authority within the confines of the controlled relief camps.[14]

The colonial statistics gathered at the time not only document the scarcity of food and the growing numbers of laboring poor, but also the rise in crime, particularly collective crime. Attacks by groups of people, not always solely the destitute, on granaries, carts transporting grain, and other sources of food rose dramatically. At the time the colonial administrators saw this as simple criminality, reinforcing the image of the famine sufferers not as victims but as threats. A more objective analysis would highlight the moral economy of these acts. Collective attacks are about acquiring relief but are also protesting and challenging the system that is causing the suffering in the first place.[15] The colonial rulers sought to maintain the status quo and ensure famine did not lead to revolution. The famished peasantry sought to survive and challenge a system which slotted them into preordained subservience.

This experiment, with relief following strict economic principles and steeped in the political dogma of the day, carried over from India to Ireland a short seven years later.

1845 to 1849 saw Western Europe's last great famine. Although the proximate cause of the Irish famine was the potato blight *Phytophthora*—which virtually destroyed the Irish people's central subsistence crop—the subsequent death by starvation of one and a half million people and the flight of a further two million as economic migrants was the result of the political and economic relationship between Ireland, the conquered state, and Britain, the conqueror.[16] From the twelfth century onward, a series of invasions had gradually brought Ireland under British control. Initial British attempts to assimilate with the Irish gave way in the mid-fourteenth century to a series of laws to enforce the separate development of the native Irish from the ruling British. By the mid-seventeenth century Catholics were legally barred from the army, the professions, commerce, land owner-ship, participation in elections, and other avenues of public life in order to consolidate control by a newly-installed Protestant elite. Although repealed in 1829, these Penal Laws, as they were known, effectively set up an apartheid system. In war-ravaged Ireland, potatoes became the crop of choice because they could be grown on poor land and with-stand the trampling of marauding armies. When the potato crop rotted in 1845, 1846, and 1847, a politically marginalized and impoverished population were robbed of the one crop they could grow in their gar-dens that would provide enough food to survive.

The state reaction at the time was initially to open up public works modeled on the Indian example, funded by the wealthy of the districts where relief works were to take place and in theory providing a subsistence wage to anyone willing to work on the construction of public goods such as roads, land improvement, and docks. The sub-sistence wages were never enough to compete with the inflated price of what little food was available, and certainly not enough to encourage its commercial importation. Indeed, at the time, Ireland was still exporting grain and did not become a net importer until two years into the famine.[17] The works, where they were completed, benefited land owners and business, not the peasantry. At their peak in March 1847, three-quarters of a million people were employed on such schemes. By the summer of that year, all the works were closed down, as it became clear that local funding was never going to provide even a fraction of the cost of running them. Direct aid in the form of soup kitchens was introduced in the spring of 1847. By July, three million "meals" a day of watery soup were being served. By September, the kitchens were closed down as funding from local authorities and charities dried up. The following winter saw massive death by starvation.

The course of the Irish famine also demonstrates two prevailing polarized views of humanitarian action. At one end of the spectrum, the Tory Prime Minister, Robert Peel, was convinced that only the massive and unimpeded importation of food, effectively mass food aid, would alleviate the famine. At the other end, the Whig or Liberal Party would not countenance any interference in the free market, believing any major attempt to prevent famine would bankrupt landowners and industry, destroy self-dependence, and ultimately slow down economic growth.[18] The Whigs came to power in 1847 and soon realized a *laissez-faire* free market response might prompt a full-scale Irish rebellion, at a time when Britain's economy was ill suited to sustain such a cost. Relief, if only in the self-interest of preserving British power, was inevitable.

The Irish experience, coming as it did on the heels of the earlier India famines, demonstrated both the necessity to address major calamity (whether for humanitarian reasons or more pragmatic ones) coupled with the difficulty of mounting and controlling such large, external interventions.

To find the first real attempt to systematically deal with this dilemma we need to go back again to India. Following the Orissa famine of 1866, the first thorough study of the cause of famine and its possible relief was carried out by a government-appointed Famine Commission. It looked not just at food supply but at markets, transport networks, and land tenure issues. It proposed a complex web of interventions to both control and supplement local market forces in preventing famine. Out of this commission—and other bodies which looked into a succession of subsequent famines and relief efforts—emerged the 1883 Famine Code of India. It identified early indicators of impending famine in the form of changes in market prices and the movement of landless laborers. Its authors advocated the trial opening of relief works to test if times were sufficiently dire to force the working peasantry to be willing to labor on public works at near subsistence wages. They recognized the pivotal role of an integrated food market in allowing the state to intervene to alleviate the worst suffering. As in the Irish famine, they also foresaw the use of free food distribution to those too sick, young or old to work.[19]

When famine broke out in British-administered Sudan in Africa in the 1920s, the Indian codes were enacted, almost verbatim. However, Sudan was not India. Indian famine victims were mostly landless laborers afflicted by rising food prices and loss of labor. In Sudan, as in most of Africa, famine victims were small-scale farmers who had first attempted a series of self-controlled responses—selling off farm implements, eating seed grain, selling cattle and land—before becoming destitute. Thus destitution in Africa was a late, not an early, sign of famine and one which called for the re-establishment of the asset base of the farmer, not just the filling of the belly of the laborer. Sudan had neither the army of bureaucrats of India, nor the well-developed transport system to administer relief and move food. In Sudan, and throughout colonial Africa, politics dictated relief. With fewer resources available, relief was focused on the urban environment where it was fear of political discontent—as much as empathy—which spurred state action.[20]

In post-independence democratic India, the colonial famine codes became further entrenched, a key marker of government accountability to citizens and a means to alleviate the most chronic suffering and correct the inability of the market to supply affordable food.[21]

The competing agendas of humanitarianism

During the emergence of modern internationally-connected nation states, notions of humanitarianism and systems to allow for humanitarian action have been shaped by constantly competing agendas:

- The agenda of compassion, reflected in private acts of charity and state acts to alleviate suffering, an agenda we shall meet again when we look at the formation of the Red Cross.
- The agenda of political change manifest in the moral economy of the "criminal acts" to acquire food in colonial India or the call to reform the Poor Laws back in the British homeland.
- The agenda of containment, in which the worst manifestations of calamity are addressed primarily to maintain the status quo, to prevent rebellion, and promote security and stability.

We will see these three agendas—compassion, change, and containment—continuing to do battle throughout the history of humanitarian action and, as we look to the future, to compete to determine the role of the humanitarian system in the twenty-first century.

Limiting the atrocities of war

So far we have examined the early history of the humanitarian system rooted in famine response. Let us now turn to its roots in war.

A Swiss businessman, Jean Henri Dunant, is commonly credited with being the founder of the modern notion and construct of humanitarian action. From his work emerged the ICRC, a global network of Red Cross and Red Crescent Societies, the principles of impartiality, independence, and neutrality in humanitarian action, and the codifying of military behavior in times of war—now collectively known as international humanitarian law (IHL).

Dunant, a product of Calvinist Geneva, was active from an early age in philanthropic ventures such as the local "League of Alms" and the Young Men's Christian Union—forerunner of today's YMCA. On 24 June 1859, aged 31, Dunant was on a business trip in northern Italy, happening to arrive in the town of Solferino to witness the aftermath of a battle between the French and Austrian armies—a battlefield and town crowded with some 40,000 wounded and dying soldiers left to fend for themselves. Dunant (crucially being neither French nor Austrian), urged commanders to allow him to organize relief for all the wounded soldiers left on the battlefield. He persuaded the women of Solferino (again Italian, not French or Austrian) and the surrounding villages to volunteer and come with him to the battlefield to provide relief. By his actions Dunant established some of the fundamental ideals and methodologies of humanitarianism. He negotiated access, he chose to act impartially, he used his position of neutrality, and he organized civil society in a voluntary, non-coerced fashion.

Upon his return to Geneva he wrote up his experiences in *A Memory of Solferino*[22]—a short essay which articulated many of the ideas which would later underpin the Red Cross and Crescent Movement. He called for local voluntary relief committees to be set up to aid the authorities in times of war and for these volunteers to be protected by law as they went about their business. By 1863, his writings and talks were having an impact. The Geneva Society for Public Welfare set up a five-man committee to consider how his ideas could be put into practice. They called themselves the International Committee for the Relief of the Wounded, organizing an international conference in October 1863 attended by representatives of 16 nations. At the conference, the International Committee for the Relief of the Wounded was transformed into the International Committee of the Red Cross and adopted the Red Cross emblem as its symbol (being the reverse of the white cross on a red background used on the Swiss flag).

It is worth quoting verbatim some of the articles that made up the conference's final resolution as they are so central to the humanitarian system that later emerged:

- Article 1. Each country shall have a Committee whose duty it shall be, in time of war and if the need arises, to assist the Army Medical

Services by every means in its power. The Committee shall organize itself in the manner which seems to it most useful and appropriate.
- Art. 3. Each Committee shall get in touch with the Government of its country, so that its services may be accepted should the occasion arise.
- Art. 4. In peacetime, the Committees and Sections shall take steps to ensure their real usefulness in time of war, especially by preparing material relief of all sorts and by seeking to train and instruct voluntary medical personnel.

In addition, the conference recommended:

- that Governments should extend their patronage to Relief Committees which may be formed, and facilitate as far as possible the accomplishment of their task;
- that in time of war the belligerent nations should proclaim the neutrality of ambulances and military hospitals, and that neutrality should likewise be recognized, fully and absolutely, in respect of official medical personnel, voluntary medical personnel, inhabitants of the country who go to the relief of the wounded, and the wounded themselves.[23]

The following year, the Swiss government convened a diplomatic conference attended by 12 nations which adopted the *Geneva Convention for the Amelioration of the Condition of the Wounded in Armies in the Field*—in effect, the first treaty forming the corpus we now know as IHL.

The newly-established International Committee of the Red Cross (all Swiss citizens) set about encouraging the organizing of relief bodies in other countries, starting with the 12 that had attended the diplomatic conference. These were the first national Red Cross and later Red Crescent societies. In 1875, the ICRC's first president, Gustave Moynier, wrote down the basic principles which he felt should guide the work of the ICRC:[24]

- *foresight*: preparations should be made in advance, to provide assistance should war break out;
- *solidarity*: whereby the Societies undertake to help each other;
- *centralization*: implying only one Society in each country;
- *mutuality*: care is given to all the wounded and the sick, irrespective of their nationality.

These fundamental principles for humanitarian work continued to evolve over the next century but it was not until 1965 that the now familiar seven *Fundamental Principles of the Red Cross and Red Crescent Movement* were finalized.

In parallel with these early attempts to codify humanitarian work, the early ICRC also used the good offices of their committee, and of other Swiss citizens they employed, to negotiate access to war wounded, initiating the relief and protection actions which are now the core mandate of the ICRC. They moved on to lobby states to curtail the worst excesses of warfare through a series of treaties forming the modern laws of war.[25] Parallel to the negotiation of the Geneva Conventions, but starting a little later in 1899, states, led by Russia, came together to negotiate limits to the means by which wars were fought culminating in the International Peace Conference of 1899 (First Hague Conference) and the Second International Peace Conference of 1907 (Second Hague Conference). Neither succeeded in their main aim of a general reduction in armaments, but they did succeed in agreeing limits to aerial bombardment, the use of submarine mines and poison gas.[26] The Hague Conventions were about how states fought wars, they were nothing to do directly with the treatment of prisoners, the wounded or civilians. In later years, the tradition of the Hague Conventions carried on through the various strategic arms limitation agreements of the Cold War and on into the 1997 Convention on the Prohibition of the Use, Stockpiling, Production and Transfer or Anti-Personnel Mines and on Their Destruction.

In 1901, nine years before his death, Henry Dunant was awarded the first Nobel Peace Prize.

World War I and the birth of NGOs

With the outbreak of World War I in 1914, the Red Cross operated for the first time as a truly international movement, visiting prisoners of war on both sides, and highlighting the plight of civilian internees. When "the war to end all wars" ended—and 8.5 million lay dead on battlefields—the Red Cross faced a quandary. If there were to be no more wars, why have national Red Cross societies standing by to act in times of war? As we shall see, Henry Davison, the president of the American Red Cross (ARC), had an answer.

Not all hostilities ended in November 1918. The Allies continued a blockade against Germany and Austria-Hungary causing intense suffering for the civilian population. Eglantyne Jebb and her sister Dorothy Buxton, born into a wealthy, well-educated, and socially active English family, had been active throughout the war in charitable work. Eglantyne had traveled to Macedonia in 1913 on behalf of the

Macedonian Relief fund, returning just before war broke out. In 1919, a pressure group "Fight the Famine Council" was set up, as the Jebb sisters sought to pressure the British government into lifting the blockade. It was clear, however, that advocacy was not enough and action was needed. On 15 April 1919, Eglantyne Jebb and colleagues established the Save the Children Fund (SCF) to raise funds to send relief to the children behind the blockades. In the same year, activists in Sweden set up a similar organization, Rädda Barnen. A year later, Jebb oversaw formation of the Geneva-based International Save the Children Union, the first recognizable trans-national humanitarian NGO. As the Allied blockade came to an end, income to the Fund rapidly dropped off but a change of tactic revived the organization. They began more targeted work, some of it among poverty-stricken children in the UK, and crucially, they realized that protection of a vulnerable group like children required law to back up charitable action. Jebb drafted the *Declaration of the Rights of the Child* and lobbied for its successful adoption by the League of Nations in 1924. The Declaration became, in effect, the mission statement of the organization, harbinger of the *Convention on the Rights of the Child* adopted by the UN in 1989.[27] The International Save the Children Alliance, as it is called today, has 27 country members, works in over a hundred countries, and in 2005 had a total annual income of just over $991 million.[28]

SCF is important to the history of the humanitarian system because it represents the first true NGO. The Red Cross, although started outside of governments, relied upon government recognition, funding, and law. SCF, however, was a fully-fledged NGO of a kind we would recognize today. It was also the first NGO to fundraise, direct its own relief actions, and lobby for international legislation to protect victims of abuse and crisis. In doing so, SCF laid down the model of the independent, activist, and operational NGO.

While WWI caused immense loss of life, the public health and economic crises that followed also brought unimaginable suffering. Polio and measles raged across Europe, and in the year the war ended, the most deadly flu pandemic ever to hit the world broke out. By the time it subsided two years later, at least 20 million people had died— although other estimates suggest 50, or even as many as 100, million had perished.[29]

The birth of global humanitarian relief

Accounts written about the misery of post-war Europe provide apocalyptic descriptions of urban starvation, mass movements of millions of demobilized troops desperately making their way home through hostile territories, and continent-wide economic and social collapse. The Ottoman Empire disintegrated, creating something akin to the pattern of Balkan states we know today. Two million Poles were on the move back to freed Poland and maybe one million Germans were returning home from across the old Austrian-Hungarian Empire. Everywhere, destitute people were on the move.[30]

Only one state survived the war with the financial, manpower, and organizational ability to even begin to address this chaos—the United States. Even as the war began, America was prominent in organizing relief to occupied Europe. The Commission for Relief to Belgium, formed in 1914, and headed by Herbert Hoover, later US President, raised over $20 million to provide famine relief in occupied—and then liberated—Belgium. As the war drew to an end, the Committee morphed into the America Relief Administration (ARA), still headed by Hoover and providing relief across Europe but with a particular eye on Russia. The Bolshevik October 1917 Revolution had ushered in a new Russia and one which now had three million troops spread across eastern Europe with no formal mechanism to get them home. As early as 1917, the ICRC had highlighted the growing problem of troop repatriation.[31] By the winter of 1920, famine was stalking Russia. The effects of war, revolution, breakdown of transport systems, and heavy rainfall combined to cause three years of famine which would eventually kill an estimated 5.1 million people.[32] Russia never appealed for assistance, but the writer Maxim Gorky published a moving account of the suffering which stimulated the ICRC and the newly-formed League of Red Cross Societies to call an urgent conference in Geneva in August 1921 at which the International Committee for Russian Relief was formed.

Earlier in the year the Norwegian explorer Fridtjof Nansen had been appointed by the League of Nations as its first High Commissioner for Refugees, a post he held till his death in 1930 (though with a very limited mandate of only administering assistance to Russian refugees).[33] He had already managed to help repatriate nearly half a million Russian refugees and devised the notion of a refugee (Nansen) passport, to give legitimacy to people seeking asylum. Nansen's ideas and championing of the refugee cause led directly, after WWII, to the formation of the short-lived International Refugee Organization (IRO) and in 1951 to the establishment of the UN High Commissioner for Refugees (UNHCR), the history of which will be described later in this chapter. Nansen seemed the natural leader to head the new relief organization and accepted the post. The League of Red Cross Societies and the International Save the Children Union were key members, but in reality the American Relief Administration and Herbert Hoover drove the operation. At its height, the ARA was feeding over 10.5 million people a day and had more than 120,000 employees in Russia. The stand-off between the Hoover-led ARA and Vladmir Lenin was in many ways a taste of things to come. The ARA demanded a full say over the use of Russia's railway system to distribute food but Lenin refused what he saw as interference in Russia's internal affairs. The "big show in Bololand," as American relief workers dubbed the US famine response mission to Russia, helped sow the seeds of the US-Soviet mistrust which fueled the Cold War for another 70 years.[34]

Herbert Hoover was not the only person to see advantages of harnessing American troops, finance, and logistical might to a major relief effort. The American Red Cross (ARC) had been active throughout the US involvement in WWI. As early as May 1917 when American President Woodrow Wilson appointed Henry Davison to chair the American Red Cross War Council, it was clear that Davison was already thinking about harnessing US resources to reconstruct Europe via what he termed a "real International Red Cross." The ARC had grown phenomenally in the early years of the war as America watched, but did not intervene, in Europe. In 1914, it had 500,000 volunteer members, a year later, 20 million. Davison saw potential for a humanitarian version of the newly-established League of Nations in which the ARC would be in the driving seat. During 1917 and 1918, Davison and his colleagues corresponded with US president Wilson and a small group of like-minded Red Cross Societies about the setting up of a League of Red Cross Societies, independent from the old Swiss ICRC. As one of Davison's supporters put it: "The League is the natural outgrowth of the worldwide activities of the American Red Cross, just as the League of Nations is the logical consequence of the entry of the United States into the war."[35]

The League not only challenged the role and authority of the old ICRC, it also implicitly challenged its notion of neutrality, then inextricably linked with the neutrality of the Swiss state. In early 1919, less than six months after Davison had first raised the notion of the League with Wilson, it became a reality. There were five founding member Societies: Britain, France, Italy, Japan, and the United States. Their focus was unashamedly public health and disaster relief and they were eager to spread the civilizing process of Red Cross activism. In April 1919, Davison invited the world's most distinguished scientists, doctors, and nurses to a conference in Cannes, France, to discuss what could be done about the unfolding health crisis gripping Europe. The conference proposed a vision of the Red Cross League which would essentially make it the health wing of the new League of Nations and central to the future health of the world.[36] The early League, however, never lived up to Davison's vision. Its first mission, to war-destroyed Poland in the summer of 1919, saw much reporting, but little action. The Russian famine of 1921–23 should have been a godsend to the new organization, but it was already hamstrung by bickering between member national Red Cross societies. Allied to this, Davison and the League were backed by the US Democratic President Wilson, but the American manpower and cash on the ground in the ARA were controlled by the Republican President-in-waiting, Herbert Hoover. Hoover was in no mood to turn his organization over to the League.

The initial American funding for the League, some $2.5 million, was by 1920 fast running out. Politics, personal rivalries, and the distrust shaping the growing stand-off between American capitalism and Soviet communism all conspired to move the League away from Davison's vision—as a US-led active and global relief body—to a self-help collective with each national society assuming leadership within its own country.

Unlike the League of Nations, the League of Red Cross Societies survived the lead-up to, and aftermath of the carnage of World War II. In 1991, it renamed itself the International Federation of Red Cross and Red Crescent Societies (IFRC). With 186 members, the IFRC is today one of the world's largest global humanitarian organizations—although in financial terms still not as large as the ICRC.

Natural disasters and the faltering beginnings of a system

Famine codes in India and the Sudan had put in place the beginnings of an international system for addressing these specific calamities. The early work of the Red Cross, and the emergence of IHL, laid the foundation for international action to address suffering in times of war, but response to suffering from natural disasters was still unspecified. In April 1906, one of the first major disasters of modern times struck the west coast of America as a shift of the San Andreas fault destroyed most of San Francisco, killing up to 3,000 people and making as many as 225,000 of the city's population of 400,000 homeless.[37] The reaction of the city and state authorities at the time is instructive. City fathers feared the disaster would shake confidence in what was then the financial hub of western America and consistently downplayed the quake's impact, reporting a mere 567 deaths, conspicuously failing to account for fatalities in the city's Chinatown. Damage was estimated at

$500,000 whereas a more realistic estimate would have been $5 billion. As news of the disaster spread across the country and to Europe, funds flowed in—from England, Canada, the federal government and magnates such as Andrew Carnegie—which eventually reached nearly $5 million. Plans to rebuild the city were rushed through and work started quickly. Building and public health standards were eased in order to speed recovery. By the time the Panama-Pacific International Exposition was held in 1915, San Francisco had recovered. Tellingly, while relief in time of international war was beginning to assume the organized nature we now take for granted, response to national and natural disasters was still seen as a local issue. All this would change with the aftermath of World War I.

Two years after the California earthquake, on 28 December 1908, southern Italy and Sicily were hit by one of Europe's largest ever earthquakes and tsunami. The towns of Messina on Sicily and neighboring Reggio on the mainland were flattened. Over 100,000 people died and 200,000 were made homeless. Giovanni Ciraolo, at the time a leading figure in the local Red Cross, was appalled by the ineffectiveness of the improvised relief. In 1919, he became president of the Italian Red Cross and, with the birth of the new League of Red Cross, found a vehicle to promote his ideas of an organized international response to natural disasters. His ideas, first articulated at the tenth International Red Cross Conference in 1920, led directly to the establishment of the first ever international organization specifically set up to respond to disaster, but it would be the League of Nations, not the League of Red Cross, that turned the idea into a reality.[38]

The League of Nations, established in Paris in 1919, ultimately collapsed as the more powerful nation states chose to ignore its attempts to curtail their expansionism. By 1940, its secretariat in Geneva was reduced to a skeleton staff and in 1946 it was formally dissolved and its properties, notably the Palais des Nations in Geneva, transferred to the new UN. During its short life, it did have some diplomatic successes, settling a border dispute between Sweden and Finland and preventing the outbreak of a Balkans war in 1925. It also adopted in 1927 a *Convention and Statute Establishing the International Relief Union* which was, in effect, the first attempt to develop an intergovernmental structure explicitly to aid victims of disaster. The Union was both to provide assistance and to coordinate the assistance of others. It was to "operate for the benefit of all stricken peoples, whatever their nationality or their race, and irrespective of any social, political or religious distinction."[39] The Convention explicitly recognized the "free cooperation" of the Red Cross Societies and of "all other official or non-official organizations that may be able to undertake the same activities."[40] The term NGO had not yet been coined and this reference to non-official organizations is the first real acknowledgement of the potential role of organizations, like the then Save the Children Fund in international relief outside of war zones.

The founding statutes of the International Relief Union (IRU) provided for funding on a voluntary basis by state or private donation—a constraint on international humanitarian action which has scarcely changed in the following 80 years. The IRU offered assistance to the Indian government in 1934 for the Orissa earthquake, but this was declined and instead assistance was channeled through the Red Cross. In 1937, when the Mississippi River caused disastrous flood damage in Ohio, US President Roosevelt similarly declined IRU assistance.[41] However, the IRU did manage to sponsor a number of scientific studies into natural disasters and outlived the League of Nations, albeit in a moribund state. By the 1950s, it existed in name only and in 1965 its member countries finally recommended the transfer of all its assets and responsibilities to the UN.

Depression and war

President Wilson's vision of a world order created through open dialogue facilitated by the League of Nations, firmly led and underwritten by the United States, was one that sat increasingly uneasily with the American people. America's half-hearted military interventions in Serbia and Russia in 1918–20, followed by the Depression and the stock market crash led to a retreat into political isolationism. When Franklin D. Roosevelt came to power in 1933, his inclination was to seek reengagement in the world, but his priority was to stop the near fatal hemorrhaging of the US economy. Hitherto, dealing with such social and economic crisis has been a state, not a federal, responsibility. Roosevelt's New Deal changed the rules, creating a novel welfare and facilitating role for the federal government. Federal "cash for work" schemes opened across the country, Washington, DC, intervened to rebuild the economy, and gradually through the late 1930s lifted America out of depression.[42]

The second Sino-Japanese war broke out in 1937, followed by war in Europe in 1939, but America remained isolationist, unready to follow Roosevelt into battle. The success of the New Deal had shown that economies could be resurrected through centrally orchestrated and facilitated actions, a lesson which was not lost on those who would seek to rebuild Europe 15 years later in the aftermath of World War II.

World War II and its legacy fundamentally shaped the humanitarian community we see today. The United Nations and its agencies were born. The Bretton Woods Institutions were created, IHL was expanded and a whole new family of NGOs evolved, to work alongside, comfortably or not, the old ICRC, the League, and the older NGOs. Much of the international apparatus we today subsume under the heading of the humanitarian system, was born out of the consequences of World War II and in particular the consequences of the Cold War— a conflict that started in the anti-Nazi WWII alliance and ended with the demise of the Soviet Union in 1991.

Visions for a new world

The vision of the world after WWII was shaped by four men: Franklin D. Roosevelt, Winston Churchill, Joseph Stalin, and later Mao Zedong. The world has turned out the way it has because they each wanted something different from this brave new world and each misread the intentions of the other three. Roosevelt wanted to build a world with a balance of power, economic not military, between the Americans and the Russians and with a strong UN guaranteeing security and a place for negotiations. Churchill understood that Britain was finished as a world power but wanted to play the Greek to the United States' Roman, with the UK as the elder sage unobtrusively stewarding the energetic new titan. Russia had lost 90 times more war dead than the United States and above all else Stalin wanted security for himself and his country. He believed that with peace, the capitalist allies would inevitably turn in on themselves, fueled by greed and suspicion as Marxist theory predicted. No need for military adventure when your enemies will weaken themselves. Mao wanted, and achieved, communist rule in China, but wanted to go further. He, like Stalin, believed in the inevitable spread of communism and so was quite willing to take Stalin's lead and ally China with Russia. Add to this, America's initial military supremacy because of its sole possession of nuclear weapons, combined with Russia's overwhelming superiority in terms of conventional military assets and the plans for a world balanced economically slid into a world balanced militarily and through ever escalating mutually assured destruction.[43]

Ironically, the analysis upon which the plans for the post-war world rested, differed little between communist Russia and capitalist Europe and America. Both saw capitalism as its own worst enemy. It created wealth and could create liberty, but, if left unchecked, generated great inequality. On both the American and the Russian side, the analysis showed that inequality fueled resentment which, in Europe had led to authoritarian regimes which in turn had sought war to justify and fuel their policies at home. On the Russian side, this was seen as historical destiny, on the Allied, as a manageable consequence. The outcome was not inevitable. Writing in 1943, the US theologian Reinhold Niebuhr, by then staunchly anti-communist, was able to write: "We [the United States] have on the whole more liberty and less equality than Russia has. Russia has less liberty and more equality. Whether democracy should be defined primarily in terms of liberty or equality is a source of unending debate."[44]

The formation of the United Nations

Roosevelt, through the New Deal, had learned that the excesses of capitalism could be constrained. As WWII unfolded, he, with Churchill and their advisors, sought to build a world version of the New Deal, essentially an international welfare net that would make the world safe for capitalism. Three institutions—the International Monetary Fund (IMF), the World Bank Group (which included five separate financial agencies) and the UN—would make future global economics depressions less likely and provide the means by which the international community could contain, and if needed defeat, future aggressors.[45] While the Soviet Union was a founding UN member, Stalin rejected membership of the IMF and the Bank, seeing both as explicitly seeking to save capitalism.

The UN was thus born out of an instrument of WWII. Its first expression was the Anglo-American Atlantic Charter of 1941. The term "United Nations" was officially used from 1942 onwards to describe the coalition of countries fighting the Axis powers. Eisenhower accepted the surrender of Fascist Italy in September 1943 in the name of the UN and later the same year, anticipating the end of the war, the United Nations War Crimes Commission and the United Nations Relief and Rehabilitation Administration (UNRRA) were both created, once again reflecting the twin roles of liberty and equality in the vision for the new world.[46] In September and October 1944, at a meeting in Dumbarton Oaks in Washington, DC, the United States, UK, Russia, and pre-communist China agreed on the overall aims, structure, and functions of the post-war version of the United Nations. Earlier that year, they had met at the Mount Washington Hotel in Bretton Woods, New Hampshire, USA, and agreed on the creation of a gold standard to control currency fluctuations, along with the struc-ture of the World Bank and the IMF (organizations now known as the

Bretton Woods Institutions). In April of the next year, delegates from 50 countries met at the United Nations Conference on International Organization and drew up the 111-article Charter of the UN. By October of that year, the five permanent members of the UN had ratified the Charter, thus allowing the new UN to come into official existence and the first General Assembly to be held in January 1946, in the Central Hall of the Palace of Westminster, London. The basic structure of the new order was finalized when, in December 1948, the UN General Assembly adopted the *Universal Declaration of Human Rights*.[47]

In short, the UN evolved out of the allied alliance of WWII with three explicit purposes:

1 to provide a structure to head off and if necessarily deal directly with future wars;
2 to introduce instruments which would mitigate the worst excesses and failings of capitalism, thus increasing equality;
3 through the Declaration of Human Rights, to promote liberty.

History had come full circle. Woodrow Wilson's vision for a US-led world of collective security, economic liberalization, and political self-determination—life, liberty and freedom—now had an institutional home, the United Nations.

The agencies of the new UN

The UN developed and has burgeoned into several different agencies over time.

UNRWA and the tragedy of Palestine

If Britain had abandoned its protection mandate for Palestine a few years later, or the fledgling UN had tried harder to find a political, rather than economic, solution to Palestine, then today the world's longest running, most protracted, and most tragic refugee crisis might be a central part of the humanitarian cause, rather than a seemingly endless political quagmire.

In 1947, Britain gave up its struggle to reconcile Arabs and Jews in Palestine, handing over responsibility to the new United Nations. In November 1947, the UN passed a resolution seeking partition of mandate Palestine into Jewish and Arab territory. Britain continued to withdraw its troops, chaos ensued, and in May 1948 the Jewish community proclaimed its independent statehood. Israel was born and war broke out, finally ending in August 1949 through a series of UN-brokered truce agreements between Israel and its Arab neighbors.

Responding to the plight of Palestinian refugees who fled from Israel, in November 1948 the UN set up a special fund to be administered by the Director of United Nations Relief for Palestinian Refugees, an organization replaced in May 1950 by the UN Relief and Works Agency for Palestine Refugees (UNRWA). UNRWA today is still the prime channel for assistance to Palestinian refugees, more than 50 years after its birth.

By virtue of the fact that their forced displacement predates both the 1951 Refugee Treaty and the subsequent establishment of UNHCR, Palestinians find themselves in an anomalous situation—they are by far the world's largest refugee population, but are not officially included in UN refugee statistics.

UNRWA was envisaged as a two-phase operation—immediate relief to sustain the refugees and economic assistance to create jobs and aid their integration into the host countries. Returning home to what was now Israel was never considered an option. UNRWA, unlike UNHCR, has no mandate to provide protection or to seek durable solutions to the displacement of its client population. By 1960, UNRWA had abandoned any pretense at economic rehabilitation and has since then concerned itself with a relief, welfare, and education agenda, effectively a holding operation pending a political solution. Many credit UNRWA with playing a significant role, providing health care, educating the Palestinian population, and building capacity to today run its fledgling state.[48]

Refugees and UNHCR

One of the first UN agencies to take up the humanitarian mandate was the United Nations Relief and Rehabilitation Administration (UNRRA). In 1945, UNRRA assisted in the repatriation of millions of people across Europe and ran hundreds of displaced person camps in Germany. It coordinated the work of some 23 separate voluntary relief agencies. In its short three-and-a-half-year lifespan, it spent some $3.6 billion pursuing economic rehabilitation and repatriation across Europe. By 1947, strapped for cash and strongly criticized by the United States for repatriating nationals back into Eastern Europe and, in US eyes, thus strengthening the communist regimes, the organization was disbanded. UNRRA's responsibilities were handed over to the newly formed International Refugee Organization (IRO), a specialized agency of the UN.[49] The ill-fated IRO was in turn disbanded and replaced in January 1951 by the office of the UN High Commissioner for Refugees (UNHCR).

The disbanding of the IRO and the formation of UNHCR were largely a product of the changing attitudes to people on the move in Europe. Prior to 1950, people were returning, or being returned home as part of post-war rebuilding, but after 1950 the movements changed. In the eyes of the United States, the only serious funder of international relief and protection, movement was now East–West, with people fleeing Soviet-dominated Europe to the West. This movement was an intensely political matter. Massive population movements were also underway in India, Palestine, Korea, and China. UNRRA had defined refugees by national group. The IRO for the first time turned the definition of refugees around, talking of individuals fleeing persecution, regardless of origins. In essence, however, the IRO was still firmly entrenched in the politics of post-war and Cold War Europe.

The formation of UNHCR was paralleled by the drafting and signing of the *United Nations Convention Relating to the Statutes of Refugees*. The convention was adopted by the UN in July 1951 and entered into force in April 1954 as sufficient states ratified it. The Soviet Union, and all other communist countries except Yugoslavia, had withdrawn from the negotiations around the convention, seeing it as an instrument for the West to encourage people to flee the East. Indeed, much of the language of this early convention lends itself to this interpretation. One stipulation was that the convention only dealt with refugees created before 1951 and thus did not have to apply to the new flows of refugees in Africa and Asia—most notably, those from Palestine. By the mid-1960s this caveat had become untenable and, in October 1967, a protocol relating to the Status of Refugees was appended to the Convention which effectively removed the 1951 cutoff for defining refugees. UNHCR now had a legal instrument which matched its mandate and operations.

Since UNHCR's inception, politics, power-plays, and refugees have been inseparable. In the 1950s, most people on the move were in Europe fleeing communist regimes and non-functioning economies, seeking political freedom and a way out of destitution and looking to the reviving Western Europe and America. Refugees were the human face of the Cold War and their flight was a powerful political symbol in the rich West of the evils of communism. Aiding those fleeing was thus a powerful expression of the rightness of the Western cause. To this end, UNHCR found its mandate and reach constantly challenged, particularly by the United States which created its own refugee assistance mechanisms to keep the business of refugees firmly within the power play of the Cold War.[50] It was a grant from the Ford Foundation, not from nation states, that enabled the UNHCR to respond to the 1953 Berlin refugee crisis. Throughout the 1950s UNHCR transformed itself from an office of coordination towards a fundraising, operational protection, and assistance organization. It expanded beyond Europe to respond to Algerians fleeing civil war into Tunisia and Morocco.[51] With the withering of colonialism and the independence of African and Asian states, UNHCR's operation continued to expand.

The Marshall Plan

As post-war Europe morphed into Cold War Europe, rebuilding of the war-torn countries of Western Europe became as much a matter of political necessity as economic self-interest. For the United States, Europe remained a battle ground, shaped by economics and politics, not military adventure. UNRAA, in the eyes of the USA, was discredited as it sought to also assist the countries of Eastern Europe on their terms. In its place, driven largely by the State Department, came the European Recovery Program, led by the US Secretary of State, George Marshall, quickly dubbed the Marshall Plan.

The severe winter of 1946/7, coming on top of the war-time devastation and the major refugee movements, had seen real starvation in parts of northern Europe. Original hopes that Europe's economy could be rebuilt by the UK and France off the back of their colonial empires proved short-lived. Europe was not recovering from the war. Its people still lived under war-time austerity, and the only country with the wherewithal to inject capital was the United States. Its economy had boomed during the war and its infrastructure remained intact. In the summer of 1947, Secretary of State Marshall, arguing on grounds of national security, convinced US President Truman of the need to rebuild the economy of Europe, as a much-needed trading partner, and to head off the allure of communism. Initially the Marshall Plan offered assistance to Eastern Europe and the Soviet Union, but on condition that every country receiving assistance allowed its economy to be independently assessed—that is, assessed by appointees of the Marshall Plan. Stalin could not agree to this, perceiving it as a political ploy to undermine communist authority.[52] The Marshall Plan was signed into law in April 1948 and in the same year the participating countries, essentially Western Europe, Turkey, and the United States created the Organization for European Economic Cooperation, to coordinate the aid efforts. In 1961, the organization was renamed the Organization for Economic Cooperation and Development (OECD). Over the four years of the plan, in excess of $12.4 billion in aid was disbursed, mostly used by European countries to buy American goods and services. At the time, with European foreign reserves exhausted, Marshall Plan money was virtually the only source of funds Europe had for purchasing imports. The funds were not grants, but loans, repaid in local currency, held by each local government in special funds to be ploughed back into economic development. Funds were initially used for staple food supplies, then for urban, agricultural and industrial rehabilitation. As the Korean War unfolded, more funds were used to support the rehabilitation of the European military. The plan and the use Europe put it to helped raise industrial production by 35 percent and brought agricultural production back to pre-war levels. In the eyes of many, the plan allowed European governments to relax the wartime austerity programs, reducing civil discontent and curtailing support for the Communist movement. The Marshall Plan and the way Europe chose to implement it also helped fuel European unity. Many of its mechanisms were used to forge the European Coal and Steel Community, the precursor to today's European Union.

Historians argue over whether the Marshall Plan represented American generosity or hard-nosed pragmatism, securing dependency of Europe upon American goods and services and building political, military, and economic clientelism as the West faced off with the East. More recently, analysts have questioned the true importance of the plan in rebuilding Europe, pointing out that much was underway before hand, and economic growth was actually fastest in countries which were the lowest recipients of aid.

Whatever the analysis, the one critical factor that all agree on is that the success of European rehabilitation rested on it being driven and planned, if not fueled, by the governments of the affected countries and not by an external, multilateral. or unilateral power. This is a lesson that should not be lost on today's aid community.

From baggage to human capital: protecting children

The multilateral and neutral UNRRA succumbed to the realpolitik of the new Cold War, being replaced by the much more politically-driven Marshall Plan, but, at the final session of UNRRA in Geneva, delegates, particularly those from Norway and Poland, raised concerns over the fate of Europe's war-affected children. Children in famine-affected areas on both sides of the newly descended Iron Curtain were at risk. Ludwik Rajchman, the delegate for Poland, proposed using UNRRA's residual resources to create a new fund for emergency children's aid. On 11 December 1946, Resolution 57(I) of the UN General Assembly brought into existence the UN International Children's Emergency Fund. In 1953, the organization changed its name to the UN Children's Fund, but it continues to be known by its original acronym—UNICEF.

The fund was originally a strictly short-term relief venture, seeking to provide food to famine-affected children across Europe. But its founders, and in particular its first Executive Director, Maurice Pate, had a larger vision. UNICEF never received statutory contributions from member states, so it had to raise its own funds. In 1947, it set up its first National Committee in the United States to raise funds and lobby for UNICEF's work. Today, there are 37 such committees raising up to one-third of the organization's income. In 1953, the US actor, Danny Kaye became UNICEF's first Goodwill Ambassador, adding high profile celebrity endorsement to its public image. Crucially, Resolution 57(I) also called on the fund to support "child health purposes generally" leaving the door open for a more global and longer-term mandate.[53]

By 1948, communicable diseases, particularly tuberculosis, were ravaging Europe. The Scandinavian Red Cross Societies saw the potential of a mass vaccination campaign using the Bacille Calmette-Guérin (BCG) vaccine. Developed in 1921, the vaccine got off to a notorious start when initial batches proved to be contaminated and led to the death of many vaccinated children. However, in post-war Europe it seemed the only hope to stop the spread of the disease. In 1948, UNICEF launched the International Tuberculosis Campaign and upwards of eight million children across Europe, in the East and the West, were vaccinated.[54] This marked the beginning of UNICEF's long involvement in vaccination campaigns and public health, but also flagged a significant organizational difference between it and other UN bodies. UNICEF was operational, not just diplomatic and discursive. It sought to establish offices in crisis-affected countries and to work directly with government ministries. It sought alliances with non-governmental bodies, like the Red Cross Societies, and it sought independent funding through its National Committees. In 1950, when the original mandate of the Emergency Fund came to an end, its commitment to "child health purposes generally" enabled UN delegates, particularly those from the new developing country member states, led by Pakistan, to lobby for the fund's continuation in order to address the needs of children globally, not just in Europe.

Throughout the 1950s, UNICEF expanded its vaccination campaigns and found itself at the forefront of lobbying around public health issues. By the 1960s, it was championing approaches to development which were less top-down and technocentric and more people-focused. In many ways, UNICEF was a good decade ahead of international thinking. In 1960, it commissioned its first global survey of the state of children's well-being. Drawing on the work of sister UN agencies and taking a year to produce, the *Children of the Developing Countries* report was a landmark, laying out a vision for child development and well-being which argued that children's needs should be an intrinsic part of any national development plan. Children were no longer to be seen as accidental baggage, but as a country's nascent human capital.

UNICEF evolved from a temporary emergency child-feeding agency into a permanent child welfare and then child development agency. Significantly, though, in these early days it did not take up the challenge of children's rights. The 1924 *Declaration on the Rights of the Child* had been driven by the Save the Children International Union. In 1946, the SCIU, now part of the International Union of Child Welfare, started lobbying for this old League Declaration to be taken up by the new UN. However, the UN was preoccupied with the more generic human rights conventions and it was not until 1957 that the Human Rights Commission started work on a new Declaration of the Rights of the Child, which was adopted by the General Assembly in 1959. Even 20 years later, it was an NGO coalition, not UNICEF, that successfully lobbied for 1979 to be declared the International Year of the Child.

Throughout most of the Cold War, human rights were seen as a partial non-neutral issue which UNICEF shied away from for fear of jeopardizing its emergency and development work. Gradually during the 1980s UNICEF became more open to promoting children's rights, alongside children's welfare. When in 1989 the UN eventually passed a new *Convention on the Rights of the Child*, UNICEF was an integral part of the process. This convention has now become the most accepted human rights convention on record; 193 nation states ratifying it and only Somalia and the United States failing to do so.[55]

The World Food Programme

The final piece of the post-war humanitarian jigsaw puzzle got off to a late start. In 1943, US President Roosevelt had convened an international conference on food and agriculture as part of planning for the post-war world. This led, through the creation of the UN, to the founding of the Food and Agriculture Organization (FAO) in October 1945. As the Marshall Plan rolled out in Europe, the principle of using surplus production in one area of the world to bolster recovery and development in another was being established. By 1954, FAO had formulated its *Principles of Surplus Disposal* and, in the same year, the USA voted into law its Agricultural Trade Development and Assistance Act (Public Law 480) which institutionalized, and continues to govern, US food aid. In 1961, US President Kennedy established a Food for Peace office within the White House (which has now been subsumed within USAID) and appointed George McGovern, a close friend, canny politician, and presidential special assistant, as its first director. The stage was set for the creation of the World Food Programme.[56]

The year before, FAO had commissioned a study on the use of global food surpluses and was due to meet in Rome in April 1961 to share its findings. McGovern, with a small delegation from the Agriculture and State Departments, represented the US. The Rome meeting was supposed to simply debate the report, but McGovern—building on his close relationship with Kennedy and the White House—tabled a substantive proposal to set up a three-year trial multilateral food aid program limited to $100 million worth of aid, to focus on emergencies and pilot development projects. The US committed sufficient resources from its already existing food surpluses to entice others to support it so that it did not look like a wholly US instrument. The limit of $100 million and the emergency mandate also ensured this new multilateral fund did not interfere with the US bilateral food aid program, then worth some $1.3 billion. The proposal crafted a key governing and administrative role for FAO. In something of a diplomatic coup, McGovern stole the show, finessed would-be critics back home, ensured the FAO was on side, and paved the way for President Kennedy to endorse the idea at a press conference in late April 1961. The proposal was incorporated into a batch of resolutions passed by the FAO Conference in November 1961 and the following month the UN General Assembly established the WFP.

The experimental nature of those first three years was crucial. It pushed the new organization to be adventurous, but also realistic. In effect, with one year of planning it only had two years to "prove" the value of project food aid and its ability to respond to emergencies, yet in those first three years it responded to 32 emergencies and administered 116 development projects. Food aid was used in food-for-work projects to stimulate land resettlement and reform, and in special feeding programs. Countries in Asia, followed by Africa, Southern Europe and Latin America were the target recipients. In these early days on a case-by-case basis WFP sold food aid to offset the costs of internal transportation and administration. It did not have its own totally separate administration, being run out of FAO in Rome and supervised in the field by the precursor of the United Nations Development Program.

The experiment was deemed a success and WFP's mandate was extended for a further three years, again with substantial US contributions, but this time with a caveat that its contribution should be balanced by that of other countries. From 1960 through to the World Food Conference in 1974, WFP continued, with fluctuating resources, to use project food aid as a tool to promote social and economic development. It continued to be heavily reliant on US food aid surpluses and funding. From 1974 through to the mid-1980s, its use of project food aid became more proficient, but it was not until the mid-1980s and early 1990s that WFP shifted to become what it is today— primarily an agency concerned with food aid and food security in emergencies.

Responding to disaster

With the withering by the 1960s of the International Relief Union, responding to natural disasters had largely become the prerogative of nation states, backed up where wanted by the work of the League of Red Cross and Red Crescent Societies. The late 1960s and early 1970s witnessed a series of unconnected but major disasters—earthquakes, floods, and droughts—across the developing nations. In 1970, Bangladesh suffered a devastating cyclone, killing over 300,000 people. The disaster attracted global attention when George Harrison, of Beatles fame, staged a concert in New York to raise funds for the victims.

Frustrated by the lack of official and reliable information on the extent of these disasters and relief needs, the UN General Assembly in December 1971 called upon the Secretary-General to appoint a Disaster Relief Coordinator, who would report directly to him with a mandate to solicit funds, coordinate relief efforts, and provide timely information, but without a mandate to be operational. The Office of the Disaster Relief Coordinator—the UN Disaster Relief Organization (UNDRO)—was set up in Geneva in March 1972. Its mandate was always around coordination and information, but it never controlled substantial funding so in many ways, during the big crises of the 1970s and 1980s (notably the Sahel and the Horn of Africa famines) it was relegated to a minor role.[57] It did, however, work with the General Assembly to get the 1990s declared the International Decade for Natural Disaster Reduction. Developments during this decade—and the subsequent post-Millennium development of the International Strategy for Disaster Reduction—created a framework which helped bring attention back to natural disasters, disaster prevention as well as weather-related and climate change-driven disasters at a time when humanitarianism was dominated by the political and complex emergencies spawned by the end of the Cold War.[58, 59]

In 1992, UNDRO was disbanded as part of reforms by the incoming UN Secretary-General Boutros Boutros-Ghali and replaced by the Department of Humanitarian Affairs. It had a wider, more political brief than UNDRO, reflecting the prevailing focus on complex emergencies. In 1997, another round of reform transformed DHA into the Office for the Coordination of Humanitarian Affairs (OCHA).[60] OCHA's role remains one of coordination and information sharing but, as we shall see in Chapter 5, successive Emergency Relief Coordinators (ERCs) have created a bigger leadership role for the office and helped it develop somewhat of an independent voice, at arm's length from much of the political intrigue of the UN's secretariat.

The new NGOs

We give here just some examples of the many NGOs that came into existence in the twentieth century. We have picked examples of the most successful NGOs and of those whose history best illustrates the political and social forces of the time which led to their creation. In Chapter 6, we will come back to examine in more detail the work of the major international NGOs.

Oxfam

The Allied campaign in Europe during WWII was not just military but also economic, driven by the concept of total warfare. The British Ministry of Economic Warfare was charged with orchestrating all possible actions to disrupt and destroy the Nazi economy. One small part of it looked towards the occupied countries of southern Europe, including Greece, concluding that a naval blockade of its ports would divert Nazi resources from the war front into operations to feed civilians. A dubious logic at the best of times and one that did not sit well with a group of academics, religious leaders, and businessmen in

Oxford. Already disturbed by the notion of total warfare, which seemed to condemn the entire German population with almost racist-like vehemence, they regarded intentional starving of occupied nations as abhorrent.

The ICRC, working through the neutral Turkish Red Crescent, responded to the blockade by sending in a food cargo ship. It made five voyages before striking a rock and sinking in January 1942. Even with this assistance it is estimated that during the 1941–42 winter over 200,000 Greeks died of starvation.[61]

In Oxford, in 1942, a small group of radical thinkers formed the Oxford Committee for Famine Relief with the express purpose of stimulating public opinion to lift the blockage on occupied Greece. They decried the fact that bodies were being carted through the streets of Athens to mass graves in scenes not witnessed in Europe since the Great Plague.[62]

Petitions were signed and appeals made, but nothing changed. In March 1943 the committee's tactics changed, they registered as a charity, and started collecting funds to send to the still-functioning Greek Red Cross. They also managed to arrange for a ship full of dried milk from South Africa to reach the blockaded city. As the war dragged on, the committee raised funds for other countries where civilians were suffering, including Germany. They opened charity shops in Oxford, both to collect donations of used clothes and to raise funds; functions which continue today. They sought to work through already established relief organizations, notably the Red Cross, the Friends Relief Committee, and the Salvation Army. By 1948, with the war ended and the Marshall Plan rebuilding Europe, many of the groups set up in WWII to aid civilians were winding down. The Oxford group considered following suit but, seeing the collapse of the British mandate in Palestine and the 725,000 Palestinians fleeing homes now occupied by Israelis, the committee decided not to close but to broaden its mandate. In 1951, it sent funds and relief to the Indian state of Bihar in response to a major crop failure and also sent relief following the cease-fire in Korea.

Throughout this time the committee still operated under its full name, though their first full-time organizer, Robert Castle, had taken to using less unwieldy titles in his publicity. Eurorelief was used for a time and later the abbreviation "Oxfam". This stuck and in 1965 the agency officially changed its name to Oxfam.

What stands out when looking at this early institutional history are two things. First, the central role of a few founding individuals. Of the five original founders of the committee, three were still active in the organization 20 years later. Second, from its start Oxfam was fueled by a radical independence. The founder's moral stance during World War II brought them perilously close to accusations of lacking patriotism. Their *modus operandi*, while not challenging state authority, was inherently suspicious of it.

CARE

Across the Atlantic, citizens in the United States were also appalled at the suffering in post-war Europe. A consortium of 22 US charities was searching for a mechanism to move relief goods to families in Europe in a way that would avoid both the still dysfunctional European postal systems and the rampant profiteering of many commercial operations looking to expand in Europe. Arthur Ringland and Lincoln Clark (later to become founding members of CARE) hit on the idea of persuading the US government to allow the public to buy boxes of the 2.8 million army food rations which were stockpiled in the Pacific. The committee formed to do this, the Cooperative for American Remittances to Europe (CARE), sought to guarantee the personal delivery of every CARE-package with a receipt from the recipient. In many ways CARE represented a parallel, people-to-people, version of the Marshall Plan.

By 1947, the supply of original rations had dried up and CARE began putting together its own CARE-packages. CARE continued to deliver individual family food packages into Europe until 1955. In the 1950s CARE expanded into Latin America, changing its name to the Cooperative for American Relief Everywhere to reflect the expanding mandate. By the 1960s it had expanded into Africa and when US President Kennedy set up the Peace Corps in 1961, he looked to CARE to train the first volunteers.

By the 1980s, CARE had expanded not only to work internationally but to be in effect an international alliance of independent CAREs. Once again, it changed its name to Cooperative for Assistance and Relief Everywhere, to reflect this new outlook.

CARE's roots therefore are firmly within the compassionate tradition of the Red Cross. In no sense, in these early days, was it seeking to challenge the structures causing famine and poverty, nor did it seem particularly concerned to be independent. Rather, like the early American plans for the League of Red Cross, one gets a sense of a natural alliance between the state actions of the American government and the popular actions of the American people. When the Soviet blockade of Berlin in 1948 prompted the US-led airlift, CARE packages were among the first supplies to be delivered. When the blockade was lifted, CARE trucks were the first vehicles to enter West Berlin.

World Vision

World Vision—today the world's largest international humanitarian NGO—owes its beginnings to a charismatic individual, the Rev. Bob Pierce. Pierce had worked as an evangelical preacher in China in the 1940s and subsequently in Korea in 1950. Returning to the United States, he made creative use of film and brochures to raise funds through child sponsorship to send direct to missions working with children in Korea. In the 1960s his work expanded into other Asian countries and expanded globally in 1974, when the organization's Relief and Development Division was established. World Vision had always had a vision of internationalism. Indeed today it has probably done more than any other international organization, with the possible exception of the IFRC, to create a truly egalitarian global network of equal national organizations. Its mission, then and now, seeks to link Christian evangelism to social and welfare action, and its fundraising methodology remains essentially the same; a well-delivered emotional plea to the Christian population of the wealthy countries of the West.

The cast assembled

By the late 1960s, just about the full cast of what today we would term the international humanitarian system had gathered on stage—donor states, UN bodies, the Red Cross and Red Crescent, and major international NGOs. International conventions governing the treatment of prisoners and civilians in war were in place alongside refugee and human rights conventions, and mechanisms to facilitate the moving of relief goods and food aid.

What we are describing, however, is more like an eco-system than a purpose-built structure. There really is no sense of common purpose or design. The system contains many competing purposes and actors rubbing up against each other. It was on the humanitarian battlefields of the 1970s and 1980s that this system was to flex its muscles and discover its less pleasant limitations.

2 Mercy and manipulation in the Cold War

The period from the Marshall Plan to the 1960s was relatively quiet for humanitarian action. The Kennedy years, characterized in many ways by a greater involvement of US institutions in global action and certainly by the euphoria of the transition away from colonial rule in Asia and Africa, focused on development and nation-building. The Vietnam War, the greatest human tragedy of the 1960s, provoked great political turmoil, but not in terms of humanitarian intervention. The 1970s and 1980s saw relatively more humanitarian action, and was the period in which NGOs came into their own as significant humanitarian actors.

There were, nevertheless, several key events during this era that contributed strongly to the shape of the contemporary humanitarian world. Principally these included the Biafra war; the genocidal rule of the Khmer Rouge in Cambodia, and the response to the aftermath of their ouster by the Vietnamese army in 1978; and of course, famines in Africa, both in the 1970s and during the catastrophic famine in the Horn of Africa in 1983–85.

By the end of the 1980s, not only was there was a much broader public appreciation for—and involvement in—humanitarian action, but there was also a core group of humanitarian workers who would lead the endeavor for much of the ensuing generation. Many of the debates and controversies that characterize that era continue today.

Biafra, 1968–1970: humanitarianism with an independent political edge

The Nigerian civil war marked a turning point for twentieth-century humanitarianism. The Republic of Biafra, covering the southeastern quarter of the Federal Republic of Nigeria, split off from the rest of Nigeria in May 1967. Although a diverse region, Biafra was largely thought of as an ethnic Igbo nation, and contained most of the oil-rich Niger delta region. The split was complicated by many factors: colonialism, post-independent continuation of colonial administrative practices, ethnic competition, and more than a little bit of bloody conflict. Some 30,000 Igbo people living in the north were massacred in late 1966, others were expelled by local governments, and nearly a million people of Igbo origin fled to the southeast. Given the prevailing Cold War international political logic of the era, the UN did not intervene, in either a political or humanitarian mode when Biafra split from Nigeria. There was little support for the secession or the creation of a new fledgling state in Africa from either East or West—indeed, both the UK and the Soviet Union aided the Nigerian federal government during the civil war. Only a handful of countries ever recognized Biafra.

The military strategy of the federal government was to cut off not only Biafra's source of revenue (the oil) but also its overland supply lines. As a military strategy, this worked very effectively: Biafra was militarily defeated in January 1970, and its leaders fled into exile. The humanitarian consequences of the strategy, however, were profound, including widespread malnutrition and mortality. They provoked a debate the echoes of which still resound 40 years later. Though there was never an official count, estimates of the number of Biafrans who died during the man-made famine caused by the blockade run from several hundred thousand to as many as two million.[1]

In 1969, fearing that military assistance was being disguised as humanitarian aid, the Nigerian government banned the ICRC from ferrying humanitarian assistance to Biafra except on planes flying in daylight from Nigerian airfields and which were inspected prior to departure. The Biafran authorities denied permission for daytime flights. The ICRC followed well-established procedures and withdrew from the operation, while continuing to quietly lobby the federal government to reconsider and grant it access. That left the airlift to Joint Church Aid, an operation surpassed only by the 1948 Berlin airlift in volume of relief ferried and for sheer audacity in the face of obstructive authorities. Federal air raids indiscriminately hit humanitarian as well as military targets at Uli—the only functioning airfield in what remained of Biafra by 1969. However, because of both the material assistance it provided and the link to the outside world, the airlift is also credited by many analysts with prolonging the war—as well as the suffering.[2]

The independence struggle was to all intents and purposes lost by the time the news of the humanitarian crisis emerged in the international media, but the crisis spawned a propaganda campaign that probably extended the life of Biafra—and the misery of its people. The classic humanitarian choice—whether to just do the best one is able to do to meet the needs of crisis-affected people or to speak out vocally about the causes of the man-made crisis—played out in Biafra with poignancy equal to the crisis itself. A whole generation of humanitarian workers was forged in the crucible of Biafra, and several new humanitarian agencies were born out of the Biafran experience—most notably Médecins Sans Frontières (MSF) and Concern. MSF will come up again later in this book. Concern, founded in Ireland, is now Concern Worldwide and has a good reputation in emergency interventions. Though "Dunantist" in philosophy, this new kind of organization was motivated as much by a sense of solidarity with the victims of crisis as by traditional humanitarian principles. The dynamics of the humanitarian movement were permanently changed.

The contentious issues faced by humanitarian workers in Biafra still echo in contemporary debates: questions over national sovereignty versus regional self-determination; the instrumentalization of humanitarian assistance for political purposes; the physical security of humanitarian workers; maintaining political neutrality vis-à-vis belligerents while expressing solidarity with humans caught in conflict; objectively measuring the evidence versus being forced to act in an extremely information-scarce (and, in retrospect, propaganda-rich) environment; and the imperative to assist acutely disaster-affected people, but without prolonging the source of the suffering or contributing to its impact. As in later conflict emergencies, many humanitarian workers saw the Biafran people as an oppressed minority, and identified as much with their political cause as with their human suffering.

The ICRC was loudly criticized for its position—including by Bernard Kouchner who had been an ICRC doctor in Biafra and witnessed civilian massacres and the starvation caused by the blockade. He publicly compared ICRC's stance in Biafra with its stance on the Holocaust in World War II.[3] On his return to France, Kouchner and his colleagues openly condemned both the Nigerian government for the blockading tactics, and the ICRC for failing to stand up to the government. This advocacy by doctors and journalists ultimately led to the formation of a new kind of aid agency that was committed to the humanitarian imperative, but which dispensed with the niceties of national sovereignty and which would not presume that silence in the face of atrocity was the price humanitarians have to pay for neutrality. Thus Médecins Sans Frontières was born in 1971, an agency that would play a central role for decades to come, both responding to crisis and also advocating for those caught in crisis. Ultimately, however, the predicted "bloodbath" that many feared would follow a Federal military victory in Biafra never ensued.

Cambodia, 1979–1980: humanitarian action in a Cold War quagmire

Through much of the conflict in Vietnam, Cambodia had managed to remain disengaged from the war. But one of the re-supply routes for the Viet Cong—the so-called "Ho Chi Minh Trail"—ran through Cambodia, and eventually became a strategic target of American intervention, thus dragging Cambodia into the war. In 1975, as the war in Vietnam was coming to an end, a rebel group calling themselves the Khmer Rouge overran the capital and ousted the government. Within days, the Khmer Rouge had emptied Phnom Penh of its residents, forcing them at gunpoint into a Maoist peasant society in which all traces of western influence were eliminated.[4] Modern services ground to a halt; schools, hospitals, and the normal functions of government—as well as the professionals who ran them—were eliminated as the Khmer Rouge implemented their radical vision of a "Democratic Kampuchea" and a collective return to "year zero."

Between 1975 and 1979, Cambodia was virtually closed to the outside world. It is estimated that, during this time between 1.5 and 2 million Cambodians died from starvation, exhaustion, disease, or outright murder by the Khmer Rouge. Little of the detail of these events was known outside Cambodia. In November 1978, in response to increasingly serious border tensions with the Khmer Rouge, Vietnam invaded and by early January 1979 had taken Phnom Penh, and installed a new government led by former Khmer Rouge cadres who had defected to Vietnam. Evidence of massacres and widespread death was everywhere.[5]

In the geopolitical logic of the time, the new regime in Cambodia was clearly beholden to Vietnam, a client state of the Soviet Union. Though driven from the capital, the Khmer Rouge and their "Democratic Kampuchea" still held the seat at the UN, and were considered an ally of the People's Republic of China. When Vietnam invaded, the Chinese ensured that the former King, Sihanouk, who was still in Cambodia under house arrest, was taken to Beijing to denounce the Vietnamese invasion. The king became their tactical ally and apologist as they continued to stake their claim to be Cambodia's legitimate government.

As the Vietnamese army pushed the Khmer Rouge northwest, the stream of Cambodian refugees across the Thai border grew larger and larger and the military government of Thailand cracked down, refouling (forcibly repatriating) thousands of them to their almost certain death. Throughout the first half of 1979, two manifestations of a growing humanitarian problem thus emerged: a refugee crisis on the Thai/Cambodian border, which Thailand initially sought to contain within Cambodia, (meaning that the civilians caught up in the crisis were still under the political domination of the Khmer Rouge, who held the north); and a mounting famine inside Cambodia caused by the final collapse of communalized production, the war, and the utter absence of infrastructure or a functioning economy or health-care system. Both the Vietnamese-backed fledgling government in Phnom Penh and the US-backed Thai government sought to portray the humanitarian crisis in terms favorable to themselves, but ultimately dictated by Cold War objectives.[6]

Two different response mechanisms arose to attempt to deal with these problems. First, the UN designated UNICEF as its lead agency in the crisis, while the ICRC delegation in Bangkok had long and quietly tracked developments and were determined not to repeat the difficulties it had faced in Biafra. Representatives of UNICEF and the ICRC—working through contacts in the Vietnamese government— sought permission to undertake an assessment inside Cambodia. At the same time, a coalition of NGOs, led by Oxfam, formed the Consortium for Cambodia and secured a budget of $40 million for relief in Cambodia—an unprecedented sum for an NGO operation at the time, and also an amount larger than the entire global budget of Oxfam at the time.[7] The NGOs expressly rejected the Cold War ideological terms in which the humanitarian crisis had been cast. But the UN agencies were somewhat more hamstrung, falling victim to superpower vetoes in the Security Council, thus having to respect the sovereignty of member states—including the Khmer Rouge, who continued to hold the UN seat for Cambodia.

The United States did not want humanitarian assistance to be channeled through the new Vietnam-affiliated government in Phnom Penh, and so deliberately used the humanitarian crisis on the Thai border to rebuild the ability of the Khmer Rouge to counter-balance the political influence of the Vietnamese. This was done irrespective of the atrocities the Khmer Rouge had committed while in power. The United States went to extraordinary lengths to belittle the efforts of the Consortium, proclaiming loudly that any such aid would "end up in Ho Chi Minh City." So it was in the context of extreme—though largely unassessed—human need, as well as considerable super-power opposition, that the NGOs set about to mount a relief operation inside

Cambodia.[8] The ICRC/UNICEF team finally gained access to Cambodia in July 1979. Oxfam's team arrived in early August, and based on an initial positive interaction with the government, expanded operations.[9]

The Consortium was able to mount a sizable relief operation. Their terms of access required them to recognize the new regime as the legitimate government of Cambodia, and also to bring supplies into the country either by barge up the Mekong River, or by air—not over the so-called "land bridge" on the Thai border, where goods would have fallen into the hands of the Khmer Rouge. In return, the Consortium negotiated access to a widening arc around Phnom Penh and was able to distribute food, medicine and seeds, and to monitor their use.

In his memoir of this effort, Brian Walker who headed Oxfam at the time, notes that despite the scale of the operation with respect to the overall budget of his own organization, it was nevertheless "penny packets" of aid compared to the assistance later offered by the UN or the World Bank (and of course not nearly adequate to address the massive need at the time). But the point wasn't so much about whether an independent NGO consortium could mount an effort that could address the acute needs of half the population of a country—it clearly could not. The point was that the Consortium had shown the way to cut through the political impasse to address the crisis inside Cambodia, which neither the UN nor the ICRC had been able to do. Walker notes in conclusion that, "articulating humanitarianism as a kind of conscience to governments, multinationals and the general public"[10] is what NGOs proved that they can do best—and did do best in the Cold War context of post-Khmer Rouge Cambodia.

Famines in Africa—the 1970s and 1980s

Though famines now seem to be exclusively associated with Africa, this is a fairly recent development. For much of the twentieth century, famines were considered primarily an Asian phenomenon—and indeed there were famines of significant proportions in Europe during the nineteenth century. From the 1970s onward, large-scale famines in Africa began receiving attention.

The Sahel

In the middle of 1973, it became clear to the world that a large-scale famine was taking place on the southern fringes of the Sahara desert in

Africa—the culmination of five years of drought, and the harbinger of a world-wide food crisis in 1974 that led to the first World Food Conference. The world had to confront, for the first time since the 1940s, the possibility that there might not be enough food to go around for everyone. Amartya Sen was later to demonstrate that drought and an apparent global food shortage notwithstanding the crisis faced by Sahelian farmers and pastoralists had less to do with an outright food shortage than with the population's inability to access what food was available.[11] Yet, for a while in the early to mid-1970s, it appeared as though Thomas Malthus' nightmare scenario of population growth outstripping resources might finally be realized.

Though long populated, the Sahel receives barely enough rainfall in a normal year to support crop production. Periodic drought in the region is common, but following a run of exceptionally good rainfall in the 1950s and 1960s, the period from 1968 onwards was characterized first by less than average rains and then by outright drought. The drought was reported as early as 1969 and by 1972 was sufficiently serious to warrant a request for emergency assistance from donors. Only in 1973/74 was a major response mounted—predominantly by the World Food Programme and the Food and Agriculture Organization, but also by NGOs.

Kent Glenzer notes:

> A massive response followed, in which across much of the Sahel relief aid was [intended] for political purposes by African states, targeting of aid provision was amateurish, local grain markets were harmed, tens of thousands of Africans and their livestock perished, aid entrepreneurs enriched themselves, corruption was rampant, and scores of international NGOs planted permanent roots in countries in which they had never worked, many of which are still there.[12]

If Biafra was, for humanitarian action, the forerunner of the conflict-emergencies of a later era, the Sahelian famine of the early 1970s forever put the term "slow-onset" crisis on the humanitarian map. The manner in which the crisis was understood, and the pattern set by the response, had repercussions for decades. The term "famine" and the powerful images it evokes, provide a humanitarian case study of their own. Though thoroughly addressed analytically in Sen's work, famine remained curiously undefined for decades—in terms of magnitude and severity on the one hand, and manifestation on the other. Sen clearly defined famine as a problem of starvation brought about by a failure of consumption, though he recognized manifestations other than just mortality by out-right starvation. The seminal work of Alex de Waal in the 1980s on destitution and the impact of famine in terms of health rather than simple starvation, helped to better understand the manifestation of famine. The popular usage of the term was perhaps most strongly defined for the current generation by the Ethiopian famine of the mid-1980s. Recent works have helped to define famine better in terms of severity and magnitude.[13]

The scope of the crisis stretched from Mauritania and Senegal on the Atlantic to the Red Sea coast of Ethiopia, but the main impact was felt in Mali, Niger, Burkina Faso (then Upper Volta), and Chad. Estimates of mortality vary. Initial reports put the death toll at 100,000, but subsequent estimates were much higher.[14] While Sen argued conclusively that the manifestation of the famine was more significant in terms of affecting demand-side factors (i.e. access to food) more significantly than supply-side factors (i.e. aggregate supply), there remained a substantial debate over causal factors—and therefore over the longer-term implications for famine-prevention policy. Ecological factors dominated the discourse at the time,[15] while more recent analyses have emphasized political factors—both in terms of the causes of the crisis.[16] But in all the discussion over causes and mani-festations of the famine/drought, the humanitarian response itself has been largely overlooked. Much of the actual response to the famine came from international donors through national governments. Independent humanitarian agencies played bit parts, their roles in crisis response remained undefined at this time. By the standards of the day, the response was massive, if too late to prevent serious malnutrition and starvation. Stephen Devereux notes three main reasons for the failure of timely humanitarian response—poor information, poor logistical capacity, and in some cases, callous disregard for the con-sequences of the crisis.[17]

But it was the question of the availability of good information that captured the attention of policymakers at the time. For much of the unfolding of the Sahelian crisis, information about the drought—and particularly information about its impact—was limited at best.

The birth of famine early warning

Though Sen's seminal work on famine would not come out for another eight years, his analysis helped to underpin the development of famine early warning systems. Although drought played a significant role in triggering both the Biafran and Sahel crises, neither was characterized by an outright shortage of food. Indeed, in both cases, surplus-producing regions existed immediately adjacent to the hardest hit famine locations. Rather than an outright food availability decline, people hit by these crises suffered a serious decline in their access to food, or an entitlement failure. This was brought about by a variety of factors, including an inability to produce adequate food—but also a distinct repositioning of the value of labor, livestock and other assets that represented both current and future income of hard-hit groups.

Though Sen's insight was primarily theoretical, the practical consequences were that if the *process* of entitlement failure could be mapped, it should be possible to predict actual famines *events* more accurately. This observation triggered a massive literature documenting "coping strategies" or the manner in which vulnerable people and households manage shrinking food stocks, incomes, and assets in the face of drought, rising food prices, or other crises.[18] "Coping" thus came to indicate both current difficulties and a worsening situation, and early warning of greater problems to come. The combined understanding of various means of coping, together with improved remote sensing gave birth to the practice of famine early warning.

The link between addressing humanitarian concerns in an acute crisis ("humanitarian assistance") and addressing the causes of the chronic problems that may result in such crises ("development assistance") became enshrined in the notion of the "relief-to-development continuum"—the notion that external intervention could, and should, shift quickly from addressing short-term manifestations of a crisis to tackling its longer-term causes. To what extent this relegated improvement of the humanitarian response to a secondary consideration has been debated ever since. In theory, this application made sense in slow-onset crises, triggered by climatic factors such as drought, but underpinned by environmental degradation and economic crisis. Its application in famines with other causes has been problematic.

The seeds of slow response

With the founding of early warning has come the dilemma that, for a variety of reasons, has dogged the humanitarian endeavor ever since the Sahelian drought. In spite of relatively good early warning information, the international community remains painfully slow to respond in crises where, precisely because the onset is slow and—at least to some extent—predictable, rapid and early response should be relatively straightforward.

Glenzer's account of the crisis—and over 30 years of follow-up in an increasingly fragile environment—calls the humanitarian endeavor to counter famine in the Sahel an institutionalized "partial success." Although hundreds of thousands of lives were no doubt saved, the response did not get into high gear until tens of thousands were already dead, and despite over three decades of subsequent experience—in the Sahel and elsewhere in Africa—the speed and flexibility of humanitarian response in slow-onset crises has not dramatically improved. Sen notes the same ambivalence about the effectiveness of the humanitarian response in the Sahel in the 1970s.[19] Margie Buchanan-Smith and Susannah Davies note that lack of information is only one factor that may slow a response.[20] More often, donors simply do not trust the information that is available, or have competing objectives. Recent work (not related to the Sahel famine) shows that good humanitarian information, and even media pressure, are often insufficient to elicit a humanitarian response from donors if they do not have a clear geo-political rationale.[21]

Glenzer offers a further explanation for why this disjunction occurs. The early warning and response systems that were developed to address the Sahel crisis were set up to address the needs of external interveners, rather than those of the communities at risk or of African governments. Glenzer summarizes:

> At root, the role of the international early warning and response system was to inform African governments when they had a problem and to initiate the process through which officials back home in Washington, Ottawa, Brussels, or other European capitals made the political decisions to respond. As the 1980s ended, therefore, the international relief community had built a system founded on African incapacity, assuming African corruption, deeply tied to export markets in the North, focused on accounting for goods moved not good done, and one that constructed the problem as much larger than Africans could possibly handle on their own ... This produced debilitating gaps between those who diagnosed, those who decided, those who acted, and those whose sovereignty and human rights were at stake.[22]

Ethiopia, 1973–74 and 1984–95: disaster, regime change, and global intervention

> Dawn ... and as the sun breaks through the piercing chill of night on the plain outside of Korem it lights up a biblical famine, now, in the 20th century. This place, say workers here, is the closest thing to hell on earth ... Death is all around.[23]

Though perhaps the world rather quickly forgot about the Sahelian crisis, it was dramatically re-awakened to African famine by Michael Buerk's famous BBC broadcast and the film footage of Kenyan photographer Mohamed Amin in the autumn of 1984. Ethiopia and other parts of the Horn of Africa had also been hit by the drought that affected the Sahel, first affecting the pastoral lowlands, and later the more politically sensitive and chronically vulnerable central highland areas of Wollo and Hararghe. Failure to recognize and deal swiftly with the consequences of the famine is widely believed to have been one of the factors leading to the overthrow of Emperor Haile Selassie's feudalist rule in 1974 by a group of young army officers that came to be known as the Derg.[24] The impact of famine on the stability of the government in power was a factor that was apparently lost on the Derg themselves, but which was duly noted by the Derg's internal opponents and by donor governments around the world.

During the 1972–74 famine, it is clear that information was suppressed, that the extent of the crisis did not become clear until far too late, and that the limited response from the government was mainly politically motivated. Both factors were to recur in the 1984–85 crisis. Many observers believe that the policies of the Derg in dealing with the 1984–85 crisis (both the role of the army in causing the crisis, and the subsequent failure to control it) ultimately led to its overthrow at the hands of guerilla movements from Tigray and Eritrea.

While the famine in the 1970s is remembered mainly for the end of the feudal empire, the famine of the 1980s probably shaped people's view of humanitarian action more than any other single event during the Cold War. It had many complex elements:

- There was, of course, abject humanitarian suffering, captured on television for the world to see. In the end, the best estimate is about one million deaths from the famine, with close to eight million people affected—a quarter of Ethiopia's population.
- The crisis unfolded directly around Cold War competition between spheres of Western and Soviet influence. The Derg transformed Ethiopia into a Soviet client state in relatively short order during the so-called Red Terror in 1975, collectivizing rural agriculture and clamping down on private business. But most of the humanitarian response came from the West.
- Like earlier crises, this one was characterized by a dearth of accurate information—or more accurately, deliberately covered up information—about the crisis until it was far too late.

- While the crisis of 1984–85 was triggered by a massive drought, this was not the only precipitating cause. The famine was to some extent both a deliberate war strategy and the obvious consequence of that strategy. As the Derg fought opponents in Eritrea and Tigray, its military used food as a weapon,[25] triggering by 1984 both massive displacement—internally and across the border into Sudan—and disruption of agricultural production.[26]

The humanitarian agencies refrained from making such an accusation at the time. But aid was systematically diverted or manipulated by the Derg, who in turn were able to keep both donors and agencies from doing much about it—fearful as the agencies were of losing access to famine-affected populations were they to publicly highlight any diversion. De Waal notes that there was a silent agreement between the agencies and the Derg whereby the agencies maintained a "hands-off" policy towards the war in return for unfettered access to famine-affected populations outside the war zone.[27]

The response of the Derg to the famines of earlier eras was to collectivize rural agricultural production, and to resettle large segments of the rural population—often in a forced manner—in less densely populated and less environmentally degraded areas.[28] Jason Clay and Bonnie Holcombe suggested that forced resettlement was another component of the war strategy. Forced resettlement not only abused human rights by its very nature, it also put people into situations where there was no rural infrastructure in terms of health, education, or local governance. When the crisis inevitably affected these areas too, there were neither local government nor kinship-based structures for families to fall back on. In many ways, although forever labeled a natural disaster because of the role of climatic factors in triggering the crisis, the Ethiopian famine was a "complex emergency" both in terms of causal factors and the political economy of the crisis' impact. However one looks at it, while there is no doubt that the drought played a factor, the Ethiopia famine of 1984–85 was not just a natural disaster.

Finally, and probably most importantly in terms of the change to the humanitarian enterprise, there was a massive international response that included not only the usual humanitarian agencies and actors. The Ethiopian famine became a *cause célèbre* among millions of ordinary people worldwide and led to unprecedented fundraising and awareness-raising by celebrities including, most famously, the rock star Bob Geldof. He organized the Band Aid initiative by recording and selling a popular song about the famine[29] and went on to organize the Live Aid concert on 13 July 1985. Watched by an estimated 1.5 billion viewers, Live Aid raised $140 million for both immediate famine relief and for later recovery programs. Buerk's famous broadcast from Korem and Geldof's global rock concert both underlined the power of television for humanitarian action. And both brought a new level of awareness of humanitarian crises to global audiences.

Reflecting on the Ethiopian famine, former Oxfam worker Tony Vaux notes that during this era, humanitarianism became "popular"— and that was part of the difficulty in taking the political reality into account. The political manipulation behind the Ethiopian famine defied easy classification. Vaux admits that aid agencies were naïve, but also reflects on why it took so long for the famine to come to everyone's attention, and what might have happened had Amin and Buerk not made their (somewhat coincidental) trip to Wollo?

Reflecting a certain degree of ambivalence towards de Waal's analysis, Vaux notes that, faced with acute suffering, many humanitarian workers

> feel it is a waste of time to complain about the abstract politics that caused it. Instead we want the world to feel what we feel, a sense of bereavement, the loss of people and happiness, the recognition that we have been diminished by what we have seen ... It needs to be said that that compassion is not a means to an end, but an end in itself, and some of the greatest work of aid agencies is not what they intend, but what their staff do out of their own humanity. But ... when the suffering is caused by the actions of other people, the principle of humanity should extend towards understanding. If the cause is an act of man, it is better not to call it an act of God.[30]

Vaux notes that the "act of God" idea was allowed to prevail—politics were kept out of the reporting and the imagery. The "biblical" famine of Buerk's BBC report didn't mention (or record) the Derg's fighter-bombers as they flew overhead northward into Tigray to bomb not only their enemies in the Tigrayan People's Liberation Front, but also food markets and population centers. Nor did Amin's cameras record the rocket launchers just outside the famine camps of Korem. Challenging the political causes *as well as* responding to humanitarian needs was the reason why MSF had been founded. True to their calling, MSF France did withdraw from their humanitarian work in Ethiopia (apparently only days before they would have been kicked out by the Derg). But the challenge of not only speaking truth to power, but also providing assistance to those who need it, arose yet again in

1984/85, and remains one of the unresolved challenges of humanitarian action.

From the vantage point of 15 years of hindsight Vaux adds one more factor in the slow response. The ideology of famine response was conditioned by the experience of the Sahelian drought where the problem had been diagnosed at least to some extent as a failure of development, and the "developmentalist" school of thought reigned supreme in the aid agencies by the mid-1980s. Humanitarian response was equated with the mythical "give-a-man-a-fish" narrative, but "teach-a-man-to-fish" had become the ideology by the mid-1980s.[31] Agencies ignored real evidence of the famine because the aid response that was clearly necessary would put development programming on hold. *Humanitarianism* was about an old-fashioned kind of charity that viewed "beneficiaries" as helpless victims, whereas *development* was about a new kind of partnership in which "participants" took control of their own lives and improved them—"a hand up, not a hand-out" was the popular slogan of another agency during the era. And of course, if humanitarian action didn't fit the developmentalist ideology, neither did war—especially a predatory war of a state against its own people. Agencies, to quote Vaux, "lived in a dream world from which the famine was a rude awakening."[32]

Hence, in many ways, the story of the Ethiopian famine was about everything and everybody—the politics, the excuses and finger-pointing, the late response, the politicians and rebel movements, the journalists, aid workers, and celebrities who all weighed in. Perhaps the only missing "voice" on the famine—its causes and what the appropriate response should have been—was that of the people who suffered its effects.

3 The globalization of humanitarianism

From the end of the Cold War to the Global War on Terror

The period between 1989 and 2001 was a time of tremendous upheaval and growth for the humanitarian enterprise. Whereas during the Cold War humanitarians were often considered a group of politically naïve do-gooders, three major events in the first half of the 1990s would force major changes in the humanitarian world. These include the Balkans wars (particularly the war in Bosnia), the civil war and famine in Somalia (including the ill-fated US military intervention), and especially the Rwanda genocide and subsequent refugee crisis (particularly in Goma). The aftermath of 9/11 required further adaptations to a changed world.

The Balkans wars

While a brief period of euphoria in international relations followed the fall of the Berlin Wall in 1989, it soon became clear that both the break-up of the former Yugoslavia, and the inability of the rest of Europe to effectively prevent it, were among its consequences. Though preceded by important changes that increasingly regionalized Yugoslavia's economy, the break-up of the country was widely believed to be fueled by resurgent Serbian nationalism. The national army, which had become an instrument of Serbian nationalism, moved into Croatia and Slovenia in the summer of 1991. The war quickly ended in Slovenia, resulting in its independence, but continued in Croatia, and by early 1992 had spread to Bosnia-Herzegovina.

The Bosnian war forever put the term "ethnic cleansing" into the popular lexicon as whole areas were cleared of non-Serb populations and Muslims in particular were forcibly displaced into cordoned-off zones.[1] Large-scale displacement started in northern Bosnia in March 1992 and provision of humanitarian assistance to the displaced began shortly thereafter. While the war initially pitted Bosnian Serbs against the Muslim majority, eventually fighting embroiled Bosnia's Croat communities as well. Eventually some four million people were displaced by the fighting—all but a tiny fraction of whom remained in Bosnia, but in areas controlled by their own ethnic group. Even for those not displaced, the war caused extreme hardship, particularly during the harsh Balkan winters. At times over half the population was dependent on humanitarian assistance.[2] The war lasted until the end of 1995, when, after heavy NATO aerial bombardment, the Bosnian Serb Army had suffered significant military setbacks and agreed to peace talks.

Several things stand out about the Bosnian war. It was the first actual military combat on the European continent since 1945 and had a significantly chilling effect on the optimism that had arisen after the end of the long Cold War stand-off. Unlike humanitarian crises elsewhere in the world, reporters and aid workers alike noted "profound similarities" between themselves and the people on whom they were reporting, or whom they were meant to be aiding.[3] A resurgent Europe took it upon itself to manage the crisis, but found that there were distinctly different political allegiances and priorities, and ultimately there wasn't much of a coordinated European approach to the problem.

But more fundamentally, the one thing that other European countries could agree on was that if there was going to be a war with humanitarian consequences in Europe, it had to be contained within the former Yugoslavia and preferably within Bosnia itself. Thus the UN refugee agency, UNHCR, came to lead the humanitarian response to a crisis in which the vast majority of the victims had not crossed any international boundary, and thus were not covered under international refugee law. And, indeed, while UNCHR's mandate was the protection of refugees, in Bosnia, the primary task was relegated to the provision of assistance. While Bosnia certainly underlined the need for more adequate civilian protection mechanisms in war, few were made available and those that were available were feeble and misunderstood. In mid-1992 the UN Security Council authorized the UN Protection Force for Yugoslavia (UNPROFOR), but its remit was to protect Sarajevo airport, and enable the passage of humanitarian assistance. Even after so-called "safe areas" were established the following year in designated places in eastern and central Bosnia, those affected by conflict were offered little real protection. This reality was forever burned into international humanitarian consciousness when Serb forces massacred an estimated 8,000 Muslim men and boys inside the "safe area" of Srebrenica in 1995, even as UNPROFOR peacekeepers stood helplessly by. With a troop strength of 30,000, UNPROFOR was one of the largest UN forces of its time but its mandate was to protect humanitarian assistance intended for people affected by the war, not to provide protection for the people themselves. This restricted role underlined both the impotence of the international community to stop the war, and its equal determination to contain the spill-over effects from the war within Bosnia itself. A regional refugee crisis was to be prevented at all costs—containment of the crisis, not its resolution, was the policy objective for several years of the war.[4]

Against that background, and effectively without existing guidelines on how to deal with such a crisis, most observers credit UNHCR with a good job of coordinating the humanitarian response. The Sarajevo airlift, in particular, was able to keep the inhabitants of the city supplied with necessary food and non-food items through a protracted siege. WFP delivered over a million tons of food aid. But, in effect, the humanitarian assistance was substituted for political action to stop the war in Bosnia.

The Bosnian war caused a profound reassessment of the humanitarian principles of neutrality and impartiality. The Bosnian government complained bitterly during the war that it was subjected to the same arms embargo as the Serb army by the international community, even though the Serb army was re-supplied by Belgrade and was clearly the aggressor. Faced with the reality of what David Rieff called "UN internment camps" for displaced Bosnian Muslims, humanitarians too came to question their commitment to neutrality as either a basic operating principle or a necessary means to the end of maintaining access to affected populations. And UNHCR faced the dilemma of becoming in effect a passive participant in ethnic cleansing—by helping Muslims escape areas overrun by the Bosnian Serb Army—or else standing by and watching people being murdered.[5] These realities politicized humanitarian aid workers like no crisis since perhaps Biafra. In the aftermath of the Bosnia war the delivery of humanitarian aid was increasingly couched in the language of human rights, and humanitarian agencies increasingly devoted resources to advocacy as well as to on-the-ground operations.

The Dayton Peace Accord of 1995 ended the fighting and essentially partitioned Bosnia into separate ethnic areas. But the break-up of the former Yugoslavia continued for many more years. By the time fighting broke out in the Muslim-dominated Serbian province of Kosovo in 1999, the language of "humanitarian warfare" was in full flower. Indeed NATO responded quickly and decisively to prevent another situation like Bosnia from recurring in Kosovo. There was a short war—sparking an acute quick onset refugee crisis—but NATO air power relatively quickly brought conflict to an end. The Kosovo war not only put "humanitarian warfare" on the map, it also brought out in graphic terms the growing gap between what humanitarian donors were willing to pay for in a conflict in their own back yard (the Balkans) compared to the response to distant and untelevised places like the Democratic Republic of the Congo (DRC). Until the massive international response to the Indian Ocean tsunami of December 2004, the per capita response to the Kosovo war was the highest of any crisis on record.

Somalia

Unlike many other post-Cold War humanitarian crises of similar or even greater scale, Somalia stands out in the memory of the era and in the shaping of subsequent events. As in the history of warfare, throughout the history of humanitarian action, humanitarians have been preparing for the "last battle" rather than the "next" one. Nowhere is this linkage more pronounced—and nowhere did it have such consequences—as in the response to the crises that engulfed Somalia in 1992–1993, and the "next" crisis—the Rwanda genocide.

Like most of the crises of the 1990s, the famine that gripped Somalia in 1991/1992—and which came to grip the attention of the Western world after graphic depictions of it hit the television news—has its own history and roots, and its own consequences for the people and nation that suffered it. For much of the rest of the international community and particularly for humanitarianism, "Somalia" became a "syndrome"—symbolizing the attempts of well-meaning outsiders to intervene in a humanitarian crisis but then getting caught up in it. Walter Clarke described this syndrome as "a naïve attempt to implement benevolent intervention in a marginal third world state [that was] doomed to failure."[6] Thomas Weiss described the Somalia intervention as the demise of "Pollyannaish humanitarianism."[7]

Reconstructing the entire Somalia story is complex. The country was forged in 1960 from British and Italian colonial entities, but did not include all of the Somali people—many of whom lived across its borders in Ethiopia, Kenya, and Djibouti. Somalis attach primary importance to clan affiliation, rather than embracing a national concept. From the time he seized power in 1969 until the central state broke up following his overthrow in 1991, Somalia was ruled by Siad Barre. While he declared the clan system a thing of the past, informally Barre favored his own clan and excluded other major clans from power, cleverly manipulated the loyalties of smaller clans, and even shrewdly exploited Cold War tensions—jumping ship from the Soviet Union and embracing the West—to maintain his grip on power.[8] Inter-clan rivalry boiled over into open warfare and by the late 1980s conflict which broke out in the north had engulfed many parts of the vast country. A coalition of forces toppled the Barre regime in 1991, but it quickly became apparent that no one faction would prevail in forming a new government, and there was no formula for power sharing. Somalia quickly broke up into areas under the authority of local militia or clan leaders and all subsequent attempts to restore central government—up to the US-backed Ethiopian military intervention in early 2007—have failed.

De Waal notes that, given all the analysis of the failure of the humanitarian and military intervention, few *ex post* analyses have bothered to deal with the actual causes and consequences of the famine itself—that the actual humanitarian crisis is viewed as, at best, a foot-note. Most analyses simply chalk it up to "anarchy" and lack of the rule of law. While it is true that some highly publicized incidents of looting or interfering with food aid were instrumental in bringing the famine to the attention of the rest of the world, the famine itself was deeply rooted in the flawed institutions of the post-colonial state. The most widely affected groups were the long-marginalized riverine farm-ing communities, and people displaced by the fighting that had spread to southern Somalia in 1991. The actual fighting that deposed Barre was in some of the more fertile areas of the country—in the Bay and Shebelle regions. Long-standing land tenure disputes led many of the region's inhabitants to side with anti-Barre elements in the fighting, but their grievances were not addressed by the forces that toppled the Barre government. People were also displaced into the Shabelle valley by the fighting in Mogadishu. This combination of factors led to a rapid depletion of existing food stocks, the breakdown of intra-regional trade, and the emergence of a "looting economy." A whole growing season was lost in some areas. By early to mid 1992, it was clear there was a significant famine, though its consequences varied significantly by location.[9] Though the ICRC had long been present in the area, and had been responding to the famine in 1991, a much more major relief effort geared up in early 1992. Several influential television reports raised the profile of the crisis in the international community. Aid workers who have written about Somalia in subsequent years speak of an almost race-like imperative to get into Somalia and to be seen to be doing so.[10]

The UN, however, did not have field-based leadership in Somalia—instead operating—as it continues to do today—out of distant Nairobi and was slow to respond. By the time it got involved, humanitarian intervention was being overtaken by events on the ground. Several high profile cases of looting of aid, including the hijacking of food supply convoys by rag-tag soldiers of clan militias, were juxtaposed in the media with clips of people starving as a result of the famine. These images began to build public demand for another kind of intervention—military intervention to protect the humanitarian convoys. As Alex de Waal notes, there was a mounting "drumbeat for intervention" in Somalia.[11] There is some evidence that the worst of the crisis was already past by the middle of 1992, and the UN special representative, Mohamed Sahnoun, was making some progress in getting warring factions to negotiate. But external pressures were too strong. President George H.W. Bush (senior) was said to have been personally disturbed by images of militias interfering with aid convoys, and saw a chance to help build a post-Cold War "New World Order" through multi-lateral intervention in Somalia.[12] On the ground, some agencies—specifically CARE, but others as well—called for military intervention to tame the militias and enable food aid to get through to people affected by the famine. A UN peacekeeping force was approved in April, and by September, 500 troops had been sent to Somalia. But it soon became apparent that this was far too small a force. A US-led (and UN-sanctioned) initiative called Operation Restore Hope was set up and in December 1992 troops waded ashore—in the style of World War II hero General Douglas MacArthur—onto a Mogadishu beach where they were greeted by CNN television camera crews.[13] It was intended to be a short, intensive operation, handing over to a UN-led operation in May 1993. The timing was unfortunate as George H.W. Bush, then a lame-duck President, was set to be replaced by Bill Clinton who was much more concerned with domestic issues than his predecessor. This significant level of international interference in Somali clan politics was not well received by many of the faction leaders, particularly one of the strongest—General Mohamed Aideed of the Somali National Alliance. On 5 June 1993, his forces attacked and killed 24 Pakistani peacekeepers, elevating what had been a nagging problem to a full-blown international crisis. Ensuing attempts to capture or kill Aideed culminated in an ill-fated US Army attack on a Mogadishu hotel in October that left 18 US soldiers dead and two Blackhawk helicopters shot down. One of the dead American soldiers was dragged through the streets of Mogadishu—scenes dutifully captured by the omnipresent television cameras—while throngs of Somalis cheered wildly. As Michael Barnett notes: "For Americans whose last memory was of US soldiers delivering desperately needed food to grateful Somalis, this was a jolting change."[14]

The impact of the debacle is difficult to over-estimate. US and UN credibility was undermined and the willingness of the international community to intervene (whether to protect aid convoys or to try to directly stop the killing) was immediately in question. There were repercussions on the other side of the world. A week later, a UN technical team in Haiti, mandated to help restore a democratically-elected president, was on board a US warship when it was met by a vaguely threatening crowd on the docks of Port-au-Prince. Rather than risk a Mogadishu-style confrontation, the captain of the *USS Harlan County* weighed anchor and left the port. These images combined to present a picture of both indecisiveness and poor planning in the new US administration, and poor coordination and leadership on the part of the UN. This led directly to scaling back UN efforts to resolve the conflict in Bosnia and to policy changes in the Department of Peacekeeping Operations at the UN. These policy shifts made it possible for the UN to intervene in Rwanda in late 1993, but paralyzed it when the genocide began.

But that all begs the question of what happened subsequently in Somalia. The famine did end, and the international relief effort did save some lives. But equally the effort may have prolonged the crisis. Noting that the roots of the famine were political (not climatic or economic), Karin von Hippel points out, "Not only did international actors exacerbate the famine and civil war by sending in food aid, most of which was subsequently stolen, but they became involved in clan politics ... which contributed to further political disintegration."[15] Somalis themselves were almost completely excluded from any of the decision-making about the intervention. Even the Somali staff of international organizations complained that their own headquarters consulted only their international staff in-country.[16]

Somalia again raised the issue of the relationship between the political work of resolving conflict and the humanitarian work of addressing acute suffering. Analysts have drawn differing conclusions from the case, but the issue remains unresolved. Competition among the aid agencies effectively prevented ordinary rules of humanitarian access from being observed by agencies—fueling the conflict rather than addressing the human suffering it engendered. The assumption that the right of humanitarian access was automatic and should be protected by the international community of states has tended to privilege the needs of the interveners more than the needs of affected populations—a phenomenon de Waal refers to as "humanitarian impunity."[17]

Finally, it is very difficult to ignore the role of live, round-the-clock, television coverage of the Somalia conflict. The so-called "CNN effect" was first widely noted during the Gulf War in 1991, but was in full force during the Somalia crisis—depictions of famine-ravaged communities raised the profile of the crisis in the first place. Subsequent images of starving people, juxtaposed with clips of gun-wielding teenagers chewing *khat* (a plant whose leaves are chewed as a stimulant) and thumbing their noses at UN peacekeeping troops, led to the massive build-up of Operation Restore Hope. Images of dead US Army Rangers showed the intervention had neither restored hope nor cemented the much-vaunted "New World Order" its architects had intended. Live cable television news as an instrument of policy-making had clearly arrived.[18]

Rwanda: genocide and its aftermath

Of all the events that have shaped the contemporary humanitarian enterprise, none is more influential than the Rwandan genocide of 1994. While one of the proximate causes of the genocide was the failure of peacekeeping and a vacuum of political action, humanitarian action was implicated in its aftermath, and even in its antecedents, in ways that demanded profound changes in the organization and implementation of humanitarian action.

Many volumes have been written on the genocide, the events leading up to it, and the accounts of states, institutions and individuals caught up in trying either to halt the genocide or to make excuses for their inaction. Here we attempt to distill out the critical impacts on the humanitarian system that resulted from both the humanitarian response to the genocide, and the refugee crisis that it spawned.

From the time of independence from Belgium in 1962 until the invasion by the Rwandan Tutsi rebel group, the Rwandan Patriotic Front (RPF) from their base in Uganda in October 1990, Rwanda had been considered a poster child for development orthodoxy. The country was considered stable, if not very wealthy, and its President, Juvénal Habyarimana, democratic (though he came to power in a *coup d'état*). Although the Hutu–Tutsi rivalry that partially drove the genocide was clearly evident in the country's history, the pogroms of the late 1950s that had driven the Tutsis to Uganda in the first place were forgotten or ignored by the international community, as was the "semi-official racism" in the national political system. The country's economic data was reasonably impressive.[19] Economic growth was constant, if modest, child mortality was dropping, and the balance of payments—aided significantly by foreign aid—compared favorably to other nations in the region.

That a "development success story" (if only a modest one) could descend into the nightmare of ethnic holocaust was simply unbelievable to many who knew the country well. But "development," in this sense, was viewed as an entirely apolitical process. Hence the belief by the international community in Rwanda as a success story contributed to a collective disbelief that genocide was actually taking place in 1994, and hence to the virtually non-existent international response.

After a brief flurry of initial activity, the war settled into a relatively low-grade conflict that simmered along for three years through several cease-fire agreements, the last of which in 1993 had international backing and a UN Security Council resolution and provided for a peacekeeping force UNAMIR—the UN Assistance Mission to Rwanda. Generally, Rwanda was thought of as an "easy" case in terms of peacekeeping, in comparison with other conflicts of the time.[20] It is impossible to understand the international response to Rwanda without looking at other contemporary crises, most notably Somalia. In the aftermath of the Cold War, the political and security arms of the UN experienced a resurgence as it was called upon to intervene in many crises between 1990 and 1993. The peacekeeping budget doubled, then doubled again. The UN was having "a pretty good year"[21] until the Somalia debacle (the real debacle for the UN had been the killing of 24 Pakistani peacekeeping troops, though most of the world remembers the downing of two US helicopters and the image of an American corpse being dragged through the streets of Mogadishu). There was a strong reluctance in the aftermath of the Somalia fiasco for the international community to engage in complex internal conflicts, but Rwanda was not believed to be such a case.

There were warnings of the potential for catastrophic inter-ethnic violence in Rwanda. The commander of UNAMIR, Canadian Lieutenant General Roméo Dallaire, indicated as early as January 1994 that he had gathered intelligence indicating Hutu plans for widespread killings of Tutsis, and some of the peacekeepers, and with government knowledge. But the information was not taken seriously by leaders in UN headquarters who were reluctant to step up what was supposed to be a relatively straightforward mission. Violence increased generally in February and March and on 6 April a plane carrying both President Habyarimana and his Burundian counterpart was shot down as it landed at Kigali airport. Hard-line Hutu militants seized power, over-riding the constitutional successor to the presidency—the Prime Minister—and eventually killing her and her family. Ten Belgian peacekeepers trying to protect the Prime Minister were also killed, which had the intended effect of Belgium's withdrawal from UNAMIR just at the time when widespread and obvious killings were kicked into high gear. In response, the RPF pulled out of the ceasefire and began a concerted march towards Kigali as the only way to stop the killing of Tutsis. Two weeks later, the UN Security Council further reduced UNAMIR's strength.

Over the following three months, an estimated 800,000 Rwandans were killed, mostly Tutsis and Hutus opposed to the killings, mostly with primitive weapons like machetes, and mostly at the hands of their neighbors and acquaintances. The national army and the *Interahamwe* militias played a major role in the killings, but much of it was done by inciting the masses. The international community debated and dithered, even as bodies literally floated down rivers into other countries and Dallaire reported increasing numbers of killings inside Rwanda. In May, the Security Council finally agreed to increase UNAMIR's strength. The RPF meanwhile, had stepped up military pressure and by late May had captured the Kigali airport. As the extremist government collapsed, the Security Council finally authorized "Operation Turquoise" led by the French, to create a "safe zone" in southern Rwanda. The RPF captured all of Kigali in early July, signaling the end of both the previous government and the genocide. In the following several weeks, some two million refugees, primarily Hutus, fled to neighboring Tanzania or Zaire (now known as the DRC) fearing reprisals.[22]

Humanitarian action during the genocide itself was minimal. The ICRC maintained its presence in Rwanda through the crisis, and the UN set up a small humanitarian unit. But these were tiny operations in comparison to the scale of the slaughter, and largely powerless to do anything about it. Most other agencies left the country when the genocide began in April, and only returned in July and August. The response to the refugee crisis, however, was quite different.

Over a million refugees crossed into Zaïre, the vast majority of them into the small border town of Goma at the northern end of Lake Kivu. This massive concentration of human beings, without adequate food, water, or sanitation, completely overwhelmed the infrastructure of the town and led almost immediately to a major cholera epidemic that killed an estimated 50,000 people in just over four weeks.[23] In contrast to the inaction of the international community during the genocide itself, donors were quick to respond to the refugee crisis, with UNHCR and some 100 agencies moving into camps in both eastern Zaïre and northwestern Tanzania. Supported by a military airlift, the humanitarian operation contained the cholera epidemic and related problems over the ensuring few months, but in the general lawlessness in Zaïre, there was little to stop the former leaders of the genocide from using the refugee camps to re-group and re-arm themselves, effectively using the refugees as a human shield. When this manipulation became apparent to the humanitarian community, and particularly when it became clear that neither the UN, the Zaïre government, nor anyone else was going to intervene, some of the agencies—most notably MSF and the International Rescue Committee—pulled their operations out of eastern Zaïre, but it had little effect on the problem. David Rieff notes that the combination of idealistic but ill-informed agency staff, the inability of the UN to control the camps, and the disinterest of the major powers about the role of the ex Forces Armée Rwandaise (FAR) and the *Interahamwe* militias in the refugee camps, led to "calamitous" consequences. These included the use of the refugee camps to stage attacks against Rwanda; a mass refoulement[24] of refugees in 1996; and the extension of the Congolese civil war into a massive, multi-country conflict after Rwanda invaded the country.[25] Stockton estimates that civilian death rates were higher in that crisis than during the Goma crisis. But whereas the Goma crisis took place in the full glare of the media, subsequent military action failed to attract much attention from either the media or the international community. The overwhelming conclusion was that humanitarian aid had been subverted to support those who had caused the crisis in the first place.[26]

We need to consider several points for the purposes of this discussion. First, humanitarian assistance, both on a small scale in Rwanda itself during the genocide, but more in neighboring countries in the aftermath—particularly in Goma—was at least partially used by the international community as an alternative to concerted political action.[27] Numerous critics, including Rieff,[28] have emphatically noted that in the context of genocide, humanitarian assistance by itself cannot contain the suffering, and it does not address the causes. Most observers caution against humanitarianism trying to take on the latter role.

Second, both the international community generally and the humanitarian community in particular, failed in their analysis of a given crisis in the time when critical decisions had to be made. Sometimes this is in the refusal—as it was in Rwanda as well as other examples raised here—to see the potential for a humanitarian emergency when everyone is focused on what is conceived as a "development" problem. And, as happened in Rwanda, external analysis often seem to be more focused on the *last* crisis—its context, failings and consequences—rather than focusing on the details of the *current* crisis. So many analysts looked at Rwanda and first saw a benign but impoverished country, but once the genocide began, saw it as a "second Somalia" that Western public opinion and political interests would not support.

Third, it is often unclear whether the impartiality of humanitarian action—responding to human needs rather than to political imperatives—is clearly distinguished from impartiality in other kinds of international engagement. Many times in the run-up to the engagement, UNAMIR asked for permission to take pre-emptive action that might have derailed or significantly mitigated the genocide, but were instructed that their role was to remain "impartial"—which in this case had little to do with treating all parties fairly, but with staying out of the messiness of local political realities.

Fourth, and probably the most damaging, was the realization that humanitarian action had in fact been the pretext for enabling those who had carried out the genocide in the first place to regroup and re-arm themselves. Humanitarian assistance had addressed some of the human suffering, but had caused great harm in the process.

The aftermath of the Rwanda crisis

Because of the magnitude of the crisis and the size and problems of the response, there was an almost immediate imperative for a multi-agency evaluation of the response to the genocide. Initially proposed by the government of Denmark, the *Joint Evaluation of Emergency Assistance to Rwanda* (JEEAR) eventually included five major donors (the Scandinavian countries as well as the UK and the USA), and resulted in five major studies. These included historical perspectives on and explanations for the genocide; early warning and conflict management; humanitarian aid and its effects; post-genocide rebuilding; and a synthesis and principal recommendations.[29]

Some of the main needs that JEEAR identified included:

- strengthening human right protection mechanisms in Rwanda;
- development of a Great Lakes conflict early warning system;
- improving performance within the humanitarian sector through better standards and self-regulation;
- improving accountability in humanitarian assistance—particularly accountability to affected groups;
- improved coherence among policy objectives;
- direct prevention of genocide.

The first was primarily directed towards the government of Rwanda; the following two were directed primarily toward the political arms of the UN; and the rest toward the humanitarian community. The main outcomes of the JEEAR in the ensuing decade—which as we shall see have helped shape the way the humanitarian community organizes itself—were:

- the *Sphere Humanitarian Charter* and its *Minimum Standards for Disaster Response*;[30]
- the Active Learning Network for Accountability and Performance in Humanitarian Action (ALNAP);[31]
- the idea of a "humanitarian ombudsman" which eventually resulted in the Humanitarian Accountability Partnership.[32]

The impact of these ongoing initiatives will be discussed in detail in Chapter 7.

Rwanda also gave rise to other, related initiatives on humanitarian standards and accountability, but which did not grow directly out of JEEAR—most notably the IFRC/NGO Code of Conduct which came out in 1994, but which preceded the genocide in terms of its origins and background. Also related to the general observations of the genocide response, but not specifically a result of the JEEAR, was Mary Anderson's work on the principles of "do no harm."[33]

The main author of the humanitarian assistance report of JEEAR notes that less progress has been made in the areas of genocide prevention and early warning (although the convening of the International Criminal Tribunal for Rwanda—ICTR—was hailed as an important step in combating impunity), and that the recommendations on coherence between humanitarian assistance and political agendas was misinterpreted.[34] Indeed, a major and unresolved debate has raged over the extent to which humanitarian action should be subsumed as part of an over-arching political and security framework or, for reasons of principle and humanitarian access, must stand apart from such a framework.[35] Other spin-offs led to a heated debate and introspection within the humanitarian community over the meaning and usefulness of humanitarian principles and international humanitarian law (IHL).[36]

"Between solidarity and governance":[37] humanitarianism post-September 11th

By the dawn of the new millennium, humanitarianism had been much changed. It had become much more openly political and, due in large part to the reforms that grew out of the post-Rwanda effort, much more institutionalized. It had also expanded dramatically in terms of its funding and its profile. By the early 2000s, the budgets of single agencies began to rival the entire global expenditure on humanitarian action a mere decade or two earlier and in many cases to exceed the annual budgets of many least developed countries. These changes were summarized by the rise of a "new humanitarianism" encapsulated in many ways in a speech by Clare Short, a long-time Labour Party activist who in 1997 became Secretary of State for International Development in the incoming Blair government. "New Humanitarianism" had an altogether different take on the world from the humanitarianism first expounded by Dunant and practiced by his followers throughout the twentieth century. "New Humanitarianism" was to be about a different kind of response to human need. One that did the following:

- recognized that all aid is political, and that some of the ideals of classic humanitarianism were a little old-fashioned (none more so than the cherished classic ideal of neutrality);
- took human rights violations as seriously as it took shortfalls in meeting basic human needs;
- was acutely aware that humanitarian interventions and inputs sometimes caused as much harm as they did good, and that humanitarianism needed to be accountable for both;
- incorporated dealing both with causes and symptoms;
- was aligned with other objectives so that all resources could be brought to bear on the problem at hand (which was, of course, manifested by both causes and symptoms or effects).

Clare Short was not a humanitarian worker, but an astute politician who pulled together a number of ideas and made them work in a politically coherent manner.[38] While no single agency—whether UN, donor, or international or local NGO—was fully described by these traits, it was significant that the most openly political of the humanitarian agencies, Médecins sans Frontières, was awarded the Nobel Peace Prize in 1999. MSF, of course, completely rejected the fifth tenet of the new humanitarianism listed above, staunchly—almost jealously—protecting its independence of action. However, in many ways MSF's activist approach was in the ascendance at the close of the millennium, and the more reserved and neutral approach of the Red Cross movement seemed to be in retreat.

The attacks of 11 September 2001 changed much of the face of humanitarian action. Within weeks, a coalition of western nations led by the United States were engaged in a "global war on terror" (GWOT)—a war that by their own reckoning, would know no borders, would be fought in shadowy hinterlands of countries believed to abet international terrorism, and would be an indefinite and perhaps all-consuming effort. In short order, "humanitarian action lost its prominence and human rights concerns were wiped off the UN agenda," in the words of one long-time observer of Afghanistan.[39]

General Colin Powell, the hero of the short and decisive first war against Iraq fought in the late winter of 1991, had become Secretary of State in the administration of George W. Bush, and quickly declared US-based humanitarian agencies as a non-lethal asset in this war, or in his own words, a "force multiplier" in the fight against terrorism. Suddenly, the notion that Short had expounded as coherence—the aligning of resources towards a single strategic goal—became an idea to which humanitarians, particularly of the more pragmatic and political persuasion, became more wary: It was a double-edged sword—aligning with the foreign policies of major powers tended to insure funding from donors, but undermined independence of action.

Humanitarians had been among the few external agencies present in Afghanistan during the Taliban regime, and were not supportive of its repressive policies. Afghanistan itself had teetered on the edge of failed statehood for decades, since the overthrow of its King in the 1970s, and the long Soviet siege of the 1980s. In the 1980s, Western interests favored the Islamists, as a counter to the Soviets, and some $7 billion was funneled to their coffers by the US alone.[40] With the Soviet pull-out, however, Afghanistan descended into an internal struggle pitting different regional warlords against one another. Lacking the global organizing rubric of the Cold War, the outside world largely left Afghanistan to its own fate. The Taliban, largely believed to have emerged from the refugee *madrassa* education system in Pakistan, first appeared on the Afghan political scene in a significant way in the mid-1990s. With the assistance of elements of the Pakistani state, they slowly extended their control over much of the country, with perhaps their greatest military success coming just two days before the September 11th attack when they finally managed to assassinate Ahmed Shah Massoud, the popular commander of the "Northern Alliance," the greatest single threat to continued Taliban rule.

But following September 11th, it was clear that the Taliban were the first target in the GWOT's cross-hairs. Within 48 hours of the attack, foreign humanitarian agencies had all pulled out in anticipation of the invasion. The overthrow of the Taliban was relatively swift. By mid-November, most cities in northern Afghanistan had come under the control of the anti-Taliban Northern Coalition, provoking a widespread displacement crisis—the emphasis on ousting the Taliban and installing a Western-friendly government having completely trumped concerns for human rights.[41]

For humanitarian action, the invasion of Afghanistan resulted in the loss of independence and the effective "taking sides" in the conflict—a process that "was not immediately apparent to aid workers but was to the 'spoilers' and 'losers'—the remnants of the Taliban."[42] This appearance of "taking sides" has been complicated by the use of so-called provincial reconstruction teams. PRTs comprise military forces, working with civilians—both private contractors and international NGOs—but under military command to implement humanitarian and economic recovery activities. There ensued a debate, unresolved to the present—and compounded by the extensive subsequent use of PRTs in Iraq—about the wisdom of situational ethics in determining the independence (and/or neutrality) of humanitarian action in the face of the GWOT.[43]

The invasion of Iraq in 2003, ostensibly due to the presence of weapons of mass destruction under the control of Saddam Hussein's regime, only increased these divides. The attack on the UN compound in Baghdad in August of that year—killing among many others the senior and widely respected UN diplomat, Sérgio Vieira de Mello, who was serving as the Special Representative of the Secretary General—seemed to underline the widespread perception that the international humanitarian community had sided with Western powers, making it suspect as well as a legitimate target. The UN withdrew from Iraq following the bombing, and with it, the last pretense towards independent humanitarian action by the international community.

The wars in both Afghanistan and Iraq saw an increasing direct involvement of military actors in the provision of aid, to the point that humanitarian assistance has become a central tenet in the "hearts and minds" component of current Western counter-insurgency warfare doctrine. This presents both an opportunity and a risk for humanitarians—it has led to vastly bigger budgets for humanitarian work, but the money comes at a high risk to the independence and credibility of the agency that accepts it.[44]

In December 2001, the International Commission on Intervention and State Sovereignty (ICISS) published *The Responsibility to Protect*,[45] which challenged the diplomatic norms that have been the basis of most formal diplomacy regarding the intervention of the international community in the internal affairs of nation states since the treaty of Westphalia in the seventeenth century. Given the rising numbers of internally displaced people from the wars of the 1990s, but the continued insistence of belligerent states in those wars that internal displacement was none of the business of the international community, a panel of distinguished diplomats and politicians released this influential report. It challenged the long-standing notion that sovereignty trumped human rights in international affairs, and suggested instead that where states could not, or would not, provide adequate safeguards to the human rights of their citizens, the international community was not only authorized to intervene, it was obliged to do so.

Given the importance of this document, it is worth examining its background and principles. Based in part on the work of Francis Deng and Roberta Cohen on *Guiding Principles on Internal Displacement*, the ICISS sought not so much to undermine the principle of sovereignty as to argue that "sovereignty implies responsibility." The Canadian-led initiative also paralleled then-Secretary General Kofi Annan's "two concepts of sovereignty approach" which argued that states exist to serve people (not vice versa), and that human rights transcend claims of state sovereignty—themes outlined in the UN General Assembly debate in September 1999. This debate, however, came after the Rwanda genocide in which the international reaction was too little and too late, and in the immediate aftermath of the NATO intervention in Kosovo, described by one observer as "too much, too early."[46] The responsibility to protect (popularized as "R2P") proposed three phases of intervention: (1) the responsibility to prevent (pre-crisis); (2) the responsibility to react (to an actual crisis involving gross human rights violation); and (3) the responsibility to rebuild (particularly after a military intervention). Nevertheless, as implied by the name of the report, it was the middle phase that received the greatest attention—and proved the most controversial. And it needed to establish a threshold for intervention: "acts of such magnitude that that they shock the conscience and elicit a fundamental humanitarian impulse"[47] including large-scale loss of life (whether based on genocidal intent or not) or large-scale ethnic cleansing. The ICISS adopted four principles of intervention: (1) *right intentions* (only to avert or halt large-scale human suffering); (2) *last resort* (after all non-military options have been exhausted); (3) *proportional means* (minimum necessary to defend the human rights imperative); and (4) *reasonable prospects* (a reasonable chance of succeeding in defending the human rights imperative).

The impact of this report on humanitarian action has been mixed. It has served as an organizing principle for international intervention in civil wars and in failed or failing states with some element of success against a background of extremely difficult circumstances—for example, the intervention of UN MONUC peacekeepers in the Eastern part of the DRC.[48] At the same time, it has not provided adequate grounds for an international force to intervene in the long-running war in Darfur with adequate teeth to prevent the killing, rape, and displacement of civilians. At the end of the day, Weiss notes that the ICISS reformulated the basis for humanitarian intervention, moving from de-emphasizing the right of intervention to defending the rights of victims and the responsibility of outsiders. And it proposed a new "default setting" for future interventions to protect human rights. However, Weiss notes, the ICISS "ends where it began ... If there is political will and an operational capacity, humanitarian or other interventions will happen."[49] In any case, the ground rules for intervention had been shifted significantly.

A major study published by the Feinstein International Center in 2006 offered insights into four major issues facing the humanitarian community early in the twenty-first century: (1) the *universality* of humanitarianism; (2) the implications of *terrorism and counter-terrorism* for humanitarian action; (3) the search for *coherence* between humanitarian and political agendas; and (4) the *security* of both humanitarian workers and the populations they seek to serve.[50] The study demonstrates fundamentally that "action aimed at alleviating the suffering of the world's most vulnerable has been incorporated into a northern political and security agenda." With regard to universality, actually humanitarian action is largely perceived to be the action of northern and western agencies, motivated by something other than human need. Terrorism and the GWOT doubtlessly create the need for more humanitarian action, but to date, humanitarians have not become adept at navigating the politically charged waters of the GWOT or in advocating policies in the age of terror that do not undermine civilian human rights.

On the increased "coherence" between political and humanitarian objectives, the study notes this agenda is far from a "collaboration among equals." With the rise of integrated UN missions, and greater demands for conformity to donor objectives by humanitarian action, the danger is that "humanitarian and human rights priorities will be made subservient to political objectives" increasingly referred to as "instrumentalism." There is increasingly a need for safeguards that protect the independence of humanitarian action.

Post-9/11 conflicts are fraught with greater dangers to the security of both aid workers and civilian populations, but there is a major difference in the perception of these two groups regarding security. The study concludes: "If the disconnect between the perceived needs of intended beneficiaries and the assistance and protection actually provided continues to grow, humanitarianism as a compassionate endeavor to bring succor to people *in extremis* may become increasingly alien and suspect to those it purports to help."[51]

The Feinstein report did not include any case study material from Iraq—evidence that became available only later in 2007. But contrary to the presumed conclusion of many regarding the future of humanitarian action in the asymmetric conflicts of the global war against terrorism, the Iraq study concludes:

> The withering struggle to assist and protect Iraqis in an environment marked by unprecedented politicization has led many in the international humanitarian apparatus to prematurely concede the defeat of principled humanitarian action. *Evidence from ground level in Iraq serves both as a strong endorsement of the Dunantist ethos and as an indictment of the surrender to pragmatism.*[52]

4   States as responders and donors

In this chapter we will examine states' obligations in times of crisis toward their citizens and the citizens of other crisis-affected nations. States have a moral and legal responsibility to ensure the practice and promotion of human rights as enshrined in the Universal Declaration of Human Rights, in much of the Geneva Conventions, in the Refugee Convention, the Convention of the Rights of the Child, and so on. Much of the debate on states' roles in times of crisis is effectively an examination of how well they fulfil their obligations. In seeking to understand how well states meet these obligations, we will focus on four major countries which are repeatedly affected by crisis, man-made or not: India, Bangladesh, Ethiopia and the USA. We will then examine the role of states as donors, assisting victims in someone else's country. The main donor countries' efforts and the institutions they have set up to improve their collective donorship will be reviewed, and finally we will examine the growing role of foreign military forces in and around humanitarian response.

The obligations of states in times of natural disaster and war

Whether rich or poor, well organized or chaotic, states have obligations to their citizens. How they fulfill them in times of crisis says a lot about the relationship between the state and those under its authority. The question is simple: do states display a concern through their actions, for the well-being of their citizens, according to need— not race, ethnicity, location, political persuasion, or economic importance? With the *Responsibility to Protect* project, states have, as recently as 2005, reaffirmed their obligations not only to protect their own populations from genocide, war crimes, ethnic cleansing and crimes against humanity, but also their commitment to take collective action if national authorities fail to protect their populations. The obligation is there, but is it backed by the will and means to make it a reality?

The *Sphere Standards* drafted in the mid-1990s by international humanitarian agencies lays out obligations and expectations for agencies intervening in crises. They start with an important caveat: "We acknowledge the primary role and responsibility of the state to provide assistance when people's capacity to cope has been exceeded."[1]

In an initiative started in 2001, the International Federation of Red Cross and Red Crescent Societies (IFRC) began compiling a list of all national and international law relevant to national and international humanitarian aid. This International Disaster Response Law (IDRL) project seeks to help states build a solid legal basis for both national and international responses to disasters. The IFRC notes that:

> Too often, urgently needed international disaster response is delayed, or even prevented, by national legal and regulatory systems which are ill-equipped to deal with the needs of international relief providers. Similarly, international assistance should be conducted in a responsible and coordinated manner to minimize its impact on local resources and ensure good quality and accountability standards by both relief providers and donors. Fortunately, many of these issues can be identified and addressed before disaster strikes. This can be achieved by anticipating the likely needs of a country in disaster and identifying the potential legal and administrative challenges for the entry and coordination of international assistance. This enables appropriate steps to be taken by governments and relief providers to prevent unnecessary obstacles in the way of provision of fast and effective assistance to people affected by disaster.
>
> All too frequently, international agencies forget that their primary role is to supplement national efforts when the capacity to undertake them has been exhausted or where the state cannot, or will not, act. In theory, humanitarian assistance starts with an assessment of local and national capacity. If that capacity is overwhelmed, or if there is an urgent request to intervene or if local authorities are unwilling to provide much-needed assistance, then humanitarian aid should flow.[2]

The UN's *International Strategy for Disaster Reduction* has compiled, for just about every country in the world, a national profile outlining the national policies, strategies, and legislation concerning disaster reduction and response. In Albania, for example, the government passed legislation in 2000 providing for a "Policy on Civil Emergency Planning and Response," which created a Department of Civil Emergency Planning and Response, in the Ministry of Local Government and Decentralization, responsible for disaster reduction and response. In Zimbabwe, the Civil Protection Act of 1989 is presently being updated to establish a new Emergency Preparedness and Disaster Management Authority.

On paper, every country acknowledges its responsibilities towards its citizens in times of crisis. In practice, as we shall see later in this chapter, some are better than others in exercising that responsibility. Crises associated with societal breakdown or war provide a different scenario. In these situations, typified by the Darfur region of the Sudan in the mid-2000s, the state may actively seek to exclude humanitarian assistance or, indeed, may be part of the cause, rather than contribute to the solution, of the crisis.

In 2005, following on from work by the Canadian-led Responsibility to Protect project,[3] the UN General Assembly passed a resolution confirming states' responsibility to protect their citizens and, crucially, the responsibility of the international community to act if states fail to honor their responsibilities. To quote from the resolution:

> Each individual State has the responsibility to protect its populations from genocide, war crimes, ethnic cleansing and crimes against humanity ... The international community, through the United Nations, also has the responsibility to use appropriate diplomatic, humanitarian and other peaceful means, in accordance with Chapters VI and VIII of the Charter, to help protect populations from genocide, war crimes, ethnic cleansing and crimes against humanity. In this context, we are prepared to take collective action, in a timely and decisive manner, through the Security Council, in accordance with the Charter, including Chapter VII, on a case-by-case basis and in cooperation with relevant regional organizations as appropriate, should peaceful means be inadequate and national authorities manifestly fail to protect their populations from genocide, war crimes, ethnic cleansing and crimes against humanity.[4]

Similarly, the older and more tested Geneva Conventions call upon states to "respect and ensure respect" for the terms of the Conventions, including the treatment of civilians in times of war.

The Geneva Conventions in general and the Fourth Geneva Convention in particular, which deals with the protection of civilians in times of war, put state signatories under specific clearly stated humanitarian obligations. The Fourth Convention outlaws indiscriminate deportation or internship, indiscriminate destruction of property and the murder or torturing of civilians. This includes subjecting them to collective punishment. It calls for the protection of family and religious rights and outlaws the use of forced labor for military efforts.

When war unfolds and the state is replaced by an occupying power, then the conventions make it clear that responsibility for the well-being of the civilian population shifts to the occupying power. Article 27 of the Fourth Geneva Convention clearly defines the responsibility of states party to a conflict or states which are occupying powers:

> Protected persons are entitled, in all circumstances, to respect for their persons, their honor, their family rights, their religious convictions and practices, and their manners and customs. They shall at all times be humanely treated, and shall be protected especially against all acts of violence or threats thereof and against insults and public curiosity.[5]

We can confidently assert that it is an internationally recognized norm that states have a responsibility to assist their citizens in times of crisis and, still confidently, but a little less so, can assert that states recognize their responsibility to assist citizens of other countries when their sovereign states fail them.

With this background in mind, let us now look at how four nations—India, Bangladesh, Ethiopia, and the United States—all regularly affected by major disasters and humanitarian emergencies, seek to deal with these crises.

India

India, along with China, is one of the most disaster-prone countries in the world. Partly this is a matter of size—over 1.1 billion people in only three million square kilometers—but India is also prone to earthquakes, flooding, drought and, on the borders with its neighbors, conflict. In the 1990s, over 30 million Indians were disaster-affected each year.

In the early 2000s, India radically changed its approach to disasters. Previously the legacy of the India Famine (later called food scarcity) Codes, discussed in Chapter 1, was much in evidence. Disasters were aberrations, existing outside the paradigm of development. India's new approach starts from the premise that development cannot be sustainable unless disaster reduction and response are solidly built into the development process. To that end, the country's new National Disaster Framework lays out an approach to disaster prevention, early warning systems, disaster mitigation, preparedness and response, and human resource development which is an integral part of the country's development strategy.

Responsibility for implementing response lies at the state level—for India is a federation. Each state has a Calamity Relief Fund whose size is based on the average expenditure on response over the previous decade. Three-quarters of the funds come from the federal government and the remainder from the local state.

In the 1950s and 1960s, India was the poster child for humanitarian action. Much has changed. Barring exceptional circumstances—such as the 1999 Orissa cyclone which rendered 1.6 million people homeless and caused over \$2.5 billion of damage[6]—India has the financial and logistical capacity to respond effectively to most disasters.

India then has transitioned from a state beset by apocalyptic famines and the recipient in the twentieth century of substantial outside assistance, to a state equipped to deal with the worst suffering of disaster victims. It is well on its way to preventing and mitigating the unacceptable face of natural disaster. In 2005, it turned down offers of foreign assistance following a major earthquake—while neighboring Pakistan embraced it.

Bangladesh

In the past decade, Bangladesh has had similar success in curbing the worst impacts of natural disasters. Drought killed 1.6 million people in 1943 in what is now Bangladesh. In 1970, a major cyclone killed over 300,000 people in the coastal region of the country and in 1991 another cyclone killed 138,000. Bangladesh remains highly vulnerable to violent wind and rain but since 2000, fewer than 4,000 people have died in all natural disasters combined. This phenomenal turn-around has been achieved primarily by providing people living in cyclone-vulnerable areas with realistic response options. Cyclone warning in Bangladesh today is a sophisticated system, using satellite technology and predictive models, and depending on thousands of volunteers in the vulnerable delta regions who broadcast warning messages to the population. Crucially, a major program of cyclone shelter building has given the at-risk population an option they never used to have—somewhere to go when disaster strikes.[7] Through a mix of technology, government and civil society action, and international funding,

Bangladesh has—at least for the moment—curbed the massive mortality previously resulting from floods, storm surges and cyclones. Bangladesh's key challenge now lies in how to respond to climate change. Climatologists predict that, by the end of the century, sea level rise will threaten up to a quarter of Bangladesh's land mass with flooding from storm surges. Rapidly melting glaciers in the Himalayas which feed the rivers of Bangladesh will, at first, cause increased seasonal river flooding, but as the glaciers retreat and cease to supply seasonal melt-water, flooding will disappear. Rivers may even become seasonal which would have a devastating effect on the country's agricultural economy. Whether Bangladesh is able to adapt its economy, its governance, and its disaster mitigation and response systems fast and effectively enough to absorb these stresses is the key to the country's long-term future.

Ethiopia

Ethiopia has a long history of famine, and attracted global attention when millions died in the mid-1970s and again a decade later. Meles Zenawi—the current leader of Ethiopia, whose forces seized power from the Derg regime of Mengistu Haile Mariam in 1991—reformed Mengistu's famine relief agency and renamed it the Disaster Prevention and Preparedness Commission (DPPC). In many ways, however, little has changed. The DPPC still acts as the main gateway for humanitarian aid bodies working in Ethiopia and for the soliciting of emergency assistance. It has, in the past few years, been supplemented by a major initiative funded by the World Bank and other multilateral donors to put in place a national food security safety-net. The Productive Safety Net Program (PSNP) represents a shift from a relief and emergency response to a productive and development-oriented safety net, reminiscent of the measures used in colonial India under the famine codes. In specifically recognized famine-prone areas of the country it provides food and, increasingly, cash to support labor-intensive public works that purport to address the underlying causes of food insecurity. For those who cannot labor on the public works, it provides direct food and cash handouts. Triggered after three years of continuous reliance on food aid, the PSNP represents an attempt to break free from a continuous reliance on external voluntary food aid and to move toward a more systematic way of dealing with, and hopefully reducing, food insecurity. Whether the scheme will ultimately be successful and truly represent a new and radical approach to humanitarian crises for the 8.8 million food-insecure in Ethiopia remains to be seen. One recent analysis[8] points out that such a scheme, particularly where it is trying to substitute cash transfers for food aid, works best where markets are well integrated, thus allowing more cash in the local economy to pull in more traded food. However, if markets are not linked together or if there is genuine widespread food scarcity, then cash is of little value. What is clear though is that, in parallel with the PSNP and other initiatives to boost food production and household income, Ethiopia will continue to require periodic massive imports of food, either commercial or aid, for the foreseeable future in order to ward off famine.

The United States

Ethiopia and Bangladesh are still impoverished countries, India a fast developing one. The United States is of continental size, like India, but has never suffered from the endemic problems of pervasive poverty. It is, however, exposed to major hydro-meteorological risks, earthquakes, and forest fires. With a well-funded and trusted response system, disaster loss in the United States is usually measured in terms of its dollar value, not lives lost and populations displaced. However, Hurricane Katrina changed this pattern.

In the United States, disaster response is initially the responsibility of each state, backed up by the Federal Emergency Management Authority (FEMA). FEMA was established in 1979, merging many formerly separate authorities into one organization to deal with major disasters. In 2003, FEMA was subsumed into the US Department of Homeland Security. Today its mission is:

> to reduce the loss of life and property and protect the Nation from all hazards, including natural disasters, acts of terrorism, and other man-made disasters, by leading and supporting the Nation in a risk-based, comprehensive emergency management system of preparedness, protection, response, recovery, and mitigation.[9]

It works closely with other federal agencies, state and local emergency response services, the American Red Cross, and the US Army Corps of Engineers. Typically, FEMA responds to around 50 disaster emergencies in the United States every year.

Behind state response and FEMA lies a whole network of disaster mitigation measures. Household flood insurance, federal grants to support local emergencies, and earthquake building codes and practice drills are all part of the humanitarian disaster response system. All this is possible both because the state is economically wealthy and because the system of governance has a real sense of responsibility for, and accountability to, its population.

The biggest test of America's disaster response system came in 2005 when Hurricane Katrina struck New Orleans. Katrina was not just a challenge to the inhabitants of New Orleans and the federal and Louisiana state disaster response systems. It was also the first real test of the National Response Plan, developed by the US Department of Homeland Security and designed to deal with the aftermath of disaster, including terrorist attack. Over 1,800 people lost their lives to the hurricane, the largest US hurricane death toll since 1928. Infrastructure damage is estimated to be around $81 billion. Two weeks after the hurricane struck, over a million people had fled the area, the largest displacement since the US Civil War. Faced with such a massive disaster which disrupted not only the city but also virtually every system that the disaster responders relied upon, there is little wonder that a newly developed and untested system failed.[10] In the summer of 2007, at least 85,000 families displaced by the disaster were still living in "temporary" trailer parks in the states surrounding New Orleans, emulating the experiences of Kobe in Japan, a major industrial port hit by an earthquake in 1996. City authorities there thought they would have everyone re-housed in a year but five years later trailers were still occupied, mostly by the elderly, mentally ill, and destitute.

In 2007 the response to widespread devastating fires in southern California was better by orders of magnitude. Both the state and the federal systems responded faster and more coherently. But even as they did so, New Orleans was still looking like the aftermath of war with vast areas of the city still in total disrepair, services not restored, and communities in tatters. Does New Orleans need its own Marshall Plan? And more disturbingly, how can the richest nation on earth commit massive funding to the rebuilding of Iraq—a state on the receiving end of its greatest overseas adventure since World War II—and yet let one of its own oldest cities slip into destitution?

As these examples have shown, states can and do take systematic steps to address both disaster prevention and response at home. But, as with India and Ireland in the 1800s, moving from addressing the effects of disaster to addressing its causes and long term consequences is politically and economically often a bridge too far for the government of the day.

States as aid donors

Most funding into international humanitarian assistance flows from a handful of predominantly Western governments. In absolute dollar value terms, the USA tops the league table of donors most years, closely followed by the European Community's Humanitarian Aid Office (ECHO). Understanding why and how donor governments act in international crises through their funding mechanisms is a crucial part of grasping why some crises are well funded and others not, why funds get channeled though NGOs in preference to local governments, and why the goal of responding globally according to need is still a long way off.

Between 2000 and 2005, spending on global humanitarian assistance continued to rise in real terms topping $18 billion in 2005,[11] against an estimated $10 billion raised in 2000. Humanitarian contributions for the aftermath of war in Iraq and Afghanistan in 2003 and for the Asian tsunami in 2005 were something of an anomaly, raising global spending above its trend line in those years. The tsunami response in 2005 precipitated a massive spike in overall humanitarian contributions, adding additional funding of $5.5 billion in contributions from the public to NGOs, the Red Cross, and UN agencies.[12]

The USA remains the single largest donor, contributing some 33 percent of global government funding in 2005, followed by the European Union with 15 percent, Japan with 7 percent and France and the UK each with 6 percent.[13]

Africa receives the largest share of humanitarian assistance as a region (as recorded in 2004), and in volume terms, humanitarian aid to Africa has steadily increased since 1998. The Middle East, including Israel, has received an estimated one-fifth of humanitarian assistance since 2003, making it the second largest regional recipient of humanitarian aid.

In 2004, six countries received an estimated half of all humanitarian assistance: Iraq (16 percent), Sudan (11 percent), Palestine (8 percent), Ethiopia (6 percent), Afghanistan (6 percent), and the DRC (4 percent). The remaining 49 percent was shared among 148 countries. Over the past ten years, ten countries have consistently captured a majority share of humanitarian assistance.[14]

Globally food aid, its purchase and distribution, makes up the single biggest sector for humanitarian expenditure. In 2005, it accounted for 40 percent of global humanitarian expenditure. No other sector— water, health, protection—received above 10 percent of global funds.

In other words, humanitarian assistance is highly concentrated in terms of its source, its destination, and the services it buys. These patterns of concentration cannot be explained by relative humanitarian need alone. The politics of foreign policy, of domestic policy and of supply all conspire to warp the global humanitarian picture from one that is impartial and needs-driven and needs-driven to a less perfect landscape of supply and demand, realpolitik, security, and justice.

The United States

The United States administers humanitarian support through two offices. First, within USAID, humanitarian aid flows through the Bureau for Democracy, Conflict, and Humanitarian Assistance, and through it to the Office of Foreign Disaster Assistance (OFDA), the Food for Peace Program (FFP), and the Office for Transitional Initiatives (OTI). OFDA deals with most funding responses to emergencies. FFP administers US food aid. The final component, OTI was set up in the early 1990s to provide aid to countries recovering from crisis—particularly states emerging from the Soviet Union—though OTI now operates globally.

OFDA was born 30 years ago in response to the Skopje earthquake in what was then Yugoslavia. While OFDA's prime role is to fund humanitarian response, mostly via US-based NGOs and the UN agencies, it also conducts its own needs assessments in emergencies using its Disaster Assistance Response Teams (DARTs). A less publicized but crucial role they play has been in behind-the-scene negotiations to secure access for humanitarian agencies in complex and conflictual situations. In the 1990s, agreement on UN access protocols in Angola and Somalia were both preceded by behind-the-scene negotiations led by OFDA, essentially negotiating for sovereign states (Angola and Somalia) to give up part of their sovereignty and allow foreign aid workers access to rebel-controlled areas.[15]

FFP makes food aid and resources to ship it available through Public Law 480 Title II. It is the primary food aid donor of the US government, even though, for historical reasons, its budget comes mostly from the US Department of Agriculture. The biggest single food aid program is called PL 480 Title II—deriving its name from Public Law 480, the 1954 founding legislation for the US food aid program. Title II deals with "humanitarian" (emergency) and "project" (non-emergency food aid). By law, all food assistance must be provided in kind, it must be purchased from US sources, and 75 percent of it must be shipped on US-registered ships. This tends to mean that US food aid is very costly, and very slow to arrive in the case of sudden-onset emergencies. Attempts to reform US food aid laws have met with stiff resistance in the US Congress.

The OTI initially sought to address crises before they reached full-blown complex emergencies, but found itself at odds with the State Department which saw this as an encroachment onto its territory.[16]

The OTI has survived as a small office within USAID, mostly funding initiatives to aid the development of democracy in countries emerging from crisis.

Within the State Department the Bureau for Population, Refugees and Migration (BPRM) provides funding to agencies such as UNHCR, the International Organization for Migration (IOM), and the ICRC to work with refugees and internally displaced peoples around the world. Since 9/11, the shape of US humanitarian assistance has undergone radical change. The old offices and mechanisms mentioned above remain, but they have been radically supplemented by other channels, not least the US military, in a response to the realization that many of the countries seeking humanitarian assistance are also those intimately tied into the so-called global war on terror: Afghanistan, Pakistan, Sudan, and Somalia, to name but four prominent examples. According to the Organization for Economic Cooperation and Development (OECD), between 2002 and 2005 USAID's share of US overseas development assistance, which includes humanitarian aid, decreased from 50 percent to 39 percent, and the Department of Defense's increased from 6 to 22 percent.[17]

Humanitarian assistance, as a "hearts and minds" tool, is increasingly seen as part of the legitimate armory of the force commander in the field. Consider, as an example, the US "Commander's Emergency Response Program" (CERP). These funds, for use in Iraq and Afghanistan, are described by the US Secretary of Defense as:

> Additional resources to improve local governance, delivery of public services, and quality of life—to get angry young men off the street and into jobs where they will be less susceptible to the appeals of insurgents or militia groups. Commander's Emergency Response Program or (CERP) funds are a relatively small piece of the war-related budgets ... But because they can be dispensed quickly and applied directly to local needs, they have had a tremendous impact—far beyond the dollar value—on the ability of our troops to succeed in Iraq and Afghanistan. By building trust and confidence in Coalition forces, these CERP projects increase the flow of intelligence to commanders in the field and help turn local Iraqis and Afghans against insurgents and terrorists.[18]

The CERP funds have expanded from zero in 2003 to $136 million in 2005 and $923 million for 2007.[19]

When USAID was set up by the Kennedy administration in the 1960s it was deliberately created with a semi-independent structure, allowing it to pursue long-term development and short-term humanitarian objectives, relatively free of the diplomatic, trade and security concerns of the presiding administration. In the mid-1990s the State Department tried unsuccessfully to bring USAID under its control. Post 9/11, though, everything changed. In 2002, the Bush administration published a *National Security Strategy for the United States of America*.[20] The document, for the first time, elevated development (including humanitarian assistance) to a key foreign policy objective, along with security, and democracy building.

Building on this doctrine, that humanitarian aid was potentially a powerful foreign policy tool, in early 2006 the US Secretary of State announced a major change in the way US aid was administered through the creation of a Director of US Foreign Assistance within the State Department. The Director has authority over all State and USAID foreign assistance funding and programs. To quote from the State Department's website:

> In a time of transformational diplomacy—as America works with our partners to build and sustain democratic well-governed states—changes are necessary to meet new challenges. This reorganization will:
> - ensure that foreign assistance is used as effectively as possible to meet our broad foreign policy objectives;
> - more fully align the foreign assistance activities carried out by the Department of State and USAID; and
> - demonstrate that we are responsible stewards of taxpayer dollars.[21]

Administrations and governments come and go. However, the accelerated politicization of US foreign aid, including humanitarian assistance, is unlikely to be reversed in the near future. The pressure on Western governments to align all potential foreign policy tools towards the goal of security (economic and military) is immense. In the absence of existing legislation to ensure independence from partisan foreign policy, it is particularly difficult to see how US humanitarian assistance will be able to maintain an impartial and neutral stance.

The European Union

In a typical year, the European Union provides nearly 30 percent of global humanitarian aid primarily through its humanitarian office (ECHO). ECHO is a relative newcomer to the humanitarian funding business, established in 1992 as part of the consolidation of the political and administrative functions of the European Union. ECHO's mandate was formalized by the Council of Europe in 1996:

The Community's humanitarian aid shall comprise assistance, relief and protection operations on a non-discriminatory basis to help people in third countries, particularly the most vulnerable among them, and as a priority those in developing countries, victims of natural disasters, man-made crises, such as wars and outbreaks of fighting, or exceptional situations or circumstances comparable to natural or man-made disasters. It shall do so for the time needed to meet the humanitarian requirements resulting from these different situations.

Such aid shall also comprise operations to prepare for risks or prevent disasters or comparable exceptional circumstances.[22]

Around 60 percent of ECHO's funding is channeled through international NGOs (primarily those headquartered in European Union member states). The rest goes to UN agencies, the Red Cross Movement, and directly to disaster-affected states. In recent years ECHO has had a policy of focusing on so-called forgotten emergencies. In 2004, it was one of the major funders in Sudan, before the crisis in Darfur became a global issue.

While ECHO is a major league donor, it is peculiar in that it is relatively free from pressure to pursue a partisan foreign policy line since the European Union as a whole has a relatively undeveloped foreign policy apparatus in comparison to its individual nation states. This may change. In 2003, the European Union attempted to adopt an EU-wide constitution (while this move initially failed, its adoption is still on the agenda of many key policymakers within the European Union). The political reality is that Europe is moving towards more unified economic, military, and foreign aid policies.

The draft constitution laid out the basis of internal and foreign policy, including humanitarian aid, for the EU. Many observers, including the major coalitions of European NGOs, have expressed concerns that they discern in it an encroachment of short-term foreign policy and diplomatic agendas into the realm of humanitarian policy. In particular, they warn the EU not to bring political considerations into play when assessing which populations are most in need, nor to allow humanitarian aid to be shaped by the dictates of the fight against terrorism.[23]

Japan

In the 1960s, Japan was still a net recipient of aid, but by the 1970s had become a major trading and financial power. In the 1990s, it became one of the top global aid providers alongside the United States.[24] The methodology of Japanese assistance has developed rapidly. Prior to the early 1980s, the term non-governmental organization (NGO) was rarely used in Japan and when it was, it was applied in a derogatory fashion to anti-state and anti-corporation civic groupings. Early Japanese humanitarian assistance was characterized by direct financial contributions to countries in crisis and to UN agencies. It is only during the past 15 years that funding to Japanese NGOs, and occasional funding to local institutions, have started to rise in importance.[25]

In 2005, Japan provided $859 million in global humanitarian assistance, making it the second largest global donor that year. This amounts to about 10 percent of its global Official Development Assistance (ODA) and reflects an increase of over 250 percent in its humanitarian funding levels in the past decade.[26] Japan is a consistent funder of UN consolidated appeals for humanitarian action, channeling a quarter of its funding to them. Prior to the massive increase in bilateral funding to the Iraq government and for the 2004 tsunami appeals, Japan's humanitarian aid generally flowed through multilateral organizations and Japanese NGOs.

The Good Humanitarian Donorship (GHD) initiative

The 1990s saw much activity by operational humanitarian agencies, both NGOs and UN agencies, to put in place more professional and global standards for their work. This was partly in response to a concern that, as they become more important as agencies for implementing donor programs, they could find their independence eroded. It was also motivated by awareness that the sheer increase in their volume of work during the decade required them to become more professional.

Donors, however, were slower to respond and it was not until June 2003 that a similar initiative was prompted among the donor community. Sixteen donor governments (Australia, Belgium, Canada, Denmark, France, Finland, Germany, Ireland, Japan, Luxembourg, the Netherlands, Norway, Sweden, Switzerland, the UK, and the USA)—together with the European Union, the OECD, the International Red Cross and Red Crescent Movement, NGOs, and academics—met in Stockholm and drafted a set of 23 "principles and best practice" for donors. Core to these principles are that humanitarian assistance should be provided to save lives and alleviate suffering according to need; that funding should be adequate, predictable, and flexible; donors should be accountable and seek to learn from their experiences.[27]

This Good Humanitarian Donorship[28] has since expanded to embrace 23 donor nations, plus the European Union. The group undertakes peer reviews to track members' compliance with the stated principles and acts as a forum for discourse with the main humanitarian agencies they fund. Some of their initiatives are wonderfully pragmatic, trying to streamline the reporting systems for agencies to multiple donors. Others seek to improve donor coordination in the field. More recently, they have sought to drive forward the debate on what the future shape of humanitarian funding should be.

Military forces as humanitarian actors

International military forces have a long history of involvement in humanitarian action. The Geneva Conventions make it clear that victorious or occupying military have an obligation to take over the defeated state's responsibilities and see to the basic needs of the occupied peoples for food, shelter, water and health care. The Hague and Geneva Conventions prohibit military attacks of all kinds on civilians and their property, as we have already seen in this chapter.

With respect to occupying powers, Articles 56 and 57 of the Fourth Convention make their humanitarian duties clear:

> The Occupying Power has the duty of ensuring the food and medical supplies of the population; it should, in particular, bring in the necessary foodstuffs, medical stores and other articles if the resources of the occupied territory are inadequate ...
> ... the Occupying Power has the duty of ensuring and maintaining, with the cooperation of national and local authorities, the medical and hospital establishments and services, public health and hygiene in the occupied territory.

All states that have signed the Conventions are both bound by them and have a duty to ensure that their fellow states abide by them.

However, much military humanitarian activity today does not take place within this strict framework. Often the military force is not engaged in combat operations but is providing assistance as part of its country's foreign policy towards the crisis-stricken state. This assistance has traditionally taken the form of the provision of logistical support.

A separate role for the military is as providers of security—as peacekeepers, peace enforcers, military escorts, clearers of land mines and the like, whether under the umbrella of the UN or as national or regional military forces. In these contexts the role of external military forces is something that is negotiated and agreed upon by the warring parties. In theory, at least, such a military force is a welcome, trusted entity. In practice, however, as we see today in Darfur, Afghanistan and Iraq, such forces can be seen by the local populations, the states or dissident forces, as a part of the conflict. In such situations, military forces tend to focus first on their own security, and, second, on the security of the population in which they are embedded. As we saw in the descriptions of humanitarian operations across the past decades, access to those in need is often dictated by security concerns. In times of war or peacekeeping, the ability and willingness of military forces to provide security for civilian populations, including humanitarian workers is paramount.

UN peacekeeping and peacemaking operations, designed to enhance civilian security fall into one of two categories, commonly referred to as Chapter VI and Chapter VII operations, referring to the relevant chapters of the UN Charter.[29] Chapter VI of the Charter deals with the peaceful settlement of disputes and essentially allows for UN peace-keeping forces to be on the ground to monitor a peaceful settlement and, through their passive presence, discourage violence, i.e. Chapter VI assumes all the parties want and are willing to work for peace. Chapter VII is more robust, it deals with actions with respect to threats to peace and acts of aggression. It allows the Security Council to use force, through military forces seconded from UN members, to pacify unlawful acts of aggression. In this instance peacemakers (rather than peacekeepers) may use armed force against warring parties threatening civilians. The UN has mounted 63 peacekeeping and peacemaking operations in its history and presently has 17 active ones involving over 100,000 personnel on the ground.[30]

In more classic humanitarian terms, in the 1980s, many Western states provided transport aircraft and personnel from their air forces to fly food-drops into famine-stricken Sudan and Ethiopia.[31] At the end of the first Gulf War, allied military forces, acting to enforce a UN Security Council resolution, created a Kurdish "safe haven" in northern Iraq and then supplied it with humanitarian aid. That same year, allied forces, returning from the Gulf War, provided assistance to cyclone victims in Bangladesh.

Starting with the Kurdish safe havens and carrying on through the military operations in Somalia, the Balkans in the 1990s, in Kosovo, and today in Afghanistan and Iraq, a new sort of military-humanitarian relationship is emerging. The distinction between the two types of intervention is increasingly blurred and the military has gone beyond provision of logistical support to actively planning and executing what might otherwise be seen as humanitarian operations. Some of the sums involved are massive. The US Army reports that, since 2004, $750 million has been allocated to CERP reconstruction projects in Baghdad province alone.[32]

Increasingly the more powerful states are no longer fighting wars against the armies of other states, but rather wars against terrorist groups, drug lords, and insurgents. The received doctrine is that to win such wars one has to both have the support of the local population and cut off the insurgent, terrorist, or guerilla forces from having contact with them. In essence, the spectrum of perceived legitimate military actions has widened from the traditional coercion and enforcement to include peace-keeping, rebuilding and humanitarian operations, all aimed at creating or enforcing a state of security.[33] Hearts and minds campaigns, massive public infrastructure repair and rebuilding, provision of medical services, and food aid are all perceived as legitimate tools in these wars, whether carried out directly by the military or by their contracted parties.

The evidence for success of these campaigns is difficult to assess. As Weiss has pointed out, there is no counter-factual to judge them against (what would have happened if they had not been there) and there are few pre-set criteria to judge them against. Was the 1991 Kurdish safe haven a success because millions of Kurds were protected and fed, or a failure because it did nothing to alter the fundamental cause of Kurdish persecution—the regime in Baghdad?[34] In both Afghanistan and Iraq today, there is little direct evidence that these "soft" campaigns are doing anything to either isolate the "enemy" or ensure the good will and loyalty of the host population.

At the same time as military forces are developing the capacity of their humanitarian operations, so too are they looking to humanitarian actors to work with them, rather than apart from them. Colin Powell's famous remark, made when he was US Secretary of State, that US NGOs should act as "force multipliers" in Iraq, exemplifies the issue. If military forces are there to bring security, safety, human rights, democracy, and free enterprise to a previously oppressed people, then surely a humanitarian agency would want to work with them? Many individual humanitarian aid workers might well privately support such a cause. However, the *modus operandi* of humanitarian action as neutral and impartial *de facto* excludes humanitarian agencies from taking such a stance. If they are to be perceived as neutral, then it is necessary (but often not sufficient) to be apart from combatants—whether national or foreign military forces or insurgents. We will return to this argument later in Chapter 7 where we look at the future of humanitarian action.

It is a simple reality today that every economically active country's foreign policy agenda is focused on the security of its resource supplies and trade export markets. This is the essence of our globalized world. Of course, past colonial economic powers had the same imperative— protect your supply lines and your markets. The difference today is that in an interconnected global producing and trading system, any one country's prosperity is dependent on that of many others. The real foreign policy question is over whether security is best achieved by force and coercion or cooperation and compromise. Will humanitarian assistance become co-opted into the agenda of containment and coercion, as we saw it practiced in the nineteenth-century famines of India and Ireland in Chapter 2, or will it claim some independent space in an agenda of cooperation and compromise as states jockey to coexist?

5 International organizations

This chapter examines the main international organizations involved in humanitarian aid. Specifically, we will look at the more important parts of the UN Secretariat, at the relevant UN agencies and the moves they are making to reform the way they and their donor community works, and at the International Red Cross and Red Crescent Movement, an important player which sits somewhere between being an NGO and a governmental organization. We will also take a brief look at the various systems which have come into existence to monitor and track humanitarian aid. Finally, we will look at the international food aid system, a key and controversial component of the aid world.

The humanitarian role of the UN Secretariat and specialized agencies

Numerous agencies of the United Nations have a role in humanitarian affairs. These include the Security Council and offices within the Secretariat, as well as some of the specialized agencies. The roles of the Security Council, the Department of Peacekeeping Operations and the Office for the Coordination of Humanitarian Affairs (OCHA), as well as the UNHCR, World Food Programme (WFP), and UNICEF are highlighted below. Other UN specialized agencies with a more limited humanitarian role include the Food and Agricultural Organization—which plays a lead role in protecting agricultural productive capacities in emergencies; the UN Development Programme (UNDP)—which leads on economic recovery in the aftermath of disasters, and the World Health Organization. One non-UN international agency, the International Organization for Migration (IOM) is responsible for resettling refugees, and also for camp management in natural disasters under new coordination arrangements—the cluster approach.

The UN Security Council and Department of Peacekeeping Operations

Created with the intention of monitoring peace agreements between states in the mid-twentieth century, the international peacekeeping system (including UN and regional bodies) under the UN Security Council (SC) has developed a series of more proactive and robust capacities over the past few decades. The impact of the SC in complex emergencies is substantial. It has the power to draw attention to various conflicts and abuses (potentially increasing aid and political attention to those states), impose sanctions upon states (which may target leaders or have adverse effects upon populations), and empower peacekeeping missions (of various strengths and mandates) both to assist humanitarian operations already underway, and in the name of humanitarianism itself. All these actions impact ongoing crises to varying degrees.

One of its increasingly prevalent responsibilities is its response to and engagement in humanitarian emergencies. Peacekeeping responsibilities in the humanitarian arena include the protection (originally by presence alone, but now increasingly by force) of humanitarian staff and supplies and the disbursement of aid. UN peacekeepers (and in some cases soldiers of subcontracted regional bodies) are also mandated to protect civilians by securing refugee and internally displaced person (IDP) camps, creating and patrolling "safe zones" and using armed force against parties who attack civilian populations. Peacekeeping missions have varying degrees of success in all of these categories. Among their failures are the notorious inability of peacekeepers to protect aid supplies in Somalia or to prevent the massacre of civilians taken from the UN "safe zone" of Srebrenica—where, as we saw in Chapter 3, thousands of Muslim men and boys were abducted and massacred under the eyes of UN peacekeepers forbidden from using force in their protective capacities. These failures highlighted the need to empower peacekeepers to use force in their humanitarian duties, and relatively more successful contemporary peacekeeping missions, as in the Democratic Republic of Congo (DRC), indicate the added value of giving these missions the more robust "Chapter VII mandate" to use military force when required.

Additionally, humanitarian protection and assistance have emerged as the main justification for some peacekeeping operations, as observed in operations of humanitarian intervention. As we reported in Chapter 4, "The Responsibility to Protect"—a concept put forward by the International Commission on Intervention and State Sovereignty

(ICISS) in 2001—seeks to provide a legal justification for this intervention, suggesting that the maintenance of state "sovereignty" includes a responsibility to protect civilians from "serious harm" from whatever source. Should a state fail to uphold this responsibility (either by choice or lack of capacity), the international community has the responsibility to intervene for humanitarian purposes within those borders to protect civilians. A number of states have raised objection to this principle, arguing that its criteria for intervention are too ambiguous and that its challenge to sovereignty is illegal.

A number of concerns arise with regard to humanitarian-military intervention. The first is the potential for invading states to use "humanitarian intervention" as a justification for invasion when other political motivations may also be at play. A second is the blurring of the concept of the "humanitarian community," as, by introducing military bodies into humanitarian work (even solely by terminology), the traditional perception of independence and neutrality of many humanitarian organizations is threatened, particularly among local communities who may not distinguish humanitarian organizations from military bodies, putting humanitarian work and workers at risk.

The Office for the Coordination of Humanitarian Affairs (OCHA)

OCHA is the UN body delegated to coordinate the response and activities of relief agencies to humanitarian emergencies worldwide. OCHA was predated by the Department of Humanitarian Affairs (DHA) which, along with the Inter-Agency Standing Committee (IASC) (see below) was authorized by a UN General Assembly resolution in 1991. DHA was reformed into OCHA in 1998. Led by an Under-Secretary-General (also identified as the Emergency Relief Coordinator) and based in New York and Geneva, OCHA oversees the rapid deployment of UN staff to humanitarian emergencies. It coordinates humanitarian activities among all relief agencies on the ground in an effort to ensure that no populations or sectors are neglected and there is no overlap in work between organizations. Though a UN agency, OCHA's coordination efforts extend beyond the UN system to include NGOs, private organizations—such as the ICRC, bilateral organizations, and others. OCHA sometimes serves as a convening forum for coordination with host country governments during emergencies.

The ERC plays a significant role in the international relief community as a link between agencies and the Secretary General. The ERC is responsible for ensuring that all humanitarian crises are addressed (including those that fall in the gray area of responsibility between organizations, such as the protection of IDPs); advocacy of humanitarian issues (to political bodies, but also at times to the media and general public); and effective coordination of emergency humanitarian response.

This coordination is undertaken through the Inter-Agency Standing Committee. Chaired by the ERC, the IASC is made up of representatives from UN agencies, the ICRC, the IFRC, the World Bank, the International Organization for Migration (IOM) and representatives of global, US and European NGO coalitions. Together they attempt to facilitate inter-agency decision-making through organizing disaster relief, including the performance of needs assessment, consolidated appeals, field coordination, and humanitarian policies.

Though certainly effective and operational, OCHA has encountered some difficulties in its first decade, including criticism for its failure to coordinate effectively enough. Certainly one source of this difficulty may be organizational resistance to coordination. While most humanitarian organizations—both UN and NGO—support coordination in principle, their willingness to be subject to its execution can be a more tenuous matter. Some organizations that value their independence of action generally avoid coordination forums. Criticisms of OCHA's leadership capacities have also been raised, as in the Tsunami Evaluation Coalition's Synthesis Report.[1]

OCHA's budget for 2007 was nearly $160 million, most of which came from states and IASC member organizations, and only 8 percent from the regular UN budget.

The Office of the United Nations High Commissioner for Refugees (UNHCR)

As we saw in Chapter 2, UNHCR was created by the UN General Assembly in 1950 to lead and coordinate assistance to and protection of refugees internationally. Based in Geneva, the organization operates under the 1951 Refugee Convention and its 1967 protocol and is responsible for protecting the rights and well-being of refugees, including promoting their rights to seek asylum or refuge in another state and to later choose to return to their home state, remain in their state of refuge, or resettle elsewhere. Even today though, a significant number of countries, including some of the larger southern nations, have neither signed nor ratified the convention. In recent years, UNHCR's work has expanded to include assistance to and protection of internally displaced persons (IDPs)—individuals fleeing crises within their countries (including conflict), but who do not cross an international border.

UNHCR is funded almost entirely by voluntary contributions, largely from states or other international organizations. Since the 1990s, its budget has held steady at around $1 billion annually, supporting offices in over 100 countries.

Ultimately, defining who is a "refugee"—and thus who is entitled to UNHCR protection and assistance—is up to states, though UNHCR often assists in this determination. This "legal" or "diplomatic" protection includes interviewing candidates for refugee status, advising relevant departments of government and assisting in relevant legal procedures. UNHCR also advocates for strict observance of the principle of *non-refoulement*—the right of refugees not to be forcibly returned to their country of origin if their lives or freedoms are thereby endangered.

In addition to this protection, UNHCR oversees humanitarian assistance (including shelter, sanitation, food and water) to refugees. UNHCR rarely provides assistance to these populations directly, instead coordinating, supervising, and contracting this work to NGOs as implementing partners. UNHCR and WFP work jointly on the provision of food to refugee populations.

In the 1990s, UNHCR was criticized for its increasing focus on assistance at the expense of protection—UNHCR being the sole agency mandated to do the latter (with the partial exception of ICRC's role and UNICEF's work in child protection), whereas many agencies can be contracted to carry out the former. This criticism was particularly aimed at its work in Bosnia where UNHCR served as the lead organization for humanitarian response to the displaced population and also in Rwanda, where it assisted populations fleeing genocide. In recent years, UNHCR has signaled a return to, and re-strengthening of, its protection priorities.

A challenge to both of these arenas of work is that states are sometimes reluctant to permit the entry of refugees across their borders and their registration, whether for political, ethnic and/or economic reasons. As an international organization, UNHCR walks a fine line in advocating for refugee rights (protection), while ultimately having to adhere to state policies and dictates, dependent on their permission and cooperation in ultimately accessing and assisting these vulnerable populations. UNHCR is also dependent upon host country governments for the provision of security within refugee camps. Despite this need for adherence to host country policy, UNHCR has demonstrated resistance to and willingness to protest about some state policies towards refugees, such as its concerns regarding the US position towards Haitian and Iraqi refugees. In 1954 and 1981, UNHCR was awarded the Nobel Peace Prize.

The World Food Programme (WFP)

As described in Chapter 1, WFP was created in 1963, following a suggestion by US food aid advocate George McGovern at the annual FAO Conference two years earlier. Based in Rome, it was initially conceived as a three-year experimental program, but was made a permanent body in 1965. Its mission is threefold: (1) to assist populations suffering from food crises (both natural and man-made); (2) to improve nutrition worldwide (particularly among children and other extremely vulnerable populations); and (3) to assist populations to build assets and self-reliance so that they will be less vulnerable to food insecurity in the future. This latter work includes school-feeding (encouraging children—particularly girls—to attend and achieve success by providing in-school meals); addressing the challenges of HIV/AIDS; and organizing food-for-work programs (where the hungry are paid with food to build infrastructure and learn important skills). Increasingly, WFP focuses on women.

While WFP is involved in humanitarian response, nutrition, and development, its primary efforts are humanitarian. In addition to providing food aid in sudden, slow-onset and complex emergencies (often using NGOs as implementing partners), WFP also acts as the lead UN agency in humanitarian crises in the organization of logistics. It particularly assesses and addresses challenges to humanitarian response such as inadequate infrastructure and transportation, reaching beneficiaries in remote locations, and establishing communication facilities where previously there had been none. In some cases this includes airlift capability for both humanitarian aid and staff. Another strength of WFP in this capacity is its emphasis on needs-assessment (rather than aid based on donor dictation)—a strength that may be diminished with increased dependence on assistance from specific donors (the USA in particular).

WFP's budget of $2.9 billion (in 2006) is entirely dependent on voluntary contributions, most of which are provided (in cash or in kind) by states, though corporations and private donors are also well represented. In 2006, WFP distributed almost 4 million metric tons of food to about 88 million individuals in 78 countries worldwide. A multilateral organization, WFP serves to depoliticize international food aid. However, as most of its donations—particularly in food—are bilateral, the organization can be compelled towards donor countries' priorities.

For further information about food aid, see below.

The United Nations Children's Fund (UNICEF)

As we saw in Chapter 1, UNICEF was founded in 1946 to meet the post-war needs of children in Europe and China and became a permanent UN agency in 1953. The organization's mandate has since evolved, giving UNICEF responsibility to meet the needs (short- and long-term) of women and children in all developing countries through development and humanitarian assistance. It also strongly advocates for the rights of children (as outlined in the *Convention on the Rights of the Child*). Based in New York, it operates in over 190 countries at the time of writing.

UNICEF divides its work into five major categories: child survival and development (including nutrition programming); basic education and gender equality; HIV/AIDS (including prevention and treatment activities and support for orphans); child protection (from violence and abuse); and policy advocacy and partnerships (including data collection and research analysis). While it plays a strong role in humanitarian response, its development initiatives have recently expanded through its support for the child-related Millennium Development Goals (MDGs).

UNICEF's Office of Emergency Programmes (EMOPS) is responsible for information gathering and dissemination about, preparation for, and coordination during emergency relief operations. Frequently acting as the lead UN agency in humanitarian crises, UNICEF collaborates with other UN agencies, governments, and local and international NGOs to provide relief to children and families in both natural and manmade disasters. Its activities in emergencies include health, nutrition and sanitation initiatives; rehabilitating schools for immediate post-crisis use; protecting women and children from violence, including gender-based violence; family reunification; and demobilization of child and adolescent soldiers.

A UNICEF document, *Core Commitments for Children in Emergencies (CCCs)*, outlines organizational priorities for the needs of children in crises that must be addressed in the first six–eight weeks of the onset of crisis. They include assessment; vaccination; feeding and nutritional monitoring; providing safe drinking water, sanitation and hygiene; preventing separation of families; and resuming schooling. Other activities are important, but follow these first initiatives.

UNICEF is dependent entirely on voluntary contributions. The majority of this income comes from states, but a substantial amount is raised through private donations by National Committees for UNICEF and the sale of UNICEF goods. In 2005, 50 percent of the organization's income came from states, 38 percent from private donations and the rest from other organizations. In 2006, UNICEF received just under $1.8 billion in income. UNICEF was awarded the Nobel Peace Prize in 1965.

Reforming UN coordination

There have been many individual or collective efforts to improve humanitarian response, particularly since the debacle of the Rwanda genocide and the ensuing refugee crisis. In recent years—as a result of impetus from Jan Egeland, who from 2003–2006 was Under-Secretary General for Humanitarian Affairs and Emergency Relief Coordinator—the UN undertook a though review of its own operations, culminating in the 2005 *Humanitarian Response Review* (HRR).[2] Vowing to "do better to be more predictable" in humanitarian response, it highlighted gaps in response and the inequitable allocation of resources to different emergencies that had already been highlighted by an independent review published a year earlier.[3] The HRR was focused specifically on the UN and its agencies—it did not address the NGO sector or the Red Cross/Crescent Movement—although there were obvious overlaps and implications. Its main conclusion was that, in many cases, "humanitarian response provided is not good enough."[4]

Specifically, the HRR noted the need for many improvements, including better accountability to both donors and recipients; a more timely response to humanitarian emergencies; a more "global vision" for humanitarian action—in comparison to the "fragmented" vision that the commissioners found; and much better systems to support humanitarian programming in a number of areas, including preparedness, human resource management, administration systems, water and sanitation, camp management, evaluation—and particularly, coordination. Above all, the HRR found that responsibility for humanitarian protection was fragmented, the knowledge of the topic was limited, and hence the reality on the ground for civilians caught in conflict was unacceptable. This was particularly the case where IDPs were concerned—the legal status and responsibility for refugees being more clearly defined in international law.[5]

The report noted that field coordination was often dependent on the personality of the UN Humanitarian Coordinator (HC) in a given country caught in crisis—where individual leadership was adequate, so was coordination, but where this was not the case, or where UN leadership was divided on operational or policy questions, cooperation in the field tended to be poor. The report proposed a series of improvements in analysis, evaluation and accountability. Perhaps most significantly, the HRR recommended that the IASC should "identify and assign lead organizations with responsibility at sectoral level, especially in relation to IDP protection and care and develop a *cluster approach* in all priority sectors."[6]

Ultimately clusters were formed around 11 sectors or programmatic areas: shelter (led by UNHCR), health (WHO), nutrition (UNICEF), water, sanitation, hygiene—collectively known as WASH—(UNICEF), education (UNICEF, Save the Children), agriculture (FAO), early recovery (UNDP), camp management (UNHCR and IOM), telecommunications (OCHA) protection (UNHCR)[7] and logistics (WFP). Notably absent from the list of "clusters" was food security, food aid, and livelihoods.

An early evaluation of the cluster approach found that while it has improved coordination and addressed some of the gaps identified by the HRR, the performance of individual clusters was quite variable. Engagement of state actors has been mixed, and there have been no observable improvements in accountability. The new system has yet to encounter a major natural disaster on the scale of the tsunami, or a complex emergency on the scale of Darfur.

A year after the HRR, and commissioned by the Secretary-General, the UN High Level Panel on System-wide Coherence in the Areas of Development, Humanitarian Assistance, and the Environment produced a report, *Delivering as One.*[8] While this dealt with humanitarian assistance, it was more concerned with the internal coordination of the overall UN mission, including its human rights, economic development, security and environmental elements. Whereas the HRR called for greater coordination among humanitarian actors within and outside the UN system, *Delivering as One* calls for greater "coherence" among these different elements of the UN's own mission. The report is couched in the language of the MDGs, and criticizes the UN for not being results-oriented. It calls for greater consolidation of activities, elimination of duplication, multi-year centralized funding, greater attention to gender equity and environmental concerns, and a focus on outcomes—including a system-wide common evaluation mechanism to promote transparency and accountability. It also calls for unitary leadership at the country level—including oversight of the humanitarian mission. Regarding humanitarian action, the report calls for stronger coordination through the cluster system (which was only just being implemented when the report came out), greater emphasis on risk reduction and early warning, and stronger post-disaster recovery programs as well as greater emphasis on protection. While the report recognizes the need to preserve humanitarian space and humanitarian principles, it clearly sees internal coherence of UN missions as the greater priority, and thus presents some challenges for independent humanitarian action particularly with regard to the question of protection. So far "One UN" pilots have been set up in eight countries, none of which are in the midst of a humanitarian emergency, so it is too soon to judge. Tim Maurer notes that " … it is not clear how safeguards such as the principle of *non-refoulement* can continue to be guaranteed given that the process is government-owned,-signed, and -driven."[9]

Early assessments of the cluster approach to protection indicate some improvements in information systems and standards, but note that it is too soon to judge the impact on the lives of IDPs. Impact is still to some extent dependent on the leadership of particular HCs.

Reforming humanitarian funding[10]

Over the past 30 years, an increasing percentage of Official Development Assistance (ODA) has been spent on humanitarian assistance; up from around 3 percent in the 1970s to between 10 and 14 percent today. In 2005, $18 billion was raised for global humanitarian assistance,[11] though this was inflated by the tsunami response which precipitated a massive spike in overall humanitarian contributions, adding extra funding of $5.5 billion. In a typical year in the mid-2000s therefore, somewhere in the region of $10–12 billion was made available for global humanitarian assistance. According to the Global Humanitarian Assistance—an independent project designed to assist the process of mobilizing resources and ensuring the effectiveness of humanitarian aid—the official total humanitarian assistance contribution per citizen of countries belonging to the Organization for Economic Cooperation and Development in 2006 was an average $10. Contributions per country ranged widely with the United States contributing $10 per citizen, Japan a mere $2, the UK $18, Switzerland $26 and Norway $81.[12]

To put these expenditures into perspective, recent figures from the Nobel Economics Prize laureate Joseph Stiglitz suggest that the United States is spending $16bn a month on the wars in Iraq and Afghanistan alone (on top of the regular expenses of the Department of Defence)— a monthly sum almost double the annual humanitarian spend and equivalent to the entire annual budget of the UN and all its agencies.[13]

Against the global picture of growth in humanitarian spending, donors have pursued two lines of funding reforms, one through the UN system in a series of measures over the past decade, described below, and one through the Good Humanitarian Donorship Initiative described in Chapter 4. Within the UN system focus has been on moving towards a more coherent and predicable funding regime and towards improving humanitarian coordination, partly through funding mechanisms, but also through support for a number of information system initiatives. Four funding initiatives of the past decade are noteworthy, the Central Emergency Response Fund (CERF); the Common Humanitarian Fund (CHF); the Emergency Response Funds (ERFs), and the older, but still important, Consolidated Appeal Process (CAP).

CAP

CAP was a 1990s initiative aimed at pulling together at the country level the separate appeals for each of the UN agencies for funding. Initially it was simply a compiling of individual requests, but over the years has grown to allow for joint assessments and a more truly consolidated appeal which provides an overview of the humanitarian needs in-country. The CAP often covers the work of non-UN agencies, but does not formally include them. In particular the various components of the Red Cross Movement still prefer to issue their own separate appeals.

In 2005, CAP appeals targeted close to 46 million people in need.[14] An analysis of CAP data reveals that quick onset disasters received higher percentage funding than chronic disasters. Likewise, humanitarian aid funding to sectors which experience chronic issues—such as health, water, and sanitation—are routinely neglected in favor of emergency food aid.

CERF

The Central Emergency Response Fund (CERF), created in 1991, was originally designed as a $50 million fund to expedite the response of UN agencies to sudden crises ahead of receiving funds from donors. The CERF was expanded tenfold in 2005 to provide grant funding, empower UN agencies to respond more rapidly to emergencies, and to address under-funded crises.

Since its official re-launch in March 2006, the CERF has committed more than $426 million for more than 510 projects in 44 countries. As of June 2007, more than $269 million has been disbursed for rapid onset and existing crises, and $161 million went toward under-funded emergencies in 24 countries.[15]

CHF

Another significant reform mechanism is the Common Humanitarian Fund. This instrument—piloted in the Sudan and the DRC in 2006—is designed to address a critical flaw in the CAP. The CAPs were originally envisaged as a strategic planning and resource mobilization tool. CHFs were designed to remedy a structural flaw in the funding process—donors were only committing to certain projects. Their individual choices were not necessarily adding up to a coherent and rational whole. Additionally, the HC responsible for in-country delivery of the CAP had little influence over these resource allocations.

CHFs provide funds against the CAP, and allow the HC to determine resource allocation, working closely with the cluster/sectoral leads. The common fund is intended to ensure that humanitarian funds flow toward strategic priorities in the field, through quick and flexible channels. An intended strength of the common fund is a donor commitment to provide initial funding at the beginning of the year, potentially a significant step toward improving the timeliness and predictability of humanitarian financing.

ERFs

A third new mechanism, emergency response funds (ERFs) seek to offer rapidly available small grants (up to $130,000) to in-country organizations (both NGOs and UN agencies). More than $53 million has been disbursed through ERFs in the past six years. ERFs are currently operational in Liberia, Somalia, the DRC, Iraq, Ethiopia, Indonesia, and the Democratic Republic of Korea (DPRK), and may be introduced in Burundi, the Republic of Congo and Côte d'Ivoire. ERFs are still very much experimental and, in the eyes of many operational NGOs suffer from an over-cumbersome bureaucracy, negating their very purpose—the rapid disbursement of funds.

The Red Cross and Red Crescent Movement

The history of the Red Cross and Red Crescent Movement, which we outlined in Chapter 1, has led to a complex but vitally important organization in the humanitarian world. In some ways it sits between intergovernmental organizations like the UN agencies and NGOs. In terms of numbers of employees, volunteers and representation on the ground, it can claim to be the world's largest, as well as oldest humanitarian organization. To understand the movement today, one needs to understand the roles of its three constituent parts.

The International Committee of the Red Cross

The ICRC is the direct descendant of that founding committee set up by Jean Henri Dunant. The actual committee is still an all-Swiss affair of 18 leading Swiss humanitarians and policy makers. This committee, now called the ICRC Assembly, is the governing body of the organization. Its policies are carried out by the ICRC Directorate, which oversees ICRC's operation in some 80 countries involving over 12,000 employees. The ICRC sees itself as "an independent, neutral organization ensuring humanitarian protection and assistance for victims of war and armed violence." It has a permanent mandate under international humanitarian law to take impartial action for prisoners, the wounded and sick, and civilians affected by conflict.

The ICRC is funded both by contributions from the States Party to the Geneva Conventions and by more conventional fund-raising via appeals to donor governments and the general public. Thus, some of its budget each year, though voluntary, comes from states as part of their obligations under the Geneva Conventions. In 2006, ICRC's total budget was just short of $900 million: a large sum, but significantly less than the major international NGO grouping, World Vision International.

ICRC's *modus operandi* is what makes it unique. It is passionately committed to acting independently and neutrally. It will often observe, but not take part in, collaborative UN or NGO ventures. It will often work with a local Red Cross or Red Crescent Society, but not at their behest. It will always seek access to victims on the basis of need alone, investing significant resources in quietly building trust and understanding to assure access. In terms of activity on the ground, ICRC carries out relief programs for conflict-affected populations which look similar to those of other agencies. Often it will act faster than others as it programs explicitly on the basis of need, not funds raised.

In addition, though, ICRC carries out three other unique activities, stemming from its mandate under the Geneva Conventions.

It is mandated to visit prisoners of war and detainees and report back to those holding the prisoners on whether they are in compliance with their obligations under the Geneva Conventions. In 2004, over half a million people received these confidential Red Cross visits.

Linked to these visits is ICRC's tracing service which seeks to put family members in touch, via ICRC-carried letters, with their relatives, whether prisoners or those displaced by war. ICRC's tracing service contains 50 million reference files relating to 17.5 million people displaced by war.

Finally, the ICRC seeks to promote knowledge and understanding about International Humanitarian Law (IHL) and to develop new areas of humanitarian law. Thus it was central to the promotion and eventual success of the Land Mines Treaty and to discussions on the banning of Laser Weapons. In promoting IHL, the ICRC works directly with military forces and academic and research institutions to ensure that all professional soldiers are aware of their responsibilities under the law.

The national societies

Today there is a Red Cross or Red Crescent Society in nearly every country of the world, 186 national societies as of December 2007. They are local autonomous organizations, not branches of the ICRC or the International Federation of Red Cross and Red Crescent Societies (IFRC), and can only come into existence if their country has signed the Geneva Conventions and passed a law establishing a local Society as an autonomous, yet auxiliary, body to the state. Thus they are mandated by the state but seek to operate independently of it. Collectively they claim to have 97 million members and volunteers, and 300,000 employees, assisting some 233 million beneficiaries each year. They work in the fields of public health, disaster preparedness and response, blood supplies, first aid, and the promotion of IHL. In times of war they act as auxiliaries to the ICRC, under the ICRC's direction. In times of major non-conflict disaster or crisis, they appeal via their international membership organization, the IFRC, for assistance to be funneled through them from their sister Societies.

The International Federation of Red Cross and Red Crescent Societies (IFRC)

We saw in Chapter 1 how the national societies asserted their independence after World War I and established their own international federal structure, separate from the ICRC. This structure, the IFRC—whose secretariat is less than a kilometer from the ICRC's in Geneva—acts as a coordinator and promoter of international cooperation between, and public voice for, the membership. The Secretariat also seeks to support the development and capacity-building of its membership and to provide it with an international voice, both formally at international conferences and negotiations, and informally through its publications.

Humanitarian information systems

The growth of information technology and its global reach in the 1990s led to significant reform in the way the humanitarian system manages information. Coming on the heels of the popularizing of email and the Internet, the perceived failures of the aid community to prevent or respond effectively to the Rwanda genocide led to a rich development of information sharing tools. These have gone a long way to improving the effectiveness of the international humanitarian system. These systems have focused on improving the tracking of funds, the sharing of agency-generated information and the provision of one-stop-shops where anyone can quickly get a good overview of the data, analysis and opinion available around any one particular crisis or relief operation.

From famine early warning to humanitarian information systems

Chapter 3 noted the birth of famine early warning. During the 1970s and 1980s, the consensus grew that monitoring trends could in fact offer some degree of early warning—not enough to prevent crises, but at least enough to keep them from getting out of hand. Increased emphasis on technical aspects of crisis prediction has extended beyond just famines, and early warning is now an established part of the humanitarian enterprise.

Central to this story is the USAID-funded Famine Early Warning System (or FEWS) which began in the 1980s (and became FEWSNET or the Famine Early Warning System Network in 2000). FEWS and the experts who worked for it pioneered the search for early warning indicators, and eventually broadened the scope of FEWS beyond just drought and agricultural production to include conflict and other causal factors—though the organization does still have a climatic/natural disaster inclination, with heavy emphasis on remote sensing. FEWS formally functions as a data consolidating organization, making use of existing primary data collected by other organizations including national governments, though in some cases it will undertake primary data collection, particularly on vulnerability information on emerging food security problems. FEWSNET currently operates in 27 countries—all but five of which are in Sub-Saharan Africa (the other five are Afghanistan, Haiti, Nicaragua, Honduras, and Guatemala). The trajectory of the FEWS project, however, is indicative of the growth in humanitarian information systems in general. We have already mentioned recognition of the need to look comprehensively at causal factors, not just the "convenient" ones. Tracking and trying to predict the way in which conflict will cause a humanitarian crisis are considerably more difficult that predicting the impact of drought on crop production. Furthermore, early warning alone isn't very useful in the absence of baseline information against which to compare current or predicted trends. Thus there has been an increased emphasis on baseline vulnerability analysis as an integral component of humanitarian information systems.

If the purpose of early warning is fundamentally to enable a response, the information being generated must be fed into some kind of contingency planning, including the ability to rapidly assess the impact of a crisis, and to be able to respond in a timely manner. Notwithstanding the criticism of Glenzer and others in Chapter 2, humanitarian information systems now routinely link to programmatic capacity—both in terms of planning and implementation. FEWSNET remains an autonomous organization with no intervention capacity.

The World Food Programme (with the largest humanitarian implementation capacity in the world) and the Food and Agriculture Organization (with a rapidly expanding emergency response capacity) have increasingly invested in their own, in-house, information systems and analytical capacity. In WFP this began as the Vulnerability Assessment and Mapping (VAM) unit, but has since expanded to include Emergency Needs Assessment and Monitoring and Evaluation. In FAO, it has long included the Global Information Early Warning System (GIEWS) and now includes the Integrated Food Security and Humanitarian Phase Classification (IPC) and various other initiatives.

The imperative for intervention has necessitated not only the need to predict crisis and assess needs, but also the need to monitor interventions and evaluate impact. Closely related to this, particularly since the Rwanda crisis and the rise of various industry-wide initiatives to foster learning and accountability, is a well-acknowledged need for information systems to have a learning feedback loop. Information generated must be used in institutional learning and to enhance abilities to predict and respond to crises.[16]

In addition to these global institutions that are primarily focused on food security crises, there are many others, some of them regional in nature, that are more focused on conflict early warning. Perhaps the best known of these is CEWARN—the Conflict Early Warning project, operated by the Intergovernmental Authority for Development—an organization based in Djibouti with six member states from the Horn and East Africa. Given that it is run by IGAD, an agency in one of the most conflict-prone areas of the world—one member, Eritrea, has left the organization—it is not surprising that CEWARN has chosen to focus on one kind of conflict: resource-based conflict in pastoral areas, and particularly cross-border pastoral conflicts. Other, inter-state conflicts (such as between Ethiopia and Eritrea) or more highly politicized internal conflict (clan or ethnic conflict) haven't yet made it onto the official early warning agenda. Nevertheless, CEWARN has done some pioneering work in developing and monitoring conflict indicators.

Other sources of humanitarian information

Several specific sources of humanitarian information also require a mention.

Financial tracking

Tracking the funding flowing from the donors and through all these reform mechanisms are two UN information services. OCHA's FTS[17] and WFP's International Food Aid Information Service (INTERFAIS)[18] today provide the best analysis of humanitarian assistance by sector. Like all data systems they are limited to the data that is provided to them. Whereas the Global Humanitarian Assistance Reports provide good retrospective data, FTS and INTERFAIS operate in near real-time.

IRIN, ReliefWeb and HICs

The Integrated Regional Information Network (IRIN) was started by the UN in 1995, in East Africa following the Rwanda genocide. It now acts rather like a news agency for the humanitarian world in Africa, the Middle East, and Central Asia. It provides background analysis, topical stories, situation reports and the like, via a website, through email subscription, and more recently through RRS news feeds. Its website (www.irinnews.org) is one of the best sources of real-time analysis of major crises.

A related source of information is ReliefWeb, another UN-run resource for the humanitarian community. Started in 1996, ReliefWeb bills itself as "the world's leading on-line gateway to information (documents and maps) on humanitarian emergencies and disasters."[19] The site (www.reliefweb.int) enables operational agencies and researchers to have a common portal to share reports and analysis. It provides a single stop where donors and agencies alike can go to track finances, see situation reports and appeals, and download purpose-created maps for each crisis.

Another IASC initiative, started in 2003, has been the Humanitarian Information Centres (www.humanitarianinfo.org). Set up by UN missions in most countries which have recently experienced emergencies, they provide a space for sharing information about the crisis and response. They collate data and produce overview reports and pull together near real-time information specific to each crisis. They maintain contact databases and provide detailed mapping services. The key to the success of the HICs has been that they are service-driven. They do not seek to coordinate but rather provide relief workers and donors with the information they need and with a quick and convenient way of sharing it.

Alertnet

Finally, in a separate venture, also promoted after the Rwanda genocide, Reuters Foundation, the philanthropic wing of the Reuters news organization, set up Alertnet (www.alertnet.org). Similar to Reliefweb, it seeks to focus the resources of Reuters on humanitarian issues and provide aid workers and donors with well-structured and rapid access both to relevant Reuters news stories and specifically commissioned pieces.

Meeting humanitarian needs or donor objectives: fifty years of food assistance[20]

Food aid has historically been the largest single category of humanitarian assistance—a trend that continues to the present, albeit a resource that appears increasingly at risk and has been subject to shortfalls in recent years. The history of food aid is too long and complicated to detail here, but the roots of today's complex set of institutions, donors, and resources regarding food aid grew after 1945, an era when rapid increases in agricultural technology in North America—particularly mechanization, hybrid varieties, and the use of fertilizers, herbicides and insecticides—resulted in a massive increase in yields, and thus in large-scale agricultural surpluses. This rapidly became a political problem because it depressed farm-gate prices to the point that family farmers became victims of their own success, unable to survive their own technological advances.

The response was to set up a series of "price floors," below which governments would step in to purchase grain or other commodities, to ensure at least that price to farmers. As surpluses accumulated in the hands of the US and Canadian governments, rather than farmers, it quickly became clear that it was cheaper to give away the surpluses than it was to store them for some undesignated future use. Thus modern food aid was born, and for much of its existence, food aid has been more a tool to protect domestic farm prices, or to bolster the current accounts balance of payments of friendly nations, than it has had anything to do with addressing hunger or humanitarian need— although the latter has always been the "public face" of food aid.

By the 1970s, the issue of managing surpluses had largely disappeared, although it occasionally resurfaces during particularly good agricultural years. At that point the food aid program in the US became more of a political objective of a relatively small coalition of interests who grew to support the food aid business. These included companies that procured grain and other commodities on behalf of the government, the shipping industry (mandated by law to provide the bulk of the transportation for American food aid), and the NGOs that distributed (or in some cases sold) food in the recipient countries. Whereas in the early days of food aid, the most common form was government-to-government grants or very friendly loans, over time this kind of assistance—known as program food aid—has dwindled, and been replaced by much greater demand for food assistance for humanitarian purposes—emergency food aid.

A third category of food aid—project food aid—is utilized primarily by NGOs for ongoing development programs—sometimes using food directly, sometimes selling (or monetizing) the food and utilizing the cash proceeds to fund programs. Humanitarian food assistance grew rapidly from only about a million metric tons in 1980 to nearly six million tons in 2003, reflecting the increase in humanitarian emergencies during this time, and the relatively reliable availability of food assistance, combined with the reluctance of some donors to make other resources available for humanitarian response. The majority of humanitarian food aid is now channeled through the World Food Programme, though substantial quantities go directly to NGOs or, in some cases, to host country governments.

In comparison with nearly every other category of humanitarian need, there has long been the tendency for the funding and supply of most food aid requirements to be met. However, while food aid is a far bigger category than all others, there is often still not enough. In 2005, for example, there was a significant shortfall in food assistance available compared to assessed need.

For decades, food aid was seen as a means of surplus disposal—all from that donor country's internal market. This is still the case with US food aid. European and Canadian food aid is increasingly "untied" from donor source markets, meaning that money is available to purchase food for assistance elsewhere in the world—usually the recipient country if it has pockets of surplus even in the midst of a humanitarian crisis, or in a neighboring country with an exportable surplus. Called Local or Regional Purchase, this kind of food aid is believed to be less expensive, quicker to deliver, and permits the benefits of the sales to go to the developing country in which food is purchased. However, there is significant political resistance to Local and Regional Purchase from the USA, the world's largest provider of food aid.

Increasingly, cash transfers, rather than in-kind food aid, are being sought to address humanitarian food security crises. Again, there is little willingness to consider replacing the food aid budget of the US with cash transfers, but some European donors are diversifying their resource base to permit food or cash, depending on which is more appropriate. Generally, where markets are functioning and can respond to increased demand, and where adequate food is available in them, cash transfers have been shown to have greater impact. Nevertheless, it is quite unlikely that cash transfers will replace food aid in the near term.

With growing demand for higher quality food from the rapidly expanding middle classes in India and China, particularly meat and dairy products which require substantial quantities of grain as livestock feed, and more recently given the demand for grain for bio-fuels, the price of basic grains has increased dramatically since 2005. With relatively static food aid budgets, this means that the amount of food for humanitarian response has declined, leaving analysts worried about the potential impact of a large-scale food security crisis. As global food prices—and the fuel costs of moving supplies around the globe—spiraled upwards, WFP expressed concern in early 2008 that it may have to ration food aid unless donors are more generous.

6 NGOs and private action

The world of humanitarian NGOs is vast today. Many of them are transnational with budgets as large as major corporations or small states. They represent a huge range of interests and approaches and do the vast majority of the operating work of the international humanitarian system. In this chapter we will describe the global growth of the NGO phenomena and provide taxonomy for understanding the main groupings. A few of the larger NGOs will be described in detail to illustrate this taxonomy and we will also describe the key NGO coordinating bodies. Finally, the chapter will review the very real advances NGOs have led in improving the professionalism and quality of humanitarian assistance.

The joys and perils of growth

Global Humanitarian Assistance reports that the annual funding of humanitarian assistance by bilateral (government) donors over the past 35 years rose from $436 million in 1971 to $8.4 billion in 2004 and $9.2 billion in 2006.[1] Latest figures from the Organization for Economic Cooperation and Development's Development Assistance Committee (OECD-DAC) indicate that the total amount of official development assistance (ODA) provided by OECD member countries—that is aid for both long-term development and humanitarian assistance—was $104.4 billion in 2006. This was a slight drop from the "tsunami spike" which raised ODA in 2005 to its highest ever level of $107.1 billion.[2] It should be noted that even this massive figure does not quantify the total level of bilateral aid as many Muslim and other emerging donor states are not members of the OECD.

From a business model point of view this looks like rampant success, particularly post-1990 when there was a marked upwards shift in the amount of available emergency funding. This was related primarily to the ending of the Cold War and humanitarian assistance being used both to fill a foreign policy vacuum and as a response to the spate of separatist and civil wars that marked the passing of the old order. From 1990 to 2004 humanitarian aid, as a percentage share of total ODA, went up from 3.6 to 8 percent. Both in absolute and relative terms the business has grown at a massive rate.

A substantial part of this growth is being channeled through NGOs. Governments have a choice. They can transfer funds directly to the affected sister government, but often these are seen by donors as ineffective or politically suspect. They can transfer funds via UN agencies, which they do, but it must be remembered that most UN agencies work primarily by partnering with the government agencies of the affected countries—although some, notably UNICEF, the Office of UNHCR, and WFP do pass on significant funds to implementing NGOs as sub-contractors. Governments have another choice—to pass funds direct to implementing NGOs; often NGOs of their own nationality. Globally it is estimated that in the mid-2000s around $4 billion a year was flowing through the major NGOs, from government and private sources, for humanitarian assistance. This is likely to be an underestimate, for it does not capture the smaller or local NGOs. In short, NGOs have become the channel of choice, at least for donor governments and the funding public in the West.

In addition to bilateral aid, NGOs also raise their own funds from the general public. Separating out funds raised for development from those raised for humanitarian work is near impossible, but we can look at NGOs' overall incomes. They vary tremendously in their ratios of voluntary to government funding. Agencies like Médecins Sans Frontières (MSF) lay great store on the independence they achieve by being almost entirely independent of government funding while the CARE International network receives almost half of its funding from governments and therefore has far more resources than MSF to spend on crisis responses. Oxfam is somewhere in the middle. Oxfam GB report that £70.3 million of their total 2006–2007 income of £290.7 million was derived from governments.[3] Global estimates for 2005, which include the massive public and government funding in response to the Indian Ocean tsunami of December 2004, suggest that total government humanitarian aid that year exceeded $9.1 billion and private contributions (not including the unknown contributions to local NGOs or the significant amounts generated by Islamic charities) topped $6.3 billion. Ninety percent of those private contributions flowed to NGOs, the rest going predominantly to UNICEF.

Annual expenditure of major humanitarian agencies

While it is relatively easy to identify the annual budgets and expenditure of UN humanitarian agencies, it is more difficult to obtain accurate information about the combined annual budgets of major international non-governmental organizations (INGOs) as they all have many national branches/members/sections and not all consolidate their accounts in a publicly accessible form. Equally, most agencies do not report separate figures for their development spending and humanitarian spending. However, published annual reports make it possible to collate information to provide an indication of the relative financial clout of major INGO networks vis-à-vis the UN, IOM, and the Red Cross/Crescent Movement. It is clear that the largest INGO networks—in order of financial size—are World Vision, CARE, Save the Children, Oxfam, and MSF (Table 6.1).

In short, NGOs are no side show. They form the backbone of the delivery mechanism of the international humanitarian system. It should be noted that much of the funding generated by the major humanitarian UN agencies is actually disbursed by NGOs. This tremendous growth in both the size and centrality of NGOs to the humanitarian system has had consequences. We can pick out five trends of importance.

First, NGOs have had to adapt their structures. Many have effectively moved from being national to transnational organizations. Some, like World Vision, have done this by spinning off many of their former branch country offices in the south to be autonomous national organizations within the federated structure of World Vision International. Others, like the Oxfam or Save the Children families, have sought to bring their various national autonomous organizations (all northern and all essentially donors) together in closer alliances, while maintaining a branch structure in crisis-affected countries. Almost all of the large NGOs today exist in some form of international alliance, federation, network, or other such structure.

Second, as a consequence of this growth, NGOs have become much more central to the humanitarian endeavor. Formally seen as trend-setters, side-shows and external agent-provocateurs, they are now very much at the heart of the humanitarian system. They are collectively represented on the Inter-Agency Standing Committee—through powerful NGO umbrella groups such as InterAction, the International Council for Voluntary Agencies (ICVA), and the Steering Committee for Humanitarian Response (SCHR). (See below for further information.) NGOs have periodic direct access to brief the UN Security

Table 6.1 Annual reported NGO expenditure (US$) 2006

INGO Coalitions	$US
World Vision International[1]	2,103,700,000
CARE International[2]	884,206,000
International Save the Children Alliance[3]	863,094,631
OXFAM (combined expenditure of 13 affiliated agencies)[4]	858,104,000
Médecins Sans Frontières[5]	750,040,000
B. UN Agencies and International Organizations	
World Food Programme[6]	2,664,994,000
UNICEF[7]	2,343,000,000
UNHCR[8]	1,434,804,800
International Committee of the Red Cross[9]	881,375,008
International Organization for Migration (IOM)[10]	733,000,000
International Federation of Red Cross/ Crescent Societies (IFRC)[11]	488,261,000

Notes:
1 www.wvi.org/wvi/wviweb.nsf/D181644162A2E01A8825737C0075A458/$file/2006%20Annual%20Review.pdf
2 CARE has not published a consolidated financial report for 2006. This figure is the combined totals of the three largest "lead' agencies — the United States (www.care.org/newsroom/publications/annualreports/2006/annual2006_financial.pdf); Canada (http://care.ca/downloads/publ/CAREar2006e.pdf) and Australia (www.careaustralia.org.au/files/publication/FINAL%202007%20Annual%20Report.pdf). It, more or less, reflects the total annual global expenditure of the 12 CARE members (personal correspondence from CARE).
3 www.savethechildren.net/media/publications/annualreports/annualrep_2006.pdf
4 Compiled by Oxfam International, and communicated in email from Oxfam GB 2-25-08
5 www.msf.org/source/financial/2007/MSF_Financial_Report_2006.pdf
6 www.wfp.org/policies/annual_reports/documents/wfp_AR06_lowres.pdf
7 www.unicef.org/publications/files/Annual_Report_2006.pdf
8 www.unhcr.org/excom/EXCOM/44fe8cb52.pdf. It should be noted that UNHCR's 2006 expenditure reflected the effect of the tsunami spike. Its budget for 2008 is considerably less: $1,096 billion.
9 www.icrc.org/Web/Eng/siteeng0.nsf/htmlall/738EC6/$FILE/icrc_ar_06_Finances.pdf
10 www.iom.int/jahia/webdav/shared/shared/mainsite/about_iom/docs/financial_report
11 www.ifrc.org/Docs/pubs/who/ar2006-pwc.pdf

Council, and more frequently individual NGOs have access to brief and lobby the governments of their own countries.

A further trend arising from their growth and changing relationships to the state is that NGOs find themselves being co-opted not just into the global humanitarian agenda, but into much narrower agendas to support western and northern foreign policies. As former US Secretary of State Colin Powell famously put it, they can now be "force multipliers" in the Global War on Terror and promotion of foreign policy objectives. Thus the debate over the importance of independence and neutrality in humanitarian work has become more heated and much less clear than it was in the 1970s and 1980s.

A fourth trend is the way NGOs have led the way in trying to develop international standards for humanitarian work, shifting what was always perceived as a voluntary charitable sector towards a much more professionally framed workplace. This is further discussed below. For now it is sufficient to note that the creation of such standards is typical of any "industry" undergoing rapid growth amidst key concern that growth will bring chaos, loss of contracts, and increasing problems over mission and financial accountability.

Finally, increasingly complex corporate structures and the focus on standards and accountability seem to have detracted from what was once the hallmark of NGO work—ability to program to context. There is some evidence that as NGOs chase governments for grants they have become less able to nuance their programming to the particularities of each location (we will discuss this more in the final chapter). Once again, this is a common phenomenon associated with rapid growth— though sustaining that growth seems to be dependent upon getting the balance right between system-wide standards and tailoring relief programs to the specific context of each crisis. NGOs may be investing in the former at the expense of the latter, which does not bode well for their future.

A quick user's guide to some prominent humanitarian NGOs

So far we have spoken as though NGOs were a homogeneous group, albeit varying in size. This is far from the case. Humanitarian NGOs today range across an incredible and sometimes bewildering diversity of aims and objectives, modes of interventions, capacities, and loyalties. Although there are many ways of categorizing them, the literature suggests that the humanitarian world can be largely divided into at least four distinct groups—some would call them tribes.

"Principle-centered"

This group, consisting largely of those in the Dunantist tradition—the International Committee of the Red Cross and perhaps MSF and others in the "sans-frontièreist" movement, such as Pharmaciens sans Frontières[4] or Agronomes et Vétérinaires sans Frontières[5] closely adhere to the principles that defined classic humanitarianism—humanity, neutrality, impartiality, universality, and independence. In many ways this group's approach could be described as being as concerned with the means of humanitarianism (principles) as the outcomes (impact on humanitarian need). The outcomes they favor are generally a more minimalist, life-saving, kind of humanitarianism.

"Pragmatist" (or "Wilsonian")

This group is largely defined by their tendency to focus on outcomes, on impact, and relatively less on the means by which these are achieved. These agencies are not afraid to operate in politically-charged atmospheres, and tend to be aligned with the political agendas of their funders. Many would class some of the larger US agencies, who get a substantial proportion of their funding from USAID, in this category. For this reason, they can also appear to be self-serving and opportunistic.

"Solidarist"

This group grew out of the principled approach, but has gone far beyond its traditional boundaries. Generally they favor an expanded definition of humanitarianism that includes looking at underlying causes, human rights, and social transformation in addition to simply saving lives. New Humanitarianism—as we saw in Chapter 3—was in many ways the apex of the influence and thinking of this philosophy. Some organizations have no problem with humanitarian action that is not only political, but also flagrantly partisan. For example, Norwegian People's Aid concluded that one side in the Sudanese civil war—the Sudan People's Liberation Army (SPLA)—represented the legitimate political aspirations of the people of Southern Sudan, and that southern Sudanese were the aggrieved party in a conflict waged by Khartoum. They thus made it clear that their assistance was only for people in SPLA-controlled areas, and they would not abide by the ground rules of Operation Lifeline Sudan (OLS). OLS was a massive multi-year UN and NGO combined operation, coordinated in Nairobi, to deliver assistance to all in need in the region on principles of humanitarian neutrality and impartiality. This was a fairly extreme stance in the NGO world at the time—many groups that describe themselves as "solidarist" would also claim to be impartial and non-partisan when it comes to providing assistance, even if most in this group question the notion of neutrality.

"Faith-based"

Philosophically, this group cuts across the other three. Although many of these organizations have become operationally similar to those in other categories above, their fundamental principles are defined by a religious creed, not by secular principles or outcomes. World Vision and Islamic Relief[6] would be good examples from this category.

These categories are by no means mutually exclusive. For example, the *san-frontièreist* movement is without doubt a mix of principled and solidarist strains of thought. CARE International, and several of the other large US-based organizations, clearly mix "Wilsonian" pragmatism with solidarist philosophies. Islamic organizations are faith-based and often have a rather different approach to humanitarian action. For the most part the term "faith-based" tends to be associated with politically right-of-center, Christian organizations that have emerged on the scene, mostly in the past couple of decades in the United States and which, in the pragmatist tradition, adhere largely to US foreign policy objectives. But even northern faith-based organizations are difficult to describe in political terms, ranging as they do from the evangelical Samaritan's Purse—which spent just over $250 million in 2006[7]—to the more centrist World Vision (the world's largest humanitarian NGO cluster), to progressive groups such as Church World Service,[8] the American Friends Service Committee,[9] or the Mennonites.[10] The latter groups steer a course deliberately independent of, and often at odds with, US foreign policy—particularly in the Middle East.

Most US-based organizations have classically been, at root, Wilsonian in their outlook—more prone to intervene, and less genuinely "neutral" in their stance (though their political stances defy easy classification, ranging from left to right on the US political spectrum). European organizations have tended to be more solidarist in nature, with the Franco/Swiss arm of European humanitarianism remaining for the most part in the Dunantist tradition. Islamic organizations, such as the UK-based Islamic Relief, have already had a powerful impact on humanitarian action, but have a different set of core values from Western—especially Dunantist—humanitarianism. Needless to say, the operating space for Islamic organizations in mainstream humanitarian action has become somewhat more confined since September 11 as some Western governments tend to view all Islamic organizations through the same anti-terrorist lens.

Local organizations have, of course, sprung up around the world in developing countries as well. Many of these are not explicitly "humanitarian" in their outlook—often emphasizing poverty reduction or improving governance more than responding to crises. Indeed, they challenge the false dichotomy of development and relief among Western or northern agencies, viewing things more through the lens of the affected community. Now we are witnessing—particularly in the context of the GWOT—the increasing occupation of "humanitarian space" by private for-profit contractors and military actors, blurring the line between combatants and humanitarians—deliberately in some cases.

Several other points should be noted. The first and most obvious is that most of the organizations described here are not solely, or even primarily, *humanitarian* in their perspective or programming. Many would describe the fight against global poverty or a commitment to social justice as a more over-riding objective. Nevertheless, these organizations (including all those mentioned below) also have significant humanitarian capacity and programming. Additionally, there are many new or non-conventional actors on the humanitarian scene in the early twenty-first century that are not captured at all by the above rubric—including military actors, private for-profit contractors, and local organizations all over the world whose diversity is too great to capture in a few paragraphs. Again, all these may be involved in work that could be considered humanitarian, but often their primary objectives lie elsewhere. Finally, while these descriptions are useful to understand the complexity and diversity of the world of humanitarian actors, these categories are far from distinct—boundaries, if they exist at all between these categories, are very blurred and may vary over time.

A brief tour of leading NGOs

There are, quite literally, thousands of NGOs operating in the humanitarian sector. The sheer quantity of international NGOs became apparent when at least five hundred of them descended on tsunami-ravaged Aceh in early 2005. However, it is the large multinational NGOs that take the lion's share of the funding and do most of the delivering. We briefly describe here five of these multinationals to provide a sense of the scope and scale of NGO humanitarian work.

The websites for all these NGOs are referenced in the List of acronyms on p. xvi.

World Vision International

World Vision International (WVI) is a Christian relief and development organization. Founded in 1950 to care for children in Asia, World Vision's efforts have now expanded globally and include emergency relief operations, education, health care, economic development and the promotion of justice. The organization places a special emphasis on support for children and approximately half of the organization's programs are funded through child sponsorship.

CARE International

As we noted in Chapter 1, CARE International started by distributing food relief supplies to post-war Europe. Headquartered in Geneva, CARE International is today a confederation of 12 national members, each an autonomous NGO in its own right. CARE employs over 14,500 people.

International Save the Children Alliance

The International Save the Children Alliance is the world's largest independent movement for children. Founded, as we saw in Chapter 1, by British sisters Eglantyne Jebb and Dorothy Buxton, Save the Children's work includes emergency relief, long-term development assistance and advocacy for children's rights. In financial terms, Save UK is the UK's second largest development/relief agency—after Oxfam GB—reporting an income in 2006 of £163.2 million (c. $320 million).[11] The scale of the operations of Save the Children United States is similar—spending $335.5 million in 2006.[12]

OXFAM International

In Chapter 1 we described how a group of people in Oxford, England, came together to protest the intentional starving of civilians in Nazi-occupied Greece. Today the agency they founded has become Oxfam International—a confederation of thirteen independent Oxfam organizations that undertakes development, advocacy, research and humanitarian response activities in over 100 countries. Oxfam GB is, by far, its largest member. Its international secretariat is in Oxford and, like the other large NGO federations, has advocacy/fundraising offices in the centers of humanitarian power—New York, Geneva, and Brussels.

Médecins Sans Frontières (MSF)

MSF is an international independent humanitarian organization composed of 21 national sections. Each year, more than 2,500 MSF volunteer doctors, nurses, other medical professionals, logistics experts, water and sanitation engineers and administrators join 22,000 locally-hired staff to provide medical aid and to build medical infrastructures in more than 70 countries. It also works to raise global awareness of crisis situations. MSF International is headquartered in Geneva. MSF's country sections act as autonomous legal entities. The MSF International Office has no decision-making power over individual sections' operations.

NGO coordination bodies

Humanitarianism faces an interesting problem, not faced by most professions, which start by organizing nationally, then internationally. In humanitarian circles, service is typically provided by an agency based in one (usually rich) country, to many (usually poorer) countries. International alliances have formed first, with national alliances in the donor/supplying countries or in the recipient/client countries forming much later.

The International Council of Voluntary Action[13]

Formed in 1962, this alliance of northern and southern agencies, working in development, humanitarian response and human rights, has a small secretariat in Geneva. ICVA has always been at heart an advocacy grouping and a mechanism for encouraging the flow of resources from richer northern agencies to poorer but better placed southern agencies. At present it has some 70 member organizations world-wide.

Steering Committee for Humanitarian Response[14]

Formed in 1972, SCHR now has eight members—CARE, Caritas, IFRC, ICRC, the Lutheran World Federation, Oxfam, Save the Children, and the World Council of Churches—many of whom also belong to other coordination forums. In its original form it was deliberately set up to enable the chief executives of major agencies to meet biannually to discuss common problems. It has a small secretariat in Geneva. The SCHR is one of the first agency groupings to introduce and practice peer review in its programming, whereby it formally requests one member agency to review and report back on the competence of another.

VOICE[15]

A latecomer to the operational agency coordination field, Voluntary Organizations in Cooperation in Emergencies is an alliance of some 90 European humanitarian NGOs with HQ in Brussels. VOICE was formed specifically to act as a structure to allow European NGOs to speak with one voice to the European Commission, Council, and Parliament.

InterAction[16]

Headquartered in Washington, DC, InterAction is the largest coalition of US-based international NGOs, bringing together 165 agencies as a powerful lobbying alliance. A particular achievement of InterAction has been the development of a comprehensive set of competence standards for InterAction members. These *Private Voluntary Organization Standards*[17] cover the governance of an organization, its organizational integrity, finances, communications, and human resource systems. Since 1993, each InterAction member's CEO has been required to self-certify that their organization remains PVO-compliant. As the global war on terror has imposed new requirements on US not-for-profits and the Bush Administration sought to relegate US humanitarian agencies to the role of sub-contractors—InterAction has played a critical role arguing the need to maintain humanitarian space and prevent further encroachment of military and commercial assets. Many InterAction members fear that the attitudes displayed by the US Treasury as it hunts down "dual purpose" charities—NGOs allegedly engaged in charitable work but covertly supporting terrorism—indicate a basic misunderstanding of how nonprofits function, and ultimately do not help—and may even hinder—the global war on terror. The Treasury's *Anti-Terrorist Financing Guidelines: Voluntary Best Practices for U.S.-Based Charities* are in fact not voluntary, but set compliance standards which are impacting relations of trust with partner NGOs in the south. Many argue that US NGOs are being forced into assuming the untenable role of criminal investigators and enforcers of US law.

Disaster Emergency Committee[18]

In the UK, the Disaster Emergency Committee was originally formed as an alliance of a handful of the largest NGOs, in order to take advantage of an offer from the national TV broadcasters. Free air-time was offered to make general appeals in response to international emergencies, but only if they did it as one body, not as competing agencies. That was in 1963. Today it still performs this function, but in addition, with its present 13 member agencies, conducts joint evaluations of agencies' work, peer reviews, and promotes humanitarian standards.

The Inter-Agency Standing Committee (IASC)[19]

With the tumultuous global political changes at the beginning of the 1990s, the increased humanitarian role for UN agencies, and the realization that NGOs had become substantial, and no longer bit, players, the need for a more coherent global approach to humanitarian action was glaringly obvious. How to achieve it was less clear. In the end, coherent humanitarianism became a sub-set of UN reform. In 1991 the UN General Assembly passed a resolution endorsing the notion of better UN agency coordination at the country level, consolidation of UN funding appeals and establishment of the IASC. Its committee—known as the IASC Principals—is comprised of representatives from seven UN humanitarian agencies (UNICEF, WFP, UNDP, WHO, FAO, UNHCR, and the UN Population Fund UNFPA); the ICRC, IFRC, the World Bank, and IOM and the Secretary-General's Representative on the Human Rights of Internally Displaced Persons—an increasingly influential position as the humanitarian community focuses on the unmet protection and assistance needs of IDPs. The NGO community is represented by members nominated by InterAction, ICVA, and SCHR. The Principals are chaired by the Under-Secretary General and Emergency Relief Coordinator.

In recent years, the IASC has been central to another round of UN humanitarian reform—launched in 2005 to further improve the financing methods of the UN and to initiate a cooperative system for building and implementing common standards and approaches in 11 areas of humanitarian provision. This cluster approach designates, through common consent, agencies in the field to lead on each sector in each major emergency—at a global, national, and field level—and potentially represents a major move forward to a more coherent and quality-conscious approach to humanitarian response.[20]

Collective standards and the notion of professionalism

This rise in the size and complexity of NGOs, at the same time as government donors became more interested in using humanitarianism as a tool in foreign policy, also coincided with one of the system's greatest failures and biggest challenges: the genocide in Rwanda and the subsequent refugee exodus to the Democratic Republic of the Congo, Tanzania, and elsewhere. Even as early as 1991 individuals within agencies were concerned that if they did not do something collectively to start raising the bar in terms of the independence, competence and behavior of agencies and their staff, donors and host governments would enforce standards on them. Four of the initiatives conceived in this period of rapid change are still relevant today. We shall deal with them in the order in which they were conceived: the Code of Conduct, the Sphere Standards, ALNAP and HAP-International.

The Code of Conduct

The Code of Conduct, like so many initiatives in the humanitarian endeavor, was a product of its time and the experiences of the individuals who drafted it.

These individuals cut their teeth in the famine and refugee crises of the 1980s. They had seen the worst of good intentioned but incompetent individuals, the use of agencies as fronts for intelligence gathering, the proselytizing for Christianity and Islam offering food in return for conversion and yet, amidst all this, they had seen professional, honest and trustworthy behavior.

In 1991, at the Council of Delegates of the IFRC and ICRC, the French Red Cross sponsored a decision calling upon the Federation to "set up a group of experts to study the possibility of elaborating a Code of Conduct relative to Humanitarian aid in situations of natural and technological disasters."[21] The idea of a code of conduct was taken up and developed by the SCHR. At that time ICRC was not part of the SCHR, but by the end of the process were called in and helped draft the language around the use of the Code in conflict situations.

The Ten Principles of the *Code of Conduct for the International Red Cross and Red Crescent Movement and NGOs in Disaster Relief* assert principles for professional behavior among foreign aid workers in disaster situations and by extension lays down expectations on the part of the UN, host governments and donor governments. In essence, it is a code of individual professional behavior.[22]

1 The Humanitarian imperative comes first.
2 Aid is given regardless of the race, creed or nationality of the recipients and without adverse distinction of any kind. Aid priorities are calculated on the basis of need alone.
3 Aid will not be used to further a particular political or religious standpoint.
4 We shall endeavour not to act as instruments of government foreign policy.
5 We shall respect culture and custom.
6 We shall attempt to build disaster response on local capacities.
7 Ways shall be found to involve programme beneficiaries in the management of relief aid.
8 Relief aid must strive to reduce future vulnerabilities to disaster as well as meeting basic needs.
9 We hold ourselves accountable to both those we seek to assist and those from whom we accept resources.
10 In our information, publicity and advertising activities, we shall recognise disaster victims as dignified human beings, not hopeless objects.

In 1995, the Code was taken by the Red Cross to the 26th International Red Cross Conference. The resolution passed by states and the Red Cross Movement was carefully worded. They "[took] note of and [welcomed] the Code of Conduct and further [invited] all States and National Societies to encourage NGOs to both abide by the principles and spirit of the Code and consider registering their support for the Code with the International Federation."[23]

The Code thus had international recognition but remained voluntary. In the intervening years, the Code has been used in two ways. It has been used as a personal code—a set of principles to guide the behavior of aid workers. At the institutional level it has had a mixed effect. In some sense its biggest success has been to pave the way for the humanitarian charter and standards set by the Sphere project. The Code has been used by some donors as a standard they expect grant recipients to hold to.[24]

The real missed opportunity of the Code lies in its Annexes. The three Annexes speak to donor governments, host governments and UN agencies. Given the range of support the Code received on its launch these could have been a tremendous platform for advocacy. Annex 1 places prime responsibility for humanitarian action with host governments, which is where it should be. Annex two speaks to donor governments, calling on them to "provide funding with a guarantee of operational independence." Annex three promoted local and international NGOs as partners, not contracted implementers with UN agencies. This opportunity to use the Code to promote change across the humanitarian system was never taken up. Today the Code still represents the best and most widely known summation of the essence of good behavior by professional humanitarians, but remains voluntary.

The Sphere Standards[25]

Like the Code, the Sphere Standards were the brainchild of a small group of humanitarian workers within the agencies that made up the SCHR. In early 1996, they convinced the agency grouping to propose and promote the development of a set of universal standards for humanitarian relief. A year later they had sufficient funding to start work and by 1999 the first draft set of standards was published. Revised in 2004, the Sphere Standards are available in more than ten languages. The Sphere project continues to train people in the use of the standards and their promotion and is now run by a board representing 16 of the largest humanitarian NGOs. The standards are accepted and used by donors, UN agencies, host governments, NGOs and on occasions, military forces wishing to have NGOs work more closely with them.[26]

Driven by many of the same instincts as the Code of Conduct, the *Sphere Standards* attempt to lay down minimum standards for what the victims of disaster and crisis need to acquire in order to survive. To be clear, they are not standards for what agencies need to deliver. People may acquire food by trade, from family members or government, but the role of the outside agency is to make up the difference between that which people can reasonably acquire through their own resourcefulness and the basic needs of survival. It is thus fundamentally about people's rights and in particular the right to life with dignity as enshrined in the Universal Declaration of Human Rights. The Sphere Standards are prefaced by a humanitarian charter which articulates these rights in more detail and provides the link between aspirational rights and the very practical text that follows.

In its present format, Sphere lays down standards in five areas: water and sanitation; food security and nutrition; shelter and settlements; health services, as well as management and accountability. In each section the statement of standard is supported by a series of indicators which suggest how the provision of those standards may be measured and these in turn are supported by guidance notes drawn from present best practice. The standards are phrased such that they are not specific to any one culture or environment.

As well as being available on the Sphere website, the standards are published by Oxfam and have become their most successful publication. In many ways Sphere is a great success story: an example of disparate agencies coming together for the common good. It has promoted notions of professionalism and universal action by encouraging translation and promoting an impressive world-wide training initiative. Where the standards are used intelligently, they have made a significant difference to the quality of programming.

Criticisms of Sphere really fall into two categories: substantive and detailed.[27] The substantive critique is one we alluded to at the beginning of the chapter; the balance between standards and context. Some argue that the emphasis on standards has led to agencies treating programming as a technical issue rather than a highly nuanced social process. It has led, so the critiques say, to the use of ready-made, predefined solutions; and indeed there is some evidence that agencies do behave like this, but it is hard to pin the blame at the door of Sphere or any other one initiative. It is also pointed out that the standards are only relevant if the agency has access to the victims of crisis, yet denial of access is the single biggest constraint to effective humanitarian action.

On the detailed side, there is discomfort among some legal experts over the picking and choosing of rights to include in the humanitarian charter and its use of hard and soft law in the same breath. Others feel that Sphere does not say enough about protection from violence which is as integral a part of humanitarian aid as material assistance. Many also worry that practitioners all too often pass over the statement of standard and move directly to the more specific and numerical indicators, seeking only to program to these measurables.

Yet despite all these critiques, the Sphere Standards remain the single most used and read field manual for humanitarian aid workers.

ALNAP[28]

The shock that ran through the humanitarian system in the wake of the 1994 Rwanda genocide, subsequent failures to perceive and stop the massacres and then to deliver effective and impartial assistance, acted as the spur for many reform initiatives. As the relief operations to those who had fled abroad went into their second year, a group of Western government donor agencies, led by the Danes, proposed carrying out the most comprehensive and searching evaluation ever of a relief operation. It sought to look at the causes of the genocide and the mass movement out of Rwanda, the perceived failure of development programs in Rwanda and the subsequent relief operations. The *Joint Evaluation of Emergency Assistance to Rwanda* (JEEAR) assessed operations across the region, in all the countries affected and it looked at all operations, not just in one delivery sector or one class of agencies. It is still regarded as one of the best and most thorough humanitarian evaluations ever carried out.[29]

For many of those involved in JEEAR, either funding, managing or implementing, it was clear that with sufficient will to cooperate and to drive rigor upwards, evaluation could become a significant tool in improving the competence of aid delivery and the coherence of the system that delivered it.

It was this grouping of donor agencies, UN and NGOs, academics and evaluation consultants that went on in 1997 to build the Active Learning Network for Accountability and Performance in Humanitarian Action (ALNAP). Hosted by the UK's Overseas Development Institute, ALNAP seeks to promote higher standards of evaluation within its membership and beyond. It has developed a comprehensive searchable database of past evaluations and specific standards for evaluation in the humanitarian field, working from the OECD-DAC standards for evaluating development programs. Each year it publishes a reflection on the past year's global humanitarian work. It is one of the few forums where donors, operational agencies, and academics meet as equals and are able to have frank discussions on the state of the humanitarian system.

HAP-International[30]

Humanitarian Accountability Partnership-International has gone further, forming a self-policing group of agencies willing to be held accountable to agreed standards for involving beneficiaries in the humanitarian process. It defines its mission as making "humanitarian action accountable to its intended beneficiaries through self-regulation, compliance verification and quality assurance certification." HAP-International evolved out of an initiative driven by the British Red Cross in the mid-1990s to develop an ombudsman-like system for the humanitarian community—an external impartial body to whom the consumer of the humanitarian product (beneficiaries, community associations and governments, and the donor public) could address complaints and concerns over competence and quality. It was hard to take forward the idea of an ombudsman as the humanitarian system is too disparate to provide an accepted base of agreed authority. Instead, a grouping of agencies has evolved, willing to collectively develop and be publicly held accountable to a set of standards around the involvement of beneficiaries in the aid process. HAP focuses on a set of seven principles for accountability:[31]

1 Commitment to humanitarian standards and rights.
2 Setting standards and building capacity.
3 Communication with stakeholders, particularly beneficiaries and staff, about the standards adopted, programmes to be undertaken and mechanisms for addressing concerns.
4 Ensuring beneficiaries are involved in planning, implementation, monitoring and evaluation of programmes.
5 Involving beneficiaries and staff whenever standards are monitored and revised.
6 Ensuring beneficiaries and staff are able to report complaints and seek redress safely.
7 Ensuring that members require all implementation partners to abide by the HAP principles.

By early 2008, HAP-International had 21 NGOs as full members, all committed to implementing their own accountability plans, allowing for external evaluation and peer review processes.

People in Aid[32]

Agencies have also become increasingly concerned over internal accountability and how professionally they service their employees. Yet another Rwanda-inspired initiative, People in Aid seeks to set and promote best practice in human resource management, ensuring that aid workers are treated as professionals and managed in a fair and appropriate fashion. Supported by 109 members agencies across 20 countries, People in Aid has developed a widely used code of good practice for human resource managers in humanitarian agencies.

Separate from this collective initiative, many agencies have also started implementing internal accountability systems, which allow agency staff to report on perceived breaches of standards, accountability, or financial propriety. These so-called whistle-blower programs have been imitative in most major operational agencies over the past few years though they have not really been in place long enough to say anything meaningful about their effectiveness. It is, however, a major step forward that agencies recognize the need for such a mechanism.

Standards: what's next?

The plethora of initiatives to create standards and other mechanisms for improving competence in the 1990s has led to most major operational agencies now investing significantly more time in training field staff, comprehensively using evaluations and managing humanitarian workers with greater professionalism.

The presence of so many initiatives all aiming to improve the competence and professionalism of the humanitarian systems was partly driven by Rwanda, but also arose from the tremendous growth in size and power of NGOs in the 1990s. Looking ahead, we foresee two probable ways forward.

First, the free market model. The standards and tools developed collectively are already being adopted and adapted by donors and operational agencies. This process may continue and collective bodies such as the Sphere Project or ALNAP may shrink in importance, eventually going the way of the League of Nations.

A second future focuses around the collective good. Agencies and often the individuals who support, fund, manage, and promote most of the competence reform groups are often one and the same. There is no fundamental reason why many of these initiatives cannot be joined together to form the beginnings of a full international professional association for humanitarian work which, like all professional associations, would set standards, seek to develop its research and educational capacity, and develop ways to address professional negligence and malpractice. Achieving this vision would require many of the quality initiatives to willingly give up some of their autonomy. No easy task, as it would require agencies and individuals to be willing to accept a discipline from outside their own governance.

At the time of writing, it is a moot point which path is more likely, but it is clear that business as usual is not the future—too much is changing too fast for that.

7 A brave new world, a better future?

The humanitarian community faces many challenges in the twenty-first century. This book has really only skimmed the surface of the history, traditions, standards, and structures of the international humanitarian system. Its complexity of origins, multitude of players and ever-varying environment make humanitarianism a challenging system to describe and understand, and an even more challenging system to predict. This conclusion does not attempt to predict where the system will go, but rather highlights some of the critical issues and major challenges that humanitarianism has to face:

- the future of the classic humanitarian principles;
- the dilemma of determining whether to address causes of humanitarian emergencies or only their symptoms;
- challenges highlighted by the rapid growth and professionalization of humanitarian action;
- the difficulties in institutional learning and accountability in humanitarian agencies;
- dealing with the new drivers of future humanitarian crises.

These are by no means all the challenges, nor do any of the questions raised have clear or specific answers. But these are challenges that humanitarians face, affecting real decisions which must be taken, and which must be addressed on a case-by-case basis, in actual humanitarian emergencies.

The future of humanitarian principles in today's politicized environment

At the dawn of the twenty-first century, many in the humanitarian world were having second thoughts about the classic principles on which humanitarian action was based. While few doubted the humanitarian imperative itself, the notion of the universality of humanitarian action was being queried. It was increasingly realized that the vast majority of disaster-affected people come from developing nations, while the majority of humanitarian workers—or at least those in decision-making positions—were still primarily Americans and Europeans. The principle of independence was being questioned as humanitarianism became big business, its ever-increasing budgets largely funded by national government donor agencies, and increasing proportions of its efforts being undertaken by government contractors. Impartiality—or the provision of assistance based only on criteria of need—was not being questioned as a principle, but was clearly not being adhered to in practice. In part, this was because donors have a great deal more political interest in some crises than in others; and in part because of the plethora of new actors in the humanitarian business—including for-profit companies and military actors with a strategic (not humanitarian) intent. But no principle was more under fire than neutrality. In effect, the old schisms, noted in Chapter 1—between the agendas of containment, compassion, and change formed in that first period of globalization—have come back to haunt us in this present second period.[1]

Long viewed as the key to humanitarian work, neutrality had almost become a dirty word in the aftermath of the Balkans wars and the Rwanda genocide. How could humanitarian actors pretend to be neutral in the face of such evil? Predicated on the assumptions of the inter-state wars of the nineteenth and twentieth centuries, neutrality was viewed as critical for gaining access to conflict-affected populations, and for ensuring that humanitarian action was kept apolitical—and therefore helping to ensure the security of humanitarian workers since they would not be considered a threat by belligerents. (Not "taking sides in hostilities or engaging at any time in controversies of a political ... nature" is how the ICRC continues to define neutrality.) But quite apart from the questions about the utility of neutrality as a principle in non-conflict emergencies, most humanitarian analysts highlight the substantially changed nature of contemporary conflicts.

Contemporary conflict has been described as "network" or "shadow" war. No longer just between states, these wars are primarily internal to states, and non-state actors are increasingly involved. Conflicts are also more "asymmetric" in nature—with one side more militarily powerful, other parties less powerful but more nimble. This is especially the case in counter-insurgency warfare. Asymmetric conflicts are characterized by non-traditional combatants, with combatants frequently hiding in civilian populations, making the combatant/civilian distinction increasingly blurred.[2] Additionally, contemporary wars are not financed by state taxation but through war economies, aid, plunder of civilians and/or depradation of natural resources. This tends to make the logic of conflict self-perpetuating as "war economies" link illegal plunder in a war zone directly or indirectly to legal business and trade in other parts of the global economy at lower cost and higher profit than legal trade.[3]

Whereas in earlier wars the majority of casualties were soldiers, contemporary wars tend to deliberately target civilians, institutions, and livelihoods. The death toll of contemporary conflicts is now estimated to be about 90 percent civilian, and 10 percent combatants.[4]

Another feature of contemporary conflict is that it often manipulates and politicizes people's identity, causing groups to turn on each other, even when they may have lived together peacefully. Gender violence—or in the jargon deployed by humanitarians, SGBV (sexual and gender based violence)—and the use of rape as a weapon of war have become more rampant in recent conflicts. Mass rape has been documented as a systematic weapon of war in at least 34 conflicts. Rape has been used to deliberately destroy a sense of ethnic identity, for mass demoralization of "enemy" populations, and as a tool of revenge.[5]

As we outlined in Chapter 3, a New Humanitarianism was proposed in the late 1990s by the UK Department for International Development (DFID).[6] New Humanitarianism was to be a different kind of response to human need: one that did the following:

- recognized that all aid is "political" in some sense;
- took human rights violations as seriously as meeting basic human needs;
- was aware that humanitarian interventions could cause harm;
- was more accountable;
- dealt both with causes and symptoms;
- finally, and perhaps most controversially, was "coherent" or aligned with other objectives (of donors) so that all resources could be brought to bear on the problem at hand.[7]

Critical to the approach of new humanitarianism was the acceptance of advocacy and the right to protection as humanitarian tools and responsibilities. New humanitarianism clearly represented a stepping back from neutrality—as least as classically defined—and put the independence of humanitarian action into question where the "coherence" agenda was concerned.

In the aftermath of 11 September 2001, some of the tenets of new humanitarianism have been equally queried. Being seen by both belligerents and affected communities as part and parcel of a Western agenda to change the face of politics in the Middle East has been an uncomfortable—and in some cases untenable—situation for humanitarian actors in Afghanistan and Iraq. And some observers have noted that humanitarian action has been instrumentally captured as an integral part of an overall political and strategic agenda that, in itself, has little to do with humanitarian ends.[8] Others suggest that "humanitarian independence" should be context-specific—that humanitarian actors can align themselves with great powers if the former agree with the latter.[9]

Humanitarian advocacy has become a staple of many agencies' work, and agencies are increasingly deft at bridging the presumed gap between engaging in advocacy at the policy level and retaining access to affected populations. However, recent work notes that humanitarian agencies have been most effective at advocacy under circumstances where their primary role is to put a crisis on the political agenda, rather than to influence specific policies of already recognized crises.[10] Agencies, and even some donors, recognize that independence and neutrality remain critical humanitarian principles, but define neutrality in a different way. DFID, for example, defined neutrality in its humanitarian strategy simply as "not favouring any side in a conflict" but without reference to avoiding controversy. Other agencies extend this definition to holding both—or all—sides in a conflict accountable to the same standards; in other words not avoiding questions of human rights violations (which an old-fashioned view of neutrality would have suggested) but addressing violations equally, whatever party to a conflict was causing them.

As we saw in Chapter 3, some amount of space for humanitarian actors on the question of human rights violations was opened up in 2001 by *The Responsibility to Protect*, a report from the International Commission on Intervention and State Sovereignty (ICISS).[11] The authors openly challenged the prioritizing by the international community of states' right of sovereignty over the obligation to intervene when gross violations were being committed by a state or its proxies. But at the same time, the re-polarizing of global politics in the aftermath of September 11—and the "either you are with us or you are against us" political climate of the global war on terrorism—has had the effect of closing down much of the space needed for the independent action of humanitarian agencies to really implement their part of the "responsibility to protect" agenda.

Hence the future of humanitarian principles remains an open question. The independent but UN-commissioned *Humanitarian Response Review* in 2005 focused mainly on technical issues—preparedness, coordination and accountability—not on the question of principles *per se*. But it did note with some concern that existing trends constituted a compromise of independence, and recommended that UN special envoys in humanitarian emergencies "be empowered to ensure that humanitarian space is preserved and that the humanitarian principles of independence, impartiality and neutrality should all be consistently upheld."[12] The ways in which this is to be done are largely context-specific. Recent humanitarian experience, even in highly politicized contexts such as Iraq, has reaffirmed the need for these principles from the point of view of people caught in conflict crises.[13] Some observers believe that the debate over principles has essentially been overtaken by events on the ground, and that humanitarian principles will never prevail against political and strategic interests.

The dilemma of addressing effects or causes

In part, because humanitarian action often took place in something of a foreign policy vacuum in the 1990s, humanitarian actors were frequently called upon to address both the acute symptoms of humanitarian suffering and the factors causing the emergency. The mandates of humanitarian agencies gradually broadened to incorporate addressing causes as well. This was made explicit in the way that New Humanitarianism was articulated.

In the case of some humanitarian crises—famines in Africa being the classic example—it is clear, both in theory and in practice, that the "event" of a humanitarian crisis is only the tip of the iceberg. Underlying processes of chronic poverty, deteriorating natural resources, global climate change, and political marginalization are the real problems to be resolved. While the tools of humanitarian response (such as emergency food distribution or therapeutic feeding) are different from the tools of addressing underlying causes (such as livelihood diversification, resource conservation practices and political participation), there is little disagreement that the tools and approaches are complementary, and should be linked. For there is nothing contradictory about addressing both at the same time. Making that link in practice, however, remains a major challenge: evidence is strong that acute crises attract much greater attention than chronic poverty or livelihood insecurity from donors, the media, and humanitarian agencies alike.

However, in conflict-related emergencies, as the previous discussion on neutrality highlighted, there may be a choice to be made: an agency may be able to address the underlying causes of conflict or to address the humanitarian consequences of it, but it is more challenging to do both at the same time. Advocacy about the causes of a conflict has cost more than one humanitarian agency its access to affected populations as many Western NGOs are finding in Darfur today. There is some evidence that even-handed advocacy might not cost access, but it is a trade-off that humanitarian actors have to consider when working in conflict.

Whether viewed as a positive or negative development, there has been much greater emphasis in humanitarian action on dealing with the underlying causes of crisis, in addition to (or in some cases, *rather than*) dealing with effects of crises on human populations. Much of this has come together under the rubric of disaster risk reduction, encapsulated in the *Hyogo Framework for Action*.[14] Brought together by the UN, and fundamentally reliant on the action of states, the framework addresses the prevention or mitigation of virtually all causes of humanitarian emergencies *except* conflict. While the number of people affected by "natural" disasters (whether actually *caused* or just *triggered* by natural phenomena) is substantially greater than those affected by conflict in most years, the major challenges facing humanitarian action described in this book apply more to conflict situations.

Under the conditions described in the Hyogo Framework it actually is possible to invest in preventing disaster, rather than just responding to it. However, there is little evidence about the effectiveness of that investment, because little of it is actually done despite the increased highlighting of disaster risk reduction as a strategy. And preventing or reducing the risk of disaster is only one part of dealing with its long-term consequences. Seeing to it that affected populations recover in the aftermath of a major crisis is another piece of the puzzle. Understanding how to work in these transitional environments where it is not clear what is being transitioned to—or whose responsibility the transitional assistance is—constitute the other parts of the question. Some agencies emphasize "building back better" in the aftermath of disaster, implying that part of the humanitarian imperative is not only to assist in the time of acute need, but also to build the basis of stable livelihood improvement afterwards. In reality, once an acute crisis has passed—and their attention turns elsewhere—donors rarely give the country or region the help required to ensure recovery. In many post-conflict situations populations are left in a kind of limbo—not on the path to sustainable recovery, though not in acute crisis any more either. This long-term trajectory of whole populations has been described as the "normalization of crisis," particularly among chronically marginalized populations in Africa.[15] Such situations call for investment not only in disaster risk reduction, but also in longer-term support to meet basic human needs and improve livelihoods, a set of activities often described under the rubric of social protection. Social protection, like disaster risk reduction, is seen as the domain of national governments—often with donor support—but not a domain of humanitarian actors in the absence of national government for the most part. Hence in some of the most marginalized areas where states are weakest or non-existent, and where populations the most vulnerable, little is done to prevent disasters or protect human populations unless there is an acute crisis.

This state of affairs almost guarantees repeated crises, and leads to the call for humanitarian actors to take on a greater role in addressing the underlying causes of humanitarian emergencies—whether that be diversifying livelihoods in drought-prone and natural-resource-degraded communities, or peace-building and human rights-education programs in conflict-prone areas. Some observers decry this as "mission creep" or "shifting the goalposts." Nevertheless, this is the reality for humanitarian action in many places today.[16] One worry is that placing too much emphasis on prevention or addressing underlying causes in an acute crisis may come at the expense of doing what humanitarians do best—ameliorating the effects of crisis and protecting human life. A second worry is that relegating the task of prevention and recovery to humanitarian actors is simply continuing to throw a little bit of emergency funding at problem areas where policy-makers are unwilling to address the real problems. A further concern is about the mandate and legitimacy of humanitarian actors in such interventions.

The challenge of growth and deregulation

As we have seen, the humanitarian business has grown rapidly in the past two decades, with its global turnover rising from under half a billion dollars to over 12 billion.[17] It has also moved center stage. In the 1970s and much of the 1980s, it was a side-show to the real global politics of the Cold War and the wars of liberation. In the 1990s and 2000s, crises which would previously have been labeled civil war or rebellion were re-bannered as humanitarian crisis or complex emergency. The expectation that humanitarian agencies would be there and would do something noble and effective grew in the minds of states and the general public. The option for the UN, the Red Cross/ Crescent, and the NGOs not to intervene became politically unacceptable, at least for those crises that caught the public eye and hit the international political agenda. UN agencies which had previously acted almost exclusively as support structures to beleaguered national government ministries became operational. NGOs moved from being national to transnational in structure and alliances shifted from small cozy clubs to large multinational umbrellas. The notion that commitment to fight the good fight was at the heart of the endeavor was replaced by a concern for standards, accountability, and professionalism. In short, humanitarianism moved from being a quirky side-show to a center stage establishment, and with that move has come all sorts of unexpected challenges.

In the 1990s, those working to bring competence, accountability and standards to the humanitarian enterprise saw their efforts as slightly revolutionary, or at least reformist. With the benefit of a little hindsight, there is now an air of inevitability about such reforms. As we have seen, all systems and organizations—military, commercial, religious—face the same challenges when they grow rapidly. It is essentially the challenge of control. The CEO of a booming company worries about sustaining that boom but s/he worries more about losing control and direction, so put in place systems of accountability, global standards, codes of conduct, and standard operating procedures. They build new alliances with likeminded institutions and promote international associations to protect their vested interests. The humanitarian business was no different. In essence, the reforms of the 1990s were as much a direct consequence of growth as they were of a realization that commitment and concern were not enough.

This growth and institutionalization have brought three basic challenges: the challenge of financial independence, the challenge of relationship, including coordination, and the challenge of context.

Financial independence

The financial growth in international humanitarianism has largely come from the coffers of the nations of the developed North who, since the end of the Cold War, increasingly speak with one voice—the voice of economic liberalism. Foreign policy, which includes humanitarian action, is ultimately about securing trade, natural resources, markets, and the desired flow of labor. In places this is overlain by the veneer of the less than global War on Terror which, particularly in the marginalized communities where many humanitarian crises erupt, errs towards a polarizing "them and us" mentality, where aid workers individually display angst over whether they are part of "us" or "them."

It is a simple reality that many humanitarian agencies—certainly all the UN agencies (UNICEF included), the Red Cross and Crescent, and many of the major INGOs—are substantially dependent upon this northern club of nations for their bread and butter. Naturally this limits the parameters within which they can act. The anguish over so-called forgotten disasters (forgotten by the donors that is, not by those caught up in them) is largely a product of this lack of financial independence. A few NGOs are less dependent on northern governments, Médecins Sans Frontières (MSF) being the prime example, but even they are not totally financially independent. Their supporting publics have a certain expectation as to how they will behave and what they will do. Disillusion or disappoint your public, as every politician knows, and they will quickly find other causes to support.

The challenge of independence goes further than finance. Where alliances are forged, informal or formal, between states and humanitarian agencies to make common cause, those friendships, the taste for power, and the desire to use new-found leverage to change things for the good, can move agencies to work for the so-called greater common good rather than the specific needs of the vulnerable here and now. This surreptitious erosion of independence is well seen among US-based agencies. The US national political desire to promote democracy, freedom of speech and religion, and free enterprise around the world, can quickly draw in US-based agencies where individual employees are as patriotic and politically engaged as any other citizen. On the other side of the Atlantic a similar phenomenon can be seen. In the UK, a number of humanitarian agencies have been extremely successful in lobbying for changes in UK government policy and practice overseas. Individuals who started out as NGOs' lobbyists have found themselves recruited into the policy teams of government ministries: a resounding advocacy success in one way but is this a dangerous morphing? In effect, the "radical lobbyist" has become establishment and thus more prone to accepting received establishment thinking and less prone to take risks and challenge the status quo less. Move across to indigenous NGOs based in Malaysia or the Gulf and the issues are the same or even more so in societies where political conformity is the norm and strictly enforced.

Humanitarian workers are in effect required to operate a dual persona. Outside of the work environment they have political views and make judgments on the rightness or wrongness of the actions of states, war lords, corporations, and zealots. They may even practice politics, getting involved in campaigning for a presidential candidate or standing in a local council election, but all that needs to be left behind when they enter the work environment. To remain impartial, neutral, and independent, they are required not to express—either through actions, words or intent—any view on the rightness of wrongness of any political, religious or other cause. At a personal level, the need to retain this distance is intensely difficult. This is why those agencies which are able to retain a high degree of independence deliberately construct mechanisms to do so. They have principles and doctrine which all new staff must learn by heart. They require that there are always at least two agency staff present at every outside negotiation. They rotate staff around the world and between headquarters and the field.

Striving for independence is thus both central to any true attempt to be accountable to the mission and those they seek to serve, and at once an ever-changing and complex imperfect action. Of course we are never truly independent, but it is only by constantly striving for independence and being fully aware of the personal and organizational compromises we make that agencies have any chance of being humanitarian first and political second.

There is a second path, of course, no less intellectually honest—the path of commitment to a cause. That could be American security, Islam, Christianity, Buddhism or socialism. There is absolutely nothing wrong with organizing to promote any of these things, but we should not kid ourselves that we can serve two masters equally well. If you work for the cause, the cause, not the people you serve, comes first.

The challenge of relationship

As we have seen traditionally, humanitarian agencies have been of the North. They were financed, staffed and organized from the North and as they grew, they set up branches in other people's countries both to operate, and, in a number of European states, as a way of accessing European Union funding. There are notable exceptions, principally with the Red Cross and Red Crescent Societies and with some of the church agencies. But things are changing. Many agencies, concerned to demonstrate a commitment to accountability and democracy, have reorganized to convert former overseas branches into local autonomous organizations. World Vision International originating in the United States and ActionAid, originating in the UK, have both followed this route. In parallel, as the middle class starts to emerge in developing countries, local groups of concerned citizens have petitioned to set up new member-organizations to join the large federated NGOs of the North. What was a northern phenomenon is becoming global and with that come challenges. In many disaster-affected countries the coordinating meetings and bodies still reflect the old order, one for international organizations—conducted using jargon-filled English—and one for local organizations.

Within the growth of transnational NGOs there are very real dilemmas around whether they remain northern-based institutions or morph into true international federations, ceding authority and power across the federation. It is a dilemma because it means giving up power and control. It is also a dilemma because although the population of the agency federation may have become internationalized, its financial powerbase is still northern and often dominated by funds from one country.

The challenge of relationship also goes outside the agencies. Increasingly as access to crisis for international agencies becomes more difficult, they are turning to work through local institutions, community-based organizations, and the like. What should be the relationship between the external transnational humanitarian agencies and the small local grouping? Is it a partnership, is it a contractual one, is it one of control and subservience, is it one of local knowledge leading? The basic challenge here is two-fold. First, how does a previously northern-led system, which has become global, transform into a truly globally-owned system where its power structures are aligned with its principles of impartiality and independence, and with the ethos of equality, trust and mutual respect implicit in its mission? Second, how does the humanitarian business overcome the "them and us" analysis where we are the relatively well-off and well-meaning outsiders and they are the marginalized and at-risk victims? Can the humanitarian system move beyond not just its northern roots but its traditional middle-class and establishment roots to form true alliances with community-based organizations or with alliances of disaster victims? The fear is that if the system does not truly globalize, it will be increasingly difficult for it to be or be seen to be impartial, independent, and neutral.

This growth in agencies has brought with it the seemingly insoluble problem of coordination. Everyone wants coordination; no one wants to be coordinated. That is the real heart of the issue. In the minds of many agencies there is a mismatch between the protection of their independence and modifying their agendas or plans in order to coordinate better with the actions of others, a position not without a certain irony given the increasingly accepted restrictions on independence mentioned earlier. Some headway has been made. Many of the mechanisms covered in this book, aiming for greater harmony of standards or more effective information sharing are, in effect, coordination mechanisms. Likewise many of the common funding mechanisms being developed by the UN tend to act as coordinating mechanisms. At heart, however, there is still a fundamental reluctance on the part of many external agencies to accept any sort of constraining influence, from national government, UN umbrella, or local authority in the name of promoting the common good over individual freedom.

Problems of agency and system learning and accountability: standards or context?

In the struggle to contain growth, the humanitarian system constructed a whole raft of standards and accountability mechanisms, starting in the financial field but expanding—as we have seen—to individual behavior in the Red Cross/NGO Code of Conduct, to delivery standards in Sphere, and to evaluation standards in ALNAP. When these were formulated, some more radical agencies warned that this standardization was a bad move as it would lead to technical solutions not tailored to the specific disaster, and thus standards were a bad thing. In some ways they have been proved right. There is growing, as yet anecdotal, evidence that, particularly among the large, fast-growing agencies, their ability to tailor programming to the local context and to adjust programming as they learn from implementation has diminished. Agency staff report a sense of being driven to over-report success and under-report failure, as measured by the agreed deliverables in their grant contracts. Agencies report difficulty in recruiting enough skilled and experienced field staff who have the intellectual and organizational authority to adjust programming to suit the context, despite what may have previously been agreed with the funder.

This is actually an endemic problem with large rapidly growing organizations, one seen both in the computer and auto industries in the 1980s. The doubters of standards were right in that standards on their own are not enough, even if your work force is well trained and follows them. What the computer and auto industry learned was that context is everything. The standards—or the doctrine as the military might say—is absolutely essential to allow you to work in the confidence you have absorbed the collective experience of the past. However, unless you have the authority to tailor it to the moment—as a military field commander has or the head of an IBM sales team has—it is merely a constraint. That authority comes from both the power of the local program or project manager to make decisions and the skills and experience of that person.

The key challenge for humanitarian agencies is one of how to balance the need to be accountable to their donors—who increasingly demand pre-identified results with impact—and the need to tailor every intervention to best suit not just the environment of the crisis being addressed, but the evolution of that environment. Redressing the present imbalance will be a major institutional challenge to agencies over the next ten years and one that will grow as climate change and other global drivers of change force agencies to work in unfamiliar environments with unfamiliar populations.

A recent critique of humanitarian action focused specifically on the limited capacity for institutional learning among humanitarian agencies, likening von Clausewitz's famous "fog of war"—the inability of commanders in combat to understand what is going on around them—to the current "fog of humanitarianism."[18] Humanitarian agencies are often loath to take responsibility for learning when, as often happens, things go wrong in the field. Donor agencies also often don't want to hear about failures—even failures that potentially result in valuable learning. Weiss and Peter Hoffman suggest that the root of this problem is that agencies are overly action-oriented (for historically valid reasons) and have not invested in the "capacities to process information, correct errors and devise alternative strategies and tactics."[19] They note that, with a few exceptions, evaluation and policy analysis have not, at least until very recently, been priorities. They also cite the lack of conclusive evidence that ALNAP evaluations—valuable as they may be in and of themselves—are having much impact on changing agency strategy or behavior.

And even where there is some emphasis on analysis and learning, such efforts are often piecemeal. This is in part because humanitarian agencies are locked into standard procedures and responses, and don't manage information well—particularly the critical link between situational analysis and response. One manifestation of these tendencies, as we have seen, is that the humanitarian enterprise is often focusing on the last major emergency rather than analyzing the current one. Thus, the intervention in Rwanda was too little and too late for fear of "another Mogadishu;" the intervention in the civil war in the Democratic Republic of Congo was tragically insignificant for fear of "doing harm" along the lines of that done in the Goma refugee crisis. Interventions in Darfur took up to two years to adapt to the reality of the mix of genocide, assault on livelihoods, and the consequences of climate change.

Humanitarian agencies must begin to address their learning disabilities to cope with the rapid change of the new century. The final six words of a dying business are said to be "We've always done it that way!" One suspects that unless the humanitarian system can start to both truly absorb its learning and adapt in the light of it, it too may become a dying business. Part of the answer lies in greater linkage between academia and practice. Teaching hospitals, medical journals, and carefully monitored degree-level qualifications help ratchet up the quality of the medical field. We need to promote a similar move in humanitarian academia. We need more direct, properly financed links between university-based research and agency field programs. We need more journals where research and field practice can be captured. This in turn means a greater commitment from field practitioners to write up their experiences—without fear for their professional careers if their critique is judged to be overly negative. We need more than the present handful of opportunities for potential humanitarian workers to train at degree level in the profession. We need a pool of employing agencies willing to set higher academic entry standards in order to enter the humanitarian business.

Another part of the answer may lie in humanitarian workers setting their own standards. Maybe the time is right for an international professional humanitarian workers' association, equivalent to the medical or legal professional associations?

Finally, there has to be more critique from those who are the primary clients of humanitarian agencies. This could come from agency-driven initiatives like Humanitarian Accountability Partnership-International, mentioned earlier, or from host governments as the legitimate representatives of disaster victims, or from class action suits mounted by victims themselves. Any one of these mechanisms or a combination of them could be used.

Future challenges in a changing environment

We have shown throughout this book how humanitarianism and its environment have evolved and in this chapter have hinted at some of the challenges to come. But what of the operating environment, the types of crises humanitarian agencies will be called on to tackle and the populations they will be called on to serve? Is that going to change? Clearly the answer is partly no. Hurricanes, earthquakes, drought, and civil war are not going to go away. Many see a world in which these hazards and the crises they can lead to are amplified and extended through an array of global processes: climate change, economic globalization, and organized violence being key among them.

This is not the place to dwell in detail on the causes and nature of scenarios for climate change. Many others do that far more rigorously and eloquently than we have space for. What humanitarians need to grasp is the scale and nature of the change that is upon us.

Climate change—mostly human-induced but also natural—is driving a rise in sea levels around the world, rapidly altering patterns of rainfall, leading to drought in previously water-secure areas and increasing flooding in previously controlled flood plains. As research on climate change and its consequences moves forward, scientists are able to make more accurate and more localized predictions. We know now for instance that predictions of accelerated glacial melt in the Himalayas suggest that over the next generation, two rivers—the Ganges and the Brahmaputra, which spawned and sustained some of the world's greatest civilizations and which today are the lifeblood of hundreds of millions in India and Bangladesh—may dry up, seasonally if not permanently. New research published in November 2007[20] shows how a global warming of as little as 2°C will lead to significant changes in forest cover in Amazonia, increases in wildfires in the semi-arid regions of the world, and more intense droughts in West Africa.

In many regions, the nature of the environment (weather patterns and land cover) is changing more rapidly than the society and the economics of the peoples that rely on them for survival and prosperity. This mismatch between the environment and adaptation will lead to more failures of local economies and security regimes. Different climate models predict different degrees of change, but they all point in the same direction.

There will be more extremes of weather—floods, droughts, hurricanes. There will be more communities that fail to adapt quickly enough or skillfully enough to creeping change. And all of this will result in more crises and more places where crisis becomes the norm. There will of course also be locations where things get better, crops grow stronger, and change equals prosperity.

Communities living in marginal environments (climatically, politically or economically) are going to be hardest hit. Evidence to date suggests that faced with growing and seemingly uncontrollable change, many governments react by clamping down, curtailing human rights and economic freedoms. Even so-called natural disasters may take on a political dimension in the future and agencies will find themselves working with new populations in unfamiliar environments and working with increasingly large populations as climate change forces rapid and often messy adaptation.

Globalization

Climate change comes at the same time as many other global processes, often all lumped together under the banner of globalization. We can separate five interconnected processes which will affect the course of disasters and humanitarian action in the future.

First, global trade is increasingly interconnected—and not only the trade for energy and primary resources to feed the hungry beast of consumerism. It is bringing new prosperity to parts of India and China. Cell phones are allowing non-literate women traders in Darfur to get fair prices for their goods locally as they tap into a knowledge of prevailing market prices at the national level. Borana pastoralists in southern Ethiopia find that their prosperity has more to do with how Ethiopia interprets, and is constrained by, World Trade Organization (WTO) export regulations—and how Middle Eastern buyers of Ethiopian cattle interpret WTO regulations in light of the perceived shortcomings of Ethiopia's cattle vaccination system—than it is by NGO efforts to sink wells and deliver health care. Indian banks are belatedly waking up to the realization that a billion poor people each with one dollar to save is still a potential billion dollars of investment.

Second, there are qualitative changes in our ability to communicate, share, and generate knowledge globally, brought about by the Internet and broadband connectivity. This is a tremendous driver of a more level playing field—a flatter world—for those who are connected, but for those who aren't, the digital divide renders them less than spectators. In a very real sense they fall off the map.

Third, there is the tacit assumption among rich and economically powerful nations that a mix of representative government, free market economies, and reformed state structures is the norm for the future. As state capacities to deliver social welfare—education, health care or pension support—declines, there is growth in their investment in security, meaning more militarization of societies and stronger police and judicial apparatus. As well as speaking to the politics of aid, this also speaks to economics: how is humanitarian action funded—by the state, by the public, or as a profit line?

Fourth, and partly as a rebuttal of the above, but also because of the space that the above changes have created, there is a growing assertion of alternative ethnic and religious-based values and forms of governance. This is manifest mostly today in the rise of militant Islam and other forms of fundamentalism.

And, finally, globalization has also allowed for a fifth trend: the changing nature of organized violence. Rupert Smith, the just-retired head of the British armed forces, in his new book *The Utility of Force*,[21] is adamant that wars, in the classical sense for which most professional armies are designed, no long exist. The last true tank battle, he points out, was fought for the Golan Heights back in the 1970s—over 30 years ago, although some would also cite tank battles of the Iran–Iraq war in the 1980s. War today (or whatever we call it) is fought *among* the people.

All this is fueled by an ever-facilitated, ever-easy trade in small arms whose firepower and ease of use seem to increase exponentially as each decade passes. In effect, warfare has been globalized just as economies have.

None of these globalizing processes are inherently bad or good, but each of them, if left to its own devices, will tend to differentiate, creating bi-polar worlds of connected and disconnected, economically advantaged and exploited, democratically represented and disenfranchised, "them" and "us." Local and national economies have always created their chronically poor and politically marginalized groups. Now, left to their own devices, global processes that are not informed by human rights and values of equity have the ability to create a global class of dispossessed. These processes play out in today's and tomorrow's disaster environments, making the crises less severe where managed, more severe where not managed. What does all this add up to? In a phrase: chaotic change and rapid adaptation.

Change today is fast, unprecedented, and a heady mix of opportunity and risk. There is no longer a simple linear model to predict development. No more can we simply project the present forward. Rather, we have a more chaotic future where communities and the institutions that seek to serve, or exploit them, will have to adapt rapidly and with risk to an ever-changing environment. It will be a constant game to balance short-term gain (or survival) against longer-term prosperity and freedom. Rapid and ever-evolving adaptation will be the name of the game. It is not new, but it is infinitely harder and more fragile than in the past.

A few years ago there was a popular management book called *Teaching the Elephant to Dance: The Manager's Guide to Empowering Change.* That's the real message of this section. The humanitarian agencies of the future need to be far more nimble, far more aware of the constant need to readjust their structures and tactics to fight today's battles, not the textbook battles of yesterday.

The vision and goal of the work of those engaged in humanitarian assistance have not changed. Indeed, Immanuel Kant summed it up nicely nearly two hundred and fifty years ago when he wrote that "the greatest problem for the human species is that of attaining a civil society which can administer universal justice." In the eighteenth century this sounded like pure metaphysics. Today, in our globalizing world, we can glimpse its possibility, but it won't happen unless we make it happen. Those schisms between containing suffering, treating it through impartial compassion, and changing its path through robustly addressing its root causes, are still with us. The more politically powerful agendas of containment and change still threaten to drown out and replace the agenda of compassion. Yet it is self-evident that all three are needed. As long as the political and economic process causes the collateral damage of disaster and humanitarian need, the agenda of compassion, as manifest in impartial, neutral humanitarian action will still be needed. In today's globalized world, defending that space and keeping it relevant to the wars, crisis and challenges of the twenty-first century is perhaps the biggest challenge for humanitarianism.

Notes

Foreword

1 See Julie A. Mertus, *The United Nations and Human Rights: A Guide for a New Era* (London: Routledge, 2005) and Bertrand G. Ramcharan, *Contemporary Human Rights Ideas* (London: Routledge, 2008).

2 See Thomas G. Weiss and David A. Korn, *Internal Displacement: Conceptualization and its Consequences* (London: Routledge, 2006); and Gil Loescher, Alexander Betts, and James Milner, *UNHCR: The Politics and Practice of Refugee Protection Into the Twenty-First Century* (London: Routledge, 2008).

3 See David P. Forsythe and Barbara J. Rieffer-Flanagan, *The International Committee of the Red Cross: A Neutral Humanitarian Actor* (London: Routledge, 2007).

4 Michael Barnett and Thomas G. Weiss, eds, *Humanitarianism in Question: Politics, Power, Ethics* (Ithaca, NY: Cornell University Press, 2008).

5 Peter J. Hoffman and Thomas G. Weiss, *Sword & Salve: Confronting New Wars and Humanitarian Crises* (Lanham, MD: Rowman & Littlefield, 2006), 187.

6 We have strung together the titles from William Shawcross, *Deliver Us from Evil: Peacekeepers, Warlords, and a World of Endless Conflict* (New York: Simon & Schuster, 2000); David Kennedy, *The Dark Sides of Virtue: Reassessing International Humanitarianism* (Princeton, NJ: Princeton University Press, 2004); Fiona Terry, *Condemned to Repeat? The Paradox of Humanitarian Action* (Ithaca, NY: Cornell University Press, 2002); Alex de Waal, *Famine Crimes: Politics and the Disaster Relief Industry in Africa* (Oxford: James Currey, 1997); Michael Barnett, *Eyewitness to a Genocide: The United Nations and Rwanda* (Ithaca, NY: Cornell University Press, 2002); David Rieff, *A Bed for the Night: Humanitarianism in Crisis* (New York: Simon & Schuster, 2002); Arthur C. Helton, *The Price of Indifference: Refugees and Humanitarian Action in the New Century* (Oxford: Oxford University Press, 2002); and Michael Maren, *The Road to Hell: The Ravaging Effects of Foreign Aid and International Charity* (New York: Free Press, 1997).

7 Sadako Ogata, *The Turbulent Decade: Confronting the Refugee Crises of the 1990s* (New York: W.W. Norton, 2005), 25.

8 See, for example, Ben Wisner and Peter Walker, "Katrina and Goliath: Why the Greatest Military and Economic Power in the World Did Not

Protect New Orleans," *Humanitarian Exchange* no. 32 (December 2005): 46–48 and Peter Walker, "Disaster Globalization: Evaluating the Impact of Tsunami Aid," *Journal of Emergency Management* 3, no. 5 (September/October 2005): 1–4.

9 Sue Lautze and Daniel Maxwell, "Why Do Famines Persist in the Horn of Africa? Ethiopia 1999–2003," in *The "New Famines": Why Famines Persist in an Era of Globalization*, ed. Stephen Devereux (London: Routledge, 2006), 222–244; and Christopher Barrett and Daniel Maxwell, *Food Aid after Fifty Years: Recasting its Role* (London: Routledge, 2005).

Introduction

1 Charles McGlinchey and Brian Friel, *The Last of the Name* (Belfast: Blackstaff Press, 1986), 97–98.

2 The Bretton Woods Institutions consist of the World Bank, and the International Monetary Fund, both set up in 1944. The International Bank for Reconstruction and Development (IBRD) was the original World Bank, set up along with the IMF. To the IBRD have now been added the International Development Association (IDA); the International Finance Corporation (IFC); the Multilateral Investment Guarantee Agency (MIGA); and the International Centre for the Settlement of Investment Disputes (ICSID). Together these five institutions are now called the World Bank Group. For a good description of the IMF, see James Raymond Vreeland, *The International Monetary Fund (IMF): Politics of Conditional Lending* (London: Routledge, 2006). For a similar description of the workings of the World Bank, see Katherine Marshall, *The World Bank: From Reconstruction to Development to Equity* (London: Routledge, 2008).

3 UNOCHA (8 February 2007), *United Nations Ready to Assist Flood-stricken Indonesia*, Press Release, www.reliefweb.int/rw/RWB.NSF/db900SID/AMMF-6Y8GYT?OpenDocument&rc = 3&emid = FL-2007-000023-IDN.

4 Médecins Sans Frontières (9 January 2007), *MSF Issues "Top Ten" Underreported Humanitarian Stories for 2006*, www.msf.org/msfinternational/invoke.cfm?objectid = 06616F5A-5056-AA77–6CE49B621A0C195D&component = toolkit.report&method = full_html.

5 UNOCHA Financial Tracking Service, *Consolidated Appeal Report for the Central African Republic 2006*, http://ocha.unog.ch/fts/reports/daily/ocha_R3sum_A700 – 07020721.pdf.

6 USAID (24 August 2006), *USAID Awards National Capacity Development Program in Iraq*, www.usaid.gov/press/releases/2006/pr060824.html.

7 Charles Darwin, *On the Origin of Species by Means of Natural Selection, or the Preservation of Favoured Races in the Struggle for Life* (London: John Murray, 1859).

8 Thomas Huxley, *The Struggle for Existence in Human Society*, in Thomas Huxley, *Evolution and Ethics and Other Essays* (London: Macmillan & Co., 1894), 202–218.

9 Richard Dawkins, *The Selfish Gene* (Oxford: Oxford University Press, 1976).

10 Peter Kropotkin, *Mutual Aid: A Factor in Evolution* (London: William Heinemann, 1902).

11 See Lee Alan Dugatkin, *The Altruism Equation* (Princeton, NJ: Princeton University Press, 2006). This excellent collection of essays traces the history of the scientific exploration of altruism from Charles Darwin to Bill Hamilton.

12 Robert Wright, *Nonzero: The Logic of Human Destiny* (New York: Vintage Books, 2000).

13 Charles Darwin, *The Descent of Man and Selection in Relation to Sex* (New York: D. Appleton and Company, 1897), 122.

1 Origins of the international humanitarian system

1 James Henry Breasted, *Ancient Records of Egypt*, Vol. 1 (Champaign: University of Illinois Press, 2001).

2 James Legge, *The Li Ki* (Whitefish, MT: Kessinger Publishing, 2004).

3 P. Garnsey, *Famine and Food Supply in the Graeco-Roman World* (New York: Cambridge University Press, 1988), 229.

4 N. Cantor, *In the Wake of the Plague: The Black Death and the World It Made* (New York: Free Press, 2001).

5 Brian Pullan, "Catholics, Protestants, and the Poor in Early Modern Europe," *Journal of Interdisciplinary History* xxxv, no. 3 (Winter 2005): 441–456.

6 Jonathan Benthall and Jerome Bellion-Jourdan, *The Charitable Crescent: Politics and Aid in the Muslim World* (London: I.B. Tauris, 2003). See Chapter 1 (on financial worship) and Chapter 2 (on waqf and Islamic finance).

7 For a good discussion of this early history, see Michael Bonner, "Poverty and Economics in the Quar'an," *Journal of Interdisciplinary History* xxxv, no. 3 (Winter 2005): 391–406.

8 John Barns, *An Introduction to Religious Foundations in the Ottoman Empire* (Boston: Brill Academic Publishers, 1986), 83.

9 Amy Singer, "Serving Up Charity: The Ottoman Public Kitchen," *Journal of Interdisciplinary History*, xxxv, no. 3 (Winter 2005): 481–500.

10 Andrea Paras, "Once Upon a Time: Huguenots, Humanitarianism and International Society," paper presented to the Annual Meeting of the International Studies Association, Chicago: 28 February–3 March 2007.

11 Adam Khedouri, "Bury the Dead and Feed the Living: Lessons from Lisbon: An Opinion," *Revista: Harvard Review of Latin America* (Winter 2007): 19.

12 E. de Vattel, *The Law of Nations,* Book II (Luke White, 1757): 136.

13 Niall Ferguson, *The War of the World: Twentieth Century Conflict and the Descent of the West* (London: Penguin Books, 2006), 3–42.

14 M. Alamgir, *Famine in South Asia* (Westport, CT: Greenwood Press. 1980): 68.

15 S. Sharma, *Famine, Philanthropy and the Colonial State* (New York: Oxford University Press, 2001), Chapter 3.

16 Cormac O'Grada, *The Great Irish Famine* (London: Gill and Macmillan, 1989).

17 Cormac O'Grada, *Ireland Before and After the Famine: Explorations in Economic History, 1800–1925* (Manchester: Manchester University Press, 1988), 109.

18 Christine Kinealy, *This Great Calamity: The Irish Famine 1845–52* (Boulder, CO: Roberts Rinehart Publishers, 1995), 71–86.

19 Alex de Waal, "Rights and Entitlement: The Conquest of Famine in South Asia," in Alex de Waal, *Famine Crimes, Politics and the Disaster Relief Industry in Africa* (Bloomington, IN: Indiana University Press, 1997).

20 De Waal, *Famine Crimes.*

21 T. Besley and R. Burgess, "The Political Economy of Government Responsiveness: Theory and Evidence from India," *Quarterly Journal of Economics* 117, no. 4 (November 2002): 1415–1451.

22 An English translation of the original 1863 publication can be found on the ICRC's website: www.icrc.org/WEB/ENG/siteeng0.nsf/htmlall/p0361?Open Document&style = Custo_Final.4&View = defaultBody2.

23 Resolutions of the Geneva International Conference, Geneva, 26–29 October 1863, are at: www.icrc.org/IHL.nsf/52d68d14de6160e0c12563da00 5fdb1b/1548c3c0c113ffdfc125641a0059c537.

24 The Fundamental Principles of the Red Cross and Red Crescent Movement, ICRC, Geneva, 1996. www.icrc.org/Web/eng/siteeng0.nsf/html/ EA08067453343B76C1256D2600383BC4?OpenDocument&Style = Custo_ Final.3&View = defaultBody

25 For a succinct history of the early years of the Red Cross, see ICRC, *Discover the ICRC,* www.icrc.org/Web/Eng/siteeng0.nsf/htmlall/p0790/ $File/ICRC_002_0790.PDF!Open.

26 Joseph Choate, *The Two Hague Convergences* (Princeton, NJ: Princeton University Press, 1913).

27 Save the Children, *History,* http://savethechildren.org.uk/en/38_102.htm.

28 International Save the Children Alliance, *Hope and Opportunity: Annual Report 2005* (Geneva: International Save the Children Alliance, 2005).

29 Niall P.A.S. Johnson, "Updating the Accounts: Global Mortality of the 1918–1920 'Spanish' Influenza Pandemic," *Bulletin of the History of Medicine* 76, no. 1 (Spring 2002): 105–115.

30 Michael Marrus, *The Unwanted: European Refugees in the Twentieth Century* (New York: Oxford University Press, 1985).

31 Caroline Moorhead, *Dunant's Dream: War, Switzerland and the History of the Red Cross* (New York: Carroll & Graf Publishers, 1999), 266.

32 Benjamin Weissman, *Herbert Hoover and the Famine Relief to Soviet Russia: 1921–1923* (Stanford, CA: Hoover Press, 1974).

33 John Simpson, *Refugees: Preliminary Report of a Survey* (New York: Oxford University Press, 1938): 76–80.

34 Bertrand Patenaude, *The Big Show in Bololand: The American Relief Expedition to Soviet Russia in the Famine of 1921* (Palo Alto, CA: Stanford University Press, 2002).

35 Robert Olds, quoted in Caroline Moorhead, *Dunant's Dream,* 260.

36 Daphne Reid and Patrick Gilbo, *Beyond Conflict: International Federation of Red Cross and Red Crescent Societies* (Geneva: International Federation of Red Cross and Red Crescent Societies, 1997), Chapter 2.

37 Casualties and Damage after the 1906 Earthquake, USGS Earthquake Hazards Program – Northern California. http://earthquake.usgs.gov/region al/nca/1906/18april/casualties.php

38 C. Gorge, *The International Relief Union: Its Origin, Aims, Means and Future* (Geneva: International Relief Union, 1938).

39 Convention and Statute Establishing an International Relief Union, Article 3 (Geneva, 12 July 1927).

40 Convention and Statute, Article 5.
41 P. Macalister-Smith, "The International Relief Union: Reflections on the Convention Establishing an International Relief Union of July 12, 1927," *Tijdschrift voor rechtsgeschiedenis* 54, no. 2 (1986): 363–374.
42 Robert McElvaine, *The Great Depression: America 1929–1941* (New York: Three Rivers Press, 1993).
43 For an excellent review of the history of the Cold War, see John Lewis Gaddis, *The Cold War* (New York: Penguin Press, 2005).
44 Reinhold Niebuhr, "Russia and the West," *The Nation* 156 (16 January 1943): 83.
45 Gaddis, *The Cold War*, 93.
46 National Planning Association, *UNRRA: Gateway to Recovery; Planning Pamphlet 30–31* (Washington, DC: National Planning Association, 1944).
47 For a short official history of the UN, see www.un.org/abboutun/history.htm.
48 Edward Buehrig, *The UN and the Palestinian Refugees: A Study in Nonterritorial Administration* (Bloomington, IN: Indiana University Press, 1971), 9.
49 Dean Acheson, *Present at the Creation: My Years in the State Department* (New York: W.W. Norton & Company, 1969), Chapter 22.
50 Gil Loescher, *The UNHCR and World Politics: A Perilous Path* (New York: Oxford University Press, 2001), Chapter 1.
51 Alistair Horne, *A Savage War of Peace: Algeria 1954–1962* (New York: Viking Press, 1978).
52 Allen Dulles, *The Marshall Plan* (Providence, RI: Berg Publishers, 1993). (This is a reprint of Dulles' original text of 1948, written primarily to convince a skeptical American audience of the value to the United States of the Marshall Plan.)
53 For an excellent history of UNICEF, see Maggie Black, *Children First: The Story of UNICEF Past and Present* (New York: Oxford University Press, 1996).
54 George Comstock, "The International Tuberculosis Campaign: A Pioneering Venture in Mass Vaccination and Research," *Clinical Infectious Diseases* 19, no. 3 (September 1994): 528–540.
55 The Office of the High Commissioner for Human Rights keeps a record of all signings and ratifications of human rights agreements. http://www.unhchr.ch/html/menu3/b/k2crc.htm
56 For a detailed history of the formation of WFP, see John Shaw, *The UN World Food Programme and the Development of Food Aid* (New York: Palgrave Press, 2001). See Chapters 1–4 in particular.
57 United Nations, *Yearbook of the United Nations, 1985: Economic Assistance, Disasters and Emergency Relief* (New York: United Nations, 1985), 496–551.
58 David McEntire, "Reflecting on the Weaknesses of the International Community During the IDNDR: Some Implications for Research and its Application," *Disaster Prevention and Management* 6, no. 4 (1997): 221–233.
59 See ISDR's webpage for a good overview of the organization and its genesis. www.unisdr.org
60 http://www.ochaonline.un.org
61 Maggie Black, *A Cause for Our Times: Oxfam, the First 50 Years* (New York: Oxford University Press, 1992), Chapter 1.

62 Mervyn Jones, *Two Ears of Corn: Oxfam in Action* (London: Hodder and Stoughton, 1965). For the early history of Oxfam, see Chapter 3: "A Concern in Oxford."

2 Mercy and manipulation in the Cold War

1 Dan Jacobs, *The Brutality of Nations* (New York: Alfred Knopf, 1987).
2 Alex de Waal, *Famine Crimes: Politics and the Disaster Relief Industry in Africa* (Oxford: Oxford University Press, 1997).
3 Jonathan Benthall, *Disaster, Relief and the Media* (London: I.B. Tauris, 1993).
4 David Chandler, *Brother Number One: A Political Biography of Pol Pot* (Boulder, CO: Westview Press, 1993).
5 William Shawcross, *The Quality of Mercy: Cambodia, Holocaust and Modern Conscience* (New York: Simon & Schuster, 1984).
6 Shawcross, *The Quality of Mercy.*
7 Brian Walker, "NGOs Break the Cold War Impasse in Cambodia," in *Humanitarian Diplomacy,* ed. Larry Minear and Hazel Smith (Tokyo: UNU Press, 2007).
8 It should also be noted that many of the NGOs, including Oxfam, had operations in the refugee camps in Thailand, but made a point of not engaging in the cross-border operations.
9 Walker, "NGOs Break the Cold War Impasse in Cambodia."
10 Walker, "NGOs Break the Cold War Impasse in Cambodia," 149.
11 Amartya Sen, *Poverty and Famines: An Essay on Entitlements and Deprivation* (Oxford: Oxford University Press, 1981).
12 Kent Glenzer, "We Aren't the World: The Institutional Production of Partial Success," in *Niger 2005: Une Catastrophe Si Naturelle,* ed. Xavier Crombé and Jean-Hervé Jézéque (Paris: MSF, 2007).
13 These include Howe and Stephen Devereux, "Famine Scales: Towards an Instrumental Definition of 'Famine,'" Chapter 2 in *The New Famines: Why Famines Persist in an Era of Globalization,* ed. Stephen Devereux (London: Routledge, 2006) and FAO, *The Integrated Phase Classification Tool* (Nairobi: Food Security Analysis Unit for Somalia, 2006).
14 J. Seaman and J. Holt, "Markets and Famines in the Third World," *Disasters* 4, no. 3 (1980): 283–297.
15 Richard W. Franke and Barbara Chasin, *Seeds of Famine: Ecological Destruction and the Development Dilemma in the West African Sahel* (Totowa, NJ: Rowman & Allanheld, 1980).
16 Stephen Devereux, "Goats Before Ploughs: Dilemmas of Household Response Sequencing During Food Shortages," *IDS Bulletin* 24, no. 2 (1993): 52–59 and Kent Glenzer, "We Aren't the World: The Institutional Production of Partial Success."
17 Devereux, "Goats Before Ploughs," 52–59.
18 See Jane Corbett, "Famine and Household Coping Strategies," *World Development* 16, no. 9 (1988): 1099–1112; Michael Watts, *Silent Violence: Food, Famine and Peasantry in Northern Nigeria* (Berkeley, CA: University of California Press, 1983).
19 Sen, *Poverty and Famines.*

20 Margie Buchanan-Smith and Susannah Davies, *Famine Early Warning and Response: The Missing Link* (London: Intermediate Technology Publications, 1995).

21 Gorm Rye Olsen, Nils Carstensen, and Kristian Hoyen, "Humanitarian Crises: What Determines the Level of Emergency Assistance? Media Coverage, Donor Interests and the Aid Business," *Disasters* 27, no. 2 (2003): 109–126.

22 Glenzer, "We Aren't the World," 224.

23 Michael Buerk, *BBC News,* 24 October 1984.

24 De Waal, *Famine Crimes.*

25 Africa Watch, *Evil Days: 30 Years of War and Famine in Ethiopia* (New York: Human Rights Watch, 1991).

26 De Waal, *Famine Crimes.*

27 De Waal, *Famine Crimes.*

28 Jason Clay and Bonnie Holcombe, *Politics and the Ethiopian Famine* (Cambridge, MA: Cultural Survival, 1985).

29 The song was entitled "Do they know it's Christmas?" and came out in time to raise funds during the Christmas season. A later similar attempt, "We Are the World" co-written by Michael Jackson and performed by an all-star cast of musicians that called themselves USA for Africa tried an approach to raising funds through music in 1985. Both songs raised awareness about the famine as well as significant funds for famine relief.

30 Tony Vaux, *The Selfish Altruist* (London: Earthscan, 2001), 45. Emphasis added.

31 The narrative tells that giving a man a fish, feeds him for a day. Teaching him to fish feeds him for life.

32 Vaux, *The Selfish Altruist.*

3 The globalization of humanitarianism

1 The term "ethnic cleansing" does not have legal status, but refers to removing all people of a given ethnic group from a given area.

2 Nicholas Morris, "The Balkans: The Limits of Humanitarian Action," in *Humanitarian Diplomacy,* ed. Larry Minear and Hazel Smith (Tokyo: UNU Press, 2007).

3 David Rieff, *A Bed for the Night: Humanitarianism in Crisis* (New York: Simon & Schuster, 2002); Tony Vaux, *The Selfish Altruist* (London: Earthscan, 2001).

4 Rieff, *A Bed for the Night.*

5 Rieff, *A Bed for the Night.*

6 Walter Clarke and Jeffrey Herbst, eds, *Learning from Somalia: The Lessons of Armed Humanitarian Intervention* (Boulder, CO: Westview Press, 1997).

7 Thomas G. Weiss, *Military–Civilian Interactions* (Lanham, MD: Rowman and Littlefield, 1998).

8 Karin von Hippel, "The Blurring of Mandates in Somalia," in *Humanitarian Diplomacy,* ed. Larry Minear and Hazel Smith (Tokyo: UNU Press, 2007).

9 Alex de Waal, *Famine Crimes: Politics and the Disaster Relief Industry in Africa* (Oxford: Oxford University Press, 1997).

10 Vaux, *The Selfish Altruist.*

11 De Waal, *Famine Crimes.*
12 Von Hippel, "The Blurring of Mandates in Somalia."
13 Michael Barnett, *Eyewitness to a Genocide* (Ithaca, NY: Cornell University Press, 2002).
14 Barnett, *Eyewitness to a Genocide.*
15 Von Hippel, "The Blurring of Mandates in Somalia," 315. Some observers differ strongly in the assessment of how much of the food aid was actually looted. See de Waal, *Famine Crimes*, for example.
16 De Waal, *Famine Crimes.*
17 De Waal, *Famine Crimes.*
18 Piers Robinson, *The CNN Effect: The Myth of News, Foreign Policy, and Intervention* (London: Routledge, 2002).
19 Peter Uvin, *Aiding Violence* (West Hartford, CT: Kumarian Press, 1998).
20 Barnett, *Eyewitness to a Genocide.*
21 Barnett, *Eyewitness to a Genocide.*
22 For more in-depth accounts, see Philip Gourevitch, *We Wish to Inform You that Tomorrow We Will Be Killed with Our Families* (New York: Farrar, Straus, and Giroux, 1998); Johan Pottier, *Re-imagining Rwanda* (New York: Cambridge University Press, 2001); Samantha Power, *A Problem from Hell* (New York: Basic Books, 2002); Roméo Dallaire, *Shake Hands with the Devil* (New York: Carroll & Graff, 2004); and Kingsley Chiedu Moghalu, *Rwanda's Genocide: The Politics of Global Justice* (New York: Palgrave Macmillan, 2005). There are numerous other accounts as well, most by non-Rwandese authors.
23 John Borton, Adrian Wood and Raymond Apthorpe, *Evaluating International Humanitarian Action* (New York: Zed Books, 1996).
24 Refoulement is a term used in international law to refer to the forcible return of refugees to places where their lives or freedoms are threatened. Refoulement is prohibited by the 1951 Refugee Convention.
25 Fiona Fox, "New Humanitarianism: Does It Provide a Moral Banner for the 21st Century?" *Disasters* 25, no. 4 (Dec 2001): 275–289.
26 Clare Short, "Principles of a New Humanitarianism," paper delivered at the ODI/ECHO conference on Principled Aid in an Unprincipled World, 8 April 1999, London.
27 Borton, Wood, and Apthorpe, *Evaluating International Humanitarian Action.*
28 Rieff, *A Bed for the Night.*
29 Steering Committee of the Joint Evaluation of Emergency Assistance to Rwanda, *The International Response to Conflict and Genocide: Lessons from the Rwanda Experience* (Joint Evaluation of Emergency Assistance to Rwanda, March 1996). www.reliefweb.int/library/nordic
30 The Sphere Project, *The Humanitarian Charter and Minimum Standards in Disaster Response* (Geneva: The Sphere Project, 2004).
31 www.alnap.org
32 www.hapinternational.org
33 Mary Anderson, *Do No Harm: How Aid Can Support Peace — or War* (Boulder, CO: Lynne Rienner Publishers, 1999).
34 John Borton, "The Joint Evaluation of Emergency Assistance to Rwanda," in *Humanitarian Exchange* no. 26 (March 2004): 15.
35 Short, "Principles of a New Humanitarianism"; Joanna Macrae and Nicholas Leader, *The Politics of Coherence: Humanitarianism and Foreign Policy in the Post-Cold War Era* (London: Overseas Development Institute, 2000).

36 Fox, "New Humanitarianism"; Nicholas Stockton, "In Defense of Humanitarianism," *Disasters* 22, no. 4 (1998): 352–360; Rieff, *A Bed for the Night*.

37 In an influential summary, Michael Barnett, "Humanitarianism Transformed," *Perspectives on Politics* 3, no. 4 (2005): 733–740, notes that at the beginning of the twenty-first century, contemporary humanitarianism is "precariously situated between the politics of solidarity and the politics of governance" or between the idealistic but relatively marginal position of twentieth-century humanitarianism, and the power politics of the twenty-first-century repolarization of the global political economy.

38 Fox, "New Humanitarianism"; Short, "Principles of a New Humanitarianism"; Thomas Weiss, *Humanitarian Intervention: Ideas in Action* (Cambridge: Polity Press, 2007).

39 Antonio Donini, "An Elusive Quest: Integration in the Response to the Afghan Crisis," *Ethics and International Affairs* 18, no. 2 (2004): 24.

40 Ahmed Rashid, "Afghanistan: Ending the Policy Quagmire," *Columbia Journal of International Affairs* 1 (April 2001).

41 Nora Niland, *Rights, Rhetoric and Reality: Snapshot from Afghanistan* (Medford, MA: Tufts University, 2004).

42 Donini, "An Elusive Quest," 21–27.

43 See, for example, Paul O'Brien, "Old Woods, New Paths, Diverging Choices for NGOs," in Antonio Donini, Nora Niland and Karin Wermester, eds, *Nation-Building Unraveled: Aid, Peace and Justice in Afghanistan* (West Hartford, CT: Kumarian Press, 2004): 187–203.

44 Sarah Lischer, "Military Intervention and the Humanitarian 'Force Multiplier,'" *Global Governance* 13, no. 1 (2007): 99–118; Antonio Donini, Larry Minear, and Peter Walker, "The Future of Humanitarian Action: Mapping the Implications of Iraq and Other Recent Crises," *Disasters* 28, no. 2 (2004): 190–204.

45 International Commission on Intervention and State Sovereignty, *The Responsibility to Protect: Report of the International Commission on Intervention and State Sovereignty* (Ottawa: International Development Research Centre, 2001).

46 Weiss, *Humanitarian Intervention*, 88.

47 Weiss, *Humanitarian Intervention*, 104.

48 Jaya Murthy, "Mandating the Protection Cluster with the Responsibility to Protect: A Policy Recommendation Based on the Protection Cluster's Implementation in South Kivu, DRC," *Journal of Humanitarian Assistance* 5 (October 2007). Note that MONUC operates under a "Chapter 7" mandate in the Congo, meaning that it is not just there to monitor an existing peace agreement, but can engage in enforcement.

49 Weiss, *Humanitarian Intervention*, 109.

50 Donini, Minear and Walker, "The Future of Humanitarian Action," 190–204.

51 Feinstein International Center, *Humanitarian Agenda 2015 (HA 2015)—A Summary* (Medford, MA: Tufts University, 2006).

52 Greg Hansen, *Taking Sides or Saving Lives: Existential Choices for the Humanitarian Enterprise in Iraq* (Medford, MA: Tufts University, 2007), 56. Emphasis in the original.

4 States as responders and donors

1 *The Sphere Handbook* (Oxford: Oxfam Publishing, 2004), 18.

2 International Federation of the Red Cross and Red Crescent Societies, *IDRL Factsheet*, www.ifrc.org/what/disasters/IDRL/index.asp.

3 www.responsibilitytoprotect.org/

4 UN General Assembly resolution 60/1, 16 September 2005, paragraphs 138–9.

5 International Committee of the Red Cross, *Convention (IV) Relating to the Protection of Civilian Persons in Time of War* (Geneva, 12 August 1949).

6 Emergency Disaster Database, Centre for Research on the Epidemiology of Disasters, www.em-dat.net/

7 Mizan R. Khan and M. Ashiqur Rahman, "Partnership Approach to Disaster Management in Bangladesh: a Critical Policy Assessment," *Natural Hazards* 41, no. 2 (May 2007): 359–378.

8 E. Kerbed, "Moving from Emergency Food Aid to Predictable Cash Transfers: Recent Experience in Ethiopia," *Development Policy Review* 24, no. 5 (2006): 579–599.

9 www.fema.gov/about/index.shtm

10 C. Wise, "Organizing for Homeland Security after Katrina: Is Adaptive Management What's Missing?" *Public Administration Review* 66, no. 3 (May 2006): 302–318.

11 Development Initiatives, *Global Humanitarian Assistance 2006* (London: Development Initiatives, 2006), 10.

12 Development Initiatives, *Global Humanitarian Assistance 2006*, 49–50.

13 Development Initiatives, *Global Humanitarian Assistance 2006*, 18.

14 Development Initiatives, *Global Humanitarian Assistance 2006*, 14.

15 Andrew S. Natsios, *US Foreign Policy and the Four Horsemen of the Apocalypse: Humanitarian Relief in Complex Emergencies* (Westport, CT: Praeger, 1997), Chapter 3.

16 Natsios, *US Foreign Policy*, 43.

17 OECD/DAC, *Peer Review: Main Findings and Recommendations*, www. oecd.org/document/27/0,3343,en_2649_34603_37829787_1_1_1_1,00.html

18 US Secretary of Defense's Statement to the Senate Appropriates Committee, www.defenselink.mil/utility/printitem.aspx?print = http://www.defenselink. mil/speeches/speech.aspx?speechid = 1127.

19 Management of the Commander's Emergency Response Program in Iraq for Fiscal Year 2006. Report of the Office of the Inspector General. 26 April 2007 www.stormingmedia.co.uk/71/7166/A716664.html?PHPSESSID = 22e5e2dbc6d45a7b92b79798517c36d7

20 *National Security Strategy for the United States of America.* http//:www. whitehouse.gov/nsc/nss.html

21 USAID, *US Foreign Assistance Reform.* www.usaid.gov/about_usaid/dfa/

22 Council of the European Union, Council Regulation (EC) No , 20 June 1996.

23 Voluntary Organizations in Cooperation in Emergencies, *Position Paper by VOICE and Other Humanitarian and Development NGO Networks, on the Draft European Constitutional Treaty*, 18 June 2003.

24 B. Koppel and R. Orr, eds, *Japan's Foreign Aid: Power and Policy in a New Era* (Boulder, CO: Westview Press, 1993), 1.

25 Y. Nishikawa, *Japan's Changing Role in Humanitarian Crises* (London: Routledge, 2005), Chapter 3.

26 Development Initiatives, *Global Humanitarian Assistance 2006* (London: Development Initiatives, 2006), 136.

27 Good Humanitarian Donorship, *Good Humanitarian Donorship: The Challenge,* www.goodhumanitariandonorship.org/default.asp.
28 www.goodhumanitariandonorship.org
29 See the full text of the 1945 UN Charter at http://www.un.org/aboutun/charter/
30 See the web site of the UN Department of Peace Keeping. http://www.un.org/depts/dpko/dpko/bnote.htm Published December 2007.
31 Peter J. Walker, "Foreign Military Resources for Disaster Relief: An NGO Perspective," *Disasters* 16, no. 2 (June 1992): 152–159.
32 US Army Corps of Engineers, *Essayons Forward* 5, no. 2 (2008): 4 www.grd.usace.army.mil/news/Essayonsforward/documents/EF_V5N2.pdf
33 M. Pugh, "Military Intervention and Humanitarian Action: Trends and Issues," *Disasters* 22, no. 4 (Dec 1998): 39–351.
34 Thomas G. Weiss, "Research Note about Military-Civilian Humanitarianism: More Questions than Answers," *Disasters* 21, no. 2 (June 1997): 95–117.

5 International organizations

1 See Tsunami Evaluation Coalition, *Joint Evaluation of the International Response to the Indian Ocean Tsunami: Synthesis Report* (London: Overseas Development Institute, July 2006), 63. www.tsunami-evaluation.org/The+TEC+Synthesis+Report/Full+Report.htm
2 OCHA, *Humanitarian Response Review* (New York: United Nations, 2005). www.reliefweb.int/library/documents/2005/ocha-gen-02sep.pdf
3 Darcy and Hoffman, *Humanitarian Needs Assessment and Decision-Making.* HPG Briefing Paper 13. September 2003. www.odi.org.uk/hpg/papers/hpgbrief13.pdf
4 OCHA, *Humanitarian Response Review,* 9.
5 Note that the International Commission on Intervention and State Sovereignty's report, *The Responsibility to Protect* had already come out, and set the tone for some of the debate, and that during the time the report was being written, the protection crisis in Darfur had reached epic proportions.
6 OCHA, *Humanitarian Response Review,* 16. Emphasis added.
7 Only for conflict-driven IDPs—not disaster. The cluster lead for those internally displaced as a result of natural disasters is shared between UNHCR, UNICEF and the Office of the UN High Commissioner for Human Rights (OHCHR).
8 www.un.org/events/panel/resources/pdfs/HLP-SWC-FinalReport.pdf
9 Tim Maurer, "Unity in Diversity – The One UN, UNHCR and Rwanda," *Forced Migration Review* 29 (December 2007): 10–11. See other articles in the same volume (www.fmreview.org/humanitarianreform.htm) for further early assessment of UN reforms.
10 This section draws heavily on Peter Walker and Kevin Pepper, *Follow the Money: A Review and Analysis of the State of Humanitarian Funding.* A background paper for the meeting of the Good Humanitarian Donorship and Inter-Agency Standing Committee, 20 July 2007, Geneva. http://fic.tufts.edu/downloads/GHD-IASCFINALPAPER.pdf
11 Development Initiatives, *Global Humanitarian Assistance 2006* (London: Development Initiatives, 2006): 10. http://ochaonline.un.org/OchaLinkClick.aspx?link = ocha&docid = 1039804
12 www.globalhumanitarianassistance.org

13 Joseph Stiglitz and Linda Bilmes, *The Three Trillion Dollar War* (London: Allen Lane, 2008).

14 Development Initiatives, *Global Humanitarian Assistance 2006*, 28.

15 Central Emergency Response Fund, United Nations, OCHA Online, http:// ochaonline2.un.org/Default.aspx?tabid = 9932.

16 For a more complete discussion of humanitarian information systems, see Daniel Maxwell and Benjamin Watkins, "Humanitarian Information Systems and Emergencies in the Greater Horn of Africa: Logical Components and Logical Linkages," *Disasters* 27, no. 1 (March 2003): 72–90.

17 OCHA Financial Tracking Services, http://ocha.unog.ch/fts2/.

18 The International Food Aid Information System, www.wfp.org/interfais

19 ReliefWeb website, *About Reliefweb.* www.reliefweb.int/rw/hlp.nsf/db900By Key/AboutReliefWeb?OpenDocument

20 This section draws heavily on Christopher Barrett and Daniel Maxwell, *Food Aid After Fifty Years: Recasting its Role* (London: Routledge, 2005). For a more complete recount of the issues raised here, the reader should refer to this book.

6 NGOs and private action

1 www.globalhumanitarianassistance.org

2 www.oecd.org/dataoecd/17/39/40039047.gif

3 Oxfam GB Annual Report and Accounts 2006–2007: 20. www.charity-commission.gov.uk/registeredcharities/ScannedAccounts%5CEnds18%5C00 00202918_ac_20070430_e_c.pdf

4 www.psfci.org/new/indexuk.htm

5 www.avsf.org/uk/index.php

6 www.islamic-relief.com

7 www.samaritanspurse.org/glossyIncludes/pdf_files/AnnualRep_Finance.pdf

8 www.churchworldservice.org

9 www.afsc.org

10 www.mennoniteusa.org

11 www.charity-commission.gov.uk/registeredcharities/ScannedAccounts%5CE nds90%5C0000213890_ac_20070331_e_c.pdf

12 www.savethechildren.org/publications/financial/2006-financials.pdf

13 www.icva.ch

14 www.humanitarianinfo.org/iasc/content/about/schr.asp

15 www.ngovoice.org

16 www.interaction.org

17 www.interaction.org/content/pvostandards

18 www.dec.org.uk

19 www.humanitarianinfo.org/iasc

20 For official UN information on the cluster approach, visit www.humanitar ianreform.org.

21 International Red Cross and Red Crescent, *Decision 17: Humanitarian Assistance in Situations of Natural and Technological Disasters*, Council of Delegates Meeting, 1991.

22 The full text of the Code of Conduct is at: www.ifrc.org/publicat/conduct/ index.asp?navid = 09_08

166   *Notes*

23 International Red Cross and Red Crescent, *Resolution 4: Principles and action in International Humanitarian Assistance and Protection*, International Conference, 1995. www.icrc.org/Web/Eng/siteeng0.nsf/html/conf26

24 For a full history of the Code, see Peter Walker, "Cracking the Code: The Genesis, Use and Future of the Code of Conduct," *Disasters* 29, no. 4 (December 2005): 323–326. www.blackwell-synergy.com/doi/abs/10.1111/j.0361–3666.2005.00295.x

25 The full Sphere Standards, in a number of languages, along with training materials, are at: www.sphereproject.org.

26 For a full history of Sphere, see Peter Walker and Susan Purdin, "Birthing Sphere: The Early History of the Sphere Project," *Disasters* 26, no. 2 (June 2004): 100–111.

27 Jacqui Tong, "Questionable Accountability: MSF and Sphere in 2003," *Disasters* 29, no. 4 (December 2004): 176–189. See also www.alertnet.org/thefacts/reliefresources/109783801066.htm for an overview of many of the criticisms.

28 www.alnap.org

29 www.reliefweb.int/library/nordic

30 www.hapinternational.org

31 See *HAP 2007 Standard in Humanitarian Accountability and Quality Management*. www.hapinternational.org/pool/files/hap-2007-standard(1).pdf

32 www.peopleinaid.org

7 A brave new world, a better future?

1 For an excellent social science based analysis of these issues, see Michael Barnett and Thomas G. Weiss, *Humanitarianism in Question: Politics Power and Ethics* (Ithaca, NY: Cornell University Press, 2008).

2 Peter J. Hoffman and Thomas G. Weiss, *Sword and Salve: Confronting New Wars and Humanitarian Crises* (Lanham, MD: Rowman & Littlefield Publishers, 2006); Carolyn Nordstrom, *Shadows of War* (Berkeley, CA: University of California Press, 2004).

3 Mark Duffield, *Global Governance and the New Wars* (London: Zed Books, 2001); Nordstrom, *Shadows of War*.

4 Hoffman and Weiss, *Sword and Salve*; Nordstrom, *Shadows of War*.

5 Tara Gingerich and Jennifer Leaning, *The Use of Rape as a Weapon of War in the Conflict in Darfur, Sudan* (Cambridge, MA: Physicians for Human Rights, 2004). http://physiciansforhumanrights.org/library/report-2004-oct-darfurrape.html

6 http://www.publications.parliament.uk/pa/cm199899/cmselect/cmintdev/55/5511.htm

7 Fiona Fox, "New Humanitarianism: Does It Provide a Moral Banner for the 21st Century?" *Disasters* 25, no. 4 (December 2001): 275–289. www.blackwell-synergy.com/doi/abs/10.–7717.00178?journalCode = disa

8 Antonio Donini, "An Elusive Quest: Integration in the Response to the Afghan Crisis," *Ethics and International Affairs* 18, no. 2 (2004). www.cceia.org/resources/journal/18_2/special_section/005.html

9 Paul O'Brien, "Old Woods, New Paths, Diverging Choices for NGOs," in *Nation-Building Unraveled: Aid Peace and Justice in Afghanistan,* ed. Antonio Donini, Karin Wermester, and Norah Niland (Bloomfield, CT: Kumarian Press, 2004), 187–203.

10 Abby Stoddard, *Humanitarian Alert: NGO Information and its Impact on US Foreign Policy* (Bloomfield, CT: Kumarian Press, 2006).

11 *The Responsibility to Protect: Report of the International Commission on Intervention and State Sovereignty,* www.iciss.ca/report-en.asp

12 OCHA, *Humanitarian Response Review* (New York: United Nations, 2005), 11. www.reliefweb.int/library/documents/2005/ocha-gen-02sep.pdf

13 Greg Hansen, *Taking Sides or Saving Lives: Existential Choices for the Humanitarian Enterprise in Iraq* (Medford, MA: Tufts University, 2007). http://fic.tufts.edu/?pid = 10

14 International Strategy for Disaster Reduction, *Hyogo Framework for Action 2005–2015: Building the Resilience of Nations and Communities to Disasters.* www.unisdr.org/eng/hfa/hfa.htm

15 See, for example, Mark Bradbury, "Normalizing Crisis in Africa," *Disasters* 22, no. 4 (December 1998): 328–338.

16 David Rieff, *A Bed for the Night: Humanitarianism in Crisis* (New York: Simon & Schuster, 2002); Michael Barnett, "Humanitarianism Transformed," *Perspectives on Politics* 3, no. 4 (2005): 733–740; Weiss and Hoffman, *Sword and Salve.*

17 Development Initiatives. "Global Humanitarian Assistance 2006," 5. http://www.globalhumanitarianassistance.org/pdfdownloads/GHA%202006.pdf

18 Thomas G. Weiss and Peter J. Hoffman, "The Fog of Humanitarianism: Collective Action Problems and Learning-Challenged Organizations," *The Journal of Intervention and Statebuilding* 1, no. 1 (2007): 47–65.

19 Weiss and Hoffman, "The Fog of Humanitarianism," 58.

20 Inter-Governmental Panel on Climate Change, *Fourth Assessment Report.* www.ipcc.ch/ipccreports/ar4-syr.htm

21 Rupert Smith, *The Utility of Force: The Art of War in the Modern World* (New York: Vintage Press, 2007).

Select bibliography

There is a wealth of literature published on the various parts of the humanitarian system, much of which is referenced in the chapters of this book. Overview publications looking at the whole system are, unfortunately, few and far between.

We have not found any volume which pulls together the collective history of the system as we have tried to do here. Some individual agencies have published their histories. As examples see Caroline Moorhead, *Dunant's Dream: War, Switzerland and the History of the Red Cross* (New York: Carroll & Graf Publishers, 1999) for a good history of the ICRC, or Maggie Black, *A Cause for Our Times: Oxfam the First 50 Years* (New York: Oxford University Press, 1992) for a similar history of Oxfam.

Good overviews of humanitarian issues of today can be found in Peter J. Hoffman and Thomas G. Weiss, *Sword & Salve: Confronting New Wars and Humanitarian Crises* (Lanham, MD: Rowman & Littlefield, 2006). Also see Ian Smilie and Larry Minear, *The Charity of Nations: Humanitarian Action in a Calculating World* (Bloomfield, CT: Kumarian Press, 2004) and Fiona Terry, *Condemned to Repeat? The Paradox of Humanitarian Action* (Ithaca, NY: Cornell University Press, 2002).

For more personal reading which attempts to convey a sense of what it is like working within humanitarian crises, it is worth reading David Rieff, *A Bed for the Night: Humanitarianism in Crisis* (New York: Simon & Schuster, 2003) and Tony Vaux, *The Selfish Altruist: Relief Work in Famine and War* (London: Earthscan Publications, 2003).

Finally, to understand the practicalities of humanitarian aid, there is no better read than *The Sphere Handbook: Humanitarian Charter and Minimum Standards in Disaster Response*, 2nd revised edn (Oxford: Oxfam Publications, 2004).

Index

GLOBAL INSTITUTIONS SERIES

NEW TITLE

The International Olympic Committee and the Olympic System

The governance of world sport

Jean-Loup Chappelet, Swiss Graduate School of Public Administration, Switzerland and
Brenda Kübler-Mabbott

This book analyzes the International Olympic Committee, what makes the system work and whether it will survive in the twenty-first century considering the major changes that have taken place in sport over recent decades.

Selected contents: Introduction 1 A brief overview of the Olympic system 2 The International Olympic Committee 3 National Olympic Committees 4 International Sports Federations 5 Organising Committees of the Olympic Games 6 Governments and the Olympic system 7 The regulators 8 Olympic governance: some conclusions

May 2008: 216x138: 224pp
Hb: 978-0-415-43167-5: **£65.00**
Pb: 978-0-415-43168-2: **£14.99**

NEW TITLE

Internet Governance

The new frontier of global institutions

John Mathiason, Syracuse University, USA

John Mathiason tells the story of the internet governance, where the linkage between technology, information, individuals, old regulatory regimes and new approaches have led to a great experiment, what a volume produced by the United Nations Information and Communications Technology Task Force called "A Grand Collaboration."

Selected contents: Introduction 1. What is the Internet and what is governance? 2. Before the Internet 3. The non-state actors 4. Solving the domain name problem 5. Regulatory imperatives for Internet governance 6. The ICANN experiment 7. Multi-stakeholderism emerges from the World Summit on the Information Society 8. The IGF experiment begins 9. What does the frontier look like?

July 2008: 216x138: 200pp
Hb: 978-0-415-77402-4: **£65.00**
Pb: 978-0-415-77403-1: **£14.99**

Routledge
Taylor & Francis Group

To order any of these titles
Call: +44 (0) 1235 400400
Email: book.orders@routledge.co.uk

For further information visit:
www.routledge.com/politics